A HISTORY OF VIETNAM

**Recent Titles in
Contributions in Asian Studies**

Schoolmaster to an Empire: Richard Henry Brunton in Meiji Japan, 1868–1876
R. Henry Brunton, edited and annotated by Edward R. Beauchamp

Urbanizing China
Gregory Eliyu Guldin, editor

Japan and Russia: A Reevaluation in the Post-Soviet Era
William F. Nimmo

American Pioneers and the Japanese Frontier: American Experts in Nineteenth-Century
Japan
Fumiko Fujita

A HISTORY OF VIETNAM

FROM HONG BANG TO TU DUC

Oscar Chapuis

CONTRIBUTIONS IN ASIAN STUDIES, NUMBER 5

GREENWOOD PRESS
WESTPORT, CONNECTICUT • LONDON

Library of Congress Cataloging-in-Publication Data

Chapuis, Oscar
    A history of Vietnam : from Hong Bang to Tu Duc / Oscar
Chapuis.
        p.   cm. — (Contributions in Asian studies, ISSN 1053-1866 ;
    no. 5)
    Includes bibliographical references and index.
    ISBN 0-313-29622-7 (alk. paper)
    1. Vietnam—History. I. Title. II. Series.
DS556.5.C47   1995
959.7—dc20   94-48169

British Library Cataloguing in Publication Data is available.

Library of Congress Catalog Card Number: 94-48169
ISBN: 0-313-29622-7
ISSN: 1053-1866

First published in 1995

Greenwood Press, 88 Post Road West, Westport, CT 06881
An imprint of Greenwood Publishing Group, Inc.

Printed in the United States of America

The paper used in this book complies with the
Permanent Paper Standard issued by the National
Information Standards Organization (Z39.48-1984).

10 9 8 7 6 5 4 3 2 1

TO DR. AILON SHILOH

CONTENTS

ACKNOWLEDGMENTS

I am deeply indebted to the following individuals whose contributions have made this work possible:

Vo Chan for his longtime friendship and his generous assistance in all fields; Nguyen kim Nhan and her group for some Vietnamese documentations; Corinne Faye for her French materials and Becky Hembree for her delicate cartography; Angelo Lorenzo, Guy Hagen, Dalys Wright, and Andy Miller for their time to read and comment.

My love and blessing go to my two daughters, Solange and Viviane, and Viviane's husband, Robert. Their total support was most needed.

It goes without saying that I am deeply grateful to GPG and its editorial team, especially Lynn Flint, Acquisitions Editor, for her abiding interest in this project; Dina K. Rubin, Production Editor, for her meticulous coordination; and Caroline Herrick for her exceptional job in helping my prose throughout.

INTRODUCTION

As China is the main source of Asian history, students often find two major problems. The first, which relates to chronology, is acknowledged by C.P. Fitz-gerald[1] as a result of the discrepancy between the orthodox sources and the Bamboo books. The other, centered on the spelling of proper names, is, according to D.G.E. Hall, due to "various romanization systems."[2] As for the Vietnamese Quoc Ngu, the existence of diacritical marks, which changes the meaning of words, is an additional difficulty.

The traditional Asian historians were not concerned with accuracy. For them, history was part of the philosophy of *right and wrong*, and its unique function was to set *moral standards*. Within this context, what Fung Yu-Lan[3] said about Chinese philosophy applies as well to Asian history: It should be approached with intuitive mind rather than analytical spirit.

This book begins with the prehistory of both China and Vietnam, since according to the tradition, the ancestor of the Vietnamese was the Chinese emperor Shen Nung. This was a period of myths and legends. It lasted until the appearance of the historic kingdom of Au Lac, which was soon conquered by China. Nowadays, as archeology has become a major tool in historical research, there is a tendency to displace the Hung Vuong in Vietnamese textbooks with the Homo erectus, and the nature of the Asian Homo sapiens has been questioned.[4]

Throughout its long history, Vietnam had various appellations: under the Hong Bang dynasty (2879–258 BC), Vietnam was called Van Lang; under the Thuc (258–207 BC), it was Au Lac. Chao To (207–111 BC) named it Nan Yueh. When Vietnam became part of China (111 BC–AD 939), it was consecutively identified as Chiao Chih, Chiao Chou, and Annam.

Following independence, the Dinh Dynasty (AD 968-980) called their country Dai-Co-Viet. In 1054, King Ly Thanh Tong (AD 1054-1072) renamed it Dai-Viet, but later in 1138, King Ly Anh Tong (AD 1138-1175) changed it to Annam. Finally, in 1804, the current name—Vietnam—was granted by China to Gia Long (AD 1802-1819).

The existence of the kingdom of Au Lac has been denied by some Western scholars; however, the Co Loa archeological finds strongly suggest the presence of a social organization. The traditional kingdom of Au Lac was founded after the last Hung Vuong was defeated by the king of Au Viet. The Au Lac king An Duong Vuong was defeated, in turn, by Chao To, a Chinese who proclaimed himself king of Nan Yueh (Nam Viet) and chief of the barbarians to mark his separation from China. Such an appellation was not an expression of contempt since Chao To readily forsook his own culture to promote Vietnamese customs and encouraged interracial union. After Chao To, Vietnam became part of China under various appellations.

By preserving the native aristocracy, the Chinese conquerors created at the top level of Vietnamese society a duplication of classes. Internal Sino-Vietnamese antagonism among the elite ensued. This antagonism later erupted into the revolt of two gentlewomen, Trung Trac and Trung Nhi. From then on, Vietnam was more often than not a pawn on the Chinese political chessboard. In the eighteenth century, the Nguyen Hue's victory over the Ch'ing[5] marked the end of Chinese control over Vietnam. The most conspicuous result of the thousand years of Chinese rule was the inheritance of a traditional culture that could not defend itself in the face of Western technology. Nevertheless, Confucian ethics remained embedded in the Vietnamese soul and will continue to be for centuries to come, no matter what the political situation.

The first king of Vietnam, Ngo Quyen, attempted to forge a national identity by establishing a dynasty, but after reigning for five years, his dynasty fell into oblivion, leaving a chaotic situation presided over by twelve competing warlords. Not until the early Le and Ly dynasties was the Vietnamese monarchy consolidated. To secure economic independence, the Le created the first Vietnamese currency. Their victory over Champa led to the march to the south. But ultimately they lost the Mandate of Heaven because of the depravation of King Le Long Dinh. Since everyone had had enough of the descendant of Le Dai Hanh, the Ly were accepted as benevolent usurpers. They set up the democratic system of using national examinations to recruit commoners for government positions. Their dynasty came to an end when the mentally ill King Ly Hue Tong, contrary to all customs, appointed his daughter to succeed him. She soon abdicated in favor of her husband, a member of the Tran, a family of rich fishermen. In contrast with the Ly, the Tran were by no means benevolent since they set out first to exterminate their predecessors. However, their reign was a remarkable one. Their incredible victory over the Mongols kept China at bay for a long period of time, allowing the Vietnamese to resume their march to the south at the expense of Champa. Ultimately, the Le transformed their palace into a gambling casino and were overthrown by their own prime minister, Ho Qui Ly, who was probably the only person at that time capable of saving Vietnam from economic disaster. But Ho Qui Ly lost the support of the nation when

he forcefully introduced paper money to the market. This extraordinary politician, who was defeated by the Ming, ended up his career as a patrol guard in
China. And for only twenty years, Vietnam went back under Chinese domination. Despite the efforts of Le Loi and Nguyen Trai, the ultimate liberators, and
the remarkable realizations of Le Thanh Tong, Vietnam fell into the hands of
Mac usurpers. For fifty years, under the impotent heirs of Le Loi and with the
encouragement and help of western missionaries and merchants, civil war divided the North and the South.

In Vietnam as in Thailand, French missionaries resorted to armed intervention
after setbacks in religious persuasion. They had failed because " . . . receptivity
to the influence of alien religions may depend on how a people perceive the
agents through whom that religion comes to them."[6] In fact, the French missionaries were perceived as representatives of the European powers that were
trying to impose their rule on Southeast Asia. Consequently, persecutions against
Catholics were carried out with increasing brutality, thus enticing French retaliation.

In 1858, Rigault de Genouilly arrived at Tourane (Da Nang) with a contingent
of Spanish Tagals from the Philippines. After destroying Tourane, he moved to
the South where the French established direct rule.

NOTES

1. I. C. P. Fitzgerald, *China: A Short Cultural History* (New York: Praeger, 1950), p.
14.

2. D. G. E. Hall, *A History of Southeast Asia* (New York: St. Martin's Press, 1964),
p. vii.

3. Fung Yu-Lan, *A Short History of Chinese Philosophy* (New York: Macmillan,
1953), p. 23.

4. Andrew Kramer, *American Journal of Physical Anthropology* 91 (1993): 161–171.

5. The Manchu dynasty which lasted from 1644 until the beginning of the Republican
Era in 1911.

6. Alice B. Child and Irving L. Child, *Religion and Magic in the Life of Traditional
People* (Englewood Cliffs, N.J: Prentice Hall, 1993), p. 214.

MAPS

A HISTORY OF VIETNAM

THE LANDS BEFORE TIME

PREHISTORIC CHINA

In the mid-Pleistocene, Homo erectus appeared at different locations in South-east Asia. First came the Java Man, or Pithecanthropus erectus, in Indonesia, with his two cousins, the Big Java Man, or Pithecanthropus robustus, and the Java Giant, or Meganthropus palaeojavanicus. In South China, the Gigantopith-ecus, which was twice the size of a modern gorilla, dwelt in some two hundred caves in Kwangsi Province. To the north, at Chou-k'ou-Tien, there was the Sinanthropus pekinensis or Peking Man.

The search for the Peking Man began in 1921, with Dr. J. G. Andersson, from a Swedish expedition, working in the vicinity of the Chou-k'ou-Tien rail-way station, thirty-five miles southwest of Peking. In fact, the Chou-k'ou-Tien area had long been known as a hunting ground for Chinese herbalists in search of "dragon bones."[1] Later, Professor O. Zdansky found one human tooth in his 1921 Chinese collection. His discovery triggered a joint project financed by the Rockefeller Foundation and operated by the Chinese Geological Survey, which was in charge of the field work and study of fossil fauna. The study of human skeletal remains was assigned to the Peking Union Medical College. After 178,695 man-days of work and the removal of 20,000 cubic meters of earth, remains of forty-five Sinanthropus were uncovered, along with many animal bones and implements.[2] The presence of the implements led experts to conclude that the Sinanthropus was by definition man. The Sinanthropus had extended families and dwelt in caves. As skulls and limbs were found shattered, emptied of brain and marrow, the Peking Man was deemed to have been a cannibal. It practiced learned cannibalism rather than survival cannibalism.[3] According to Gordon T. Bowles, "any idea, however, that cannibalism could have had more than ritual or gourmet significance is utterly fanciful. Man would soon have eaten himself out of existence had he depended to any extent upon human meat for survival."[4] The presence of charred bones suggests that Peking Man had been able to master the use of fire.

In 1956, Pei Wen-Chung of the Chinese Academy of Sciences discovered in a cave at Ta Hsin, Kwangsi Province, three giant teeth, three to six times the size of human teeth. They came from the Gigantopithecus.[5] During World War II, the remains of the Peking Man were seized by the Japanese occupation forces and were not recovered. Fortunately, Dr. Franz Weidenreich, one of the team experts, had sent a cast of the remains to the United States.

As for the Java Man, he was discovered near the village of Trinil on the Solo River in Central Java in 1891-1892 by the Dutchman Eugene Dubois. There a stone marked P.E. (Pithecanthropus erectus) commemorates his significant find, although some critics say it stands for "probable error." Between 1931 and 1939, eight more skulls said to be Homo erectus javanensis were unearthed. Unlike Peking Man, Java Man did not undergo any significant "morphological change over a span of a million years."[6]

The fact that Chinese teeth were discovered under rather surprising circumstances—by Dr. G.H.R. von Koenigswald in a Hong Kong chemist shop and by Professor O. Zdansky among his personal collection—might have been the forerunner of further problems. Indeed, Weidenreich suggests that Java Man, Peking Man, and the Giant of Kwangsi form a continuous line, with the Java Man as the earliest in the line; however, he was opposed by the proponents of primitive gigantism. To settle the debate, Von Koenigswald proposed that the Sinanthropus and the Gigantopithecus once coexisted in South China.[7] As for Pei Wen-Chung in 1956 at Lai Pin, also in the Kwangsi Province, he found some fossils which he declared to be those of Peking Man, but later he decided they were the remains of Homo sapiens.[8] This opened a debate which two decades later took a radical turn. In the mid-1980s, cladistic methodology[9] led P. Andrew, C.B. Stringer, and B.A. Wood to classify the Asian Homo erectus a species separate from the African type and to call for removal of the Asian Homo erectus from the main line of human evolution. But in 1992, Gunter Brauer and Emma Mbua's review of the cladistic method led Andrew Kramer to conclude that "today the question of Homo Erectus taxa and affinities remains in a state of flux."[10] Be that as it may, since this book is not intended to be an anthropological work, it will not deal further with such controversies.

Over long periods of time, geological and climatic changes caused the Sinanthropus to move north for hunting subsistence. Later, in the Mesolithic period, Homo sapiens appeared and started "a drive to the south which is a recurrent theme in Southeast Asian history."[11] On the way, distinctive gene pools were formed all over the region. The Australoid, Melanesian, and Indonesian groups were followed later by the Mongoloid type. The Negrito group remained in Java, Sumatra, Borneo, and the Celebes. This resulted, as Gordon T. Bowles has written, in a "human kaleidoscope."[12] According to Bowles, the Assamese, Burmese, Thai, Cambodian, Vietnamese, and Malayan groups share a common genetic heritage.

In the Neolithic period (c. 4000–2000 BC), horticulture appeared, along with some domestication of animals. As is evidenced by the development of pottery, China became the seat of two major cultures, the Yang Shao (c. 4000 BC) and the Lung Shan (c. 2000 BC).

The Yang Shao culture, which developed along the upper reaches of the Yellow River (Huang Ho) in what are now Shensi, Shansi, and Kansu provinces, is identified by the red color of its pottery, made out of red clay from the loess deposit. It differs from the pottery of the Lung Shan culture. The form and shape of the various pottery objects depended on their end use. For example, jars for indoor use had wide mouths and large necks while those for outdoor use, such as the transport of water from a distant river to a settlement, had small mouths, narrow necks, and handles on each side for easy manipulation. Later on, jars used as funeral urns for infants were exquisitely decorated. Painting, which reached a high degree of sophistication, was another factor in distinguishing Yang Shao culture from Lung Shan.

The Lung Shan culture was found in the lower reaches of the Yellow River, in what are now Hupeh, Shangtung, Anwei, and Kiangsi provinces, and in Honan, where it coexisted with Yang Shao culture. The alluvial clay which formed the plain was originally a dark green color. During normal firing it took on a hard black tone, but through special treatment, a dark grey color was obtained to make cooking pans. Only around 1 percent of the pottery produced was pure white. The creation of fine white pottery required excellent knowledge of the use of oxidizing and reduction in the firing process. Use of the potting wheel was widespread, and the Lung Shan potters were more concerned with unusual shapes than with surface decoration. They polished their pots, but never painted them. Funeral jars were not used. The dead were buried either in a prone position or on their backs with their heads oriented toward the east. They were surrounded by a few stones and jade objects. Although jade was common, objects made of bone predominated in Lung Shan culture, and ox and deer scapulae were used in divination. Shells were also used in Lung Shan culture, as scrapers and arrow heads, and in bracelets and pendants. Shells were used in the same fashion in Vietnam. During the Lung Shan culture, a mosaic of tribes inhabited China (Map 1). In central China, in what are now Szechwan, Kweichau, Hunan, and Honan provinces, the T'ai people grew rice and raised pigs and fowl. To the north, in what is now Inner Mongolia, Turks and Mongols bred horses and camels, and they raised wheat and millet through dry agriculture. To the west, in what is now Tibet and Kansu province, sheep were raised for food and wool. To the northeast, in Manchuria and what are now Hopei and Shantung provinces, the Tungusic people domesticated pigs and planted rice. Lastly, in the east, southeast, and south, in what are now the provinces of Anwei, Chekiang, Fukien, Kwangtung, and Kwangsi, the Yueh people lived by fishing and cultivating rice.

Gradual pressure from the turbulent Mongol tribes pushed the people in the north down to central China. And some T'ai and Yueh tribes from the areas of modern Kwangsi, Fukien, and Kwangtung moved further south, taking with

Map 1
Early Civilization in China

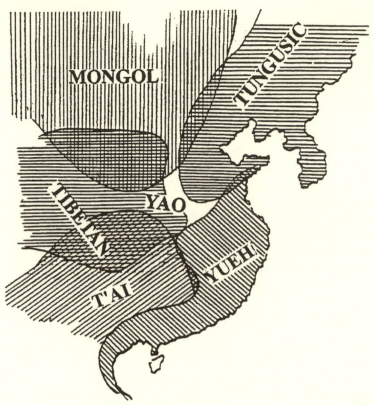

them much of their original culture. The T'ai went on to populate Thailand, Laos, and some mountainous areas between China and Vietnam. The Yueh, who settled down in the littoral plain in what are now Kwangtung-Kwangsi provinces and the Tonking area of Vietnam, were preceded by their awful reputation. To scare sea predators, they tattooed their bodies with fantastic representations of marine monsters and painted two eyes on the bows of their junks. They chewed betel, lacquered their teeth in black, and crushed rice with their bare hands. The Pai Yueh (Hundred Yueh), a branch of the Yueh, were probably the ancestors of the Vietnamese.

PREHISTORIC VIETNAM

According to Gordon T. Bowles "it is difficult to be precise about the people and history of Annam (*"peaceful south"*), now known as Vietnam."[13] The genetic pool was certainly affected by various intruding groups. The Vietnamese are biologically close to the T'ai and the Muong, and linguistically related to the Mon-Khmer. Their phenotype can be traced to Austroasian from the Sundaland (Malaya and Indonesia) and Chinese-T'ai Mongoloids who appeared in the peninsula. Later on, the introduction of Indian and Chinese culture also affected them.

The early man who lived in the mountainous regions of Langson and Ninh Binh (600,000 BC) was closely related to the Lan Tian Sinanthropus. Many of his Acheulean tools—stone shards and choppers—have been found in Thanh Hoa, in southern Vietnam (Map 2). Homo sapiens came to Vietnam around 50,000 BC.

Hoa Binh Culture

Later, in the Mesolithic period (c. 20,000–5,000 BC) in the province of Hoa Binh, early man dwelt in limestone caves near streams and rivers and indulged in gathering and big game hunting—he trapped and killed elephants and rhinoceri. He used one-sided stone axes, as well as cutters and scrapers of round and oval shapes and may have used wood and bamboo arrows for hunting. He also employed pebbles to crush roots and tubers and caught fish by hand. There are, however, no signs that he engaged in agriculture or animal domestication. The presence of Melanesian and Indonesian remains indicates northward drive.

Bac Son Culture

During the Neolithic period (c. 5,000–3,000 BC), the Bac Son civilization emerged. It is characterized by one-sided polished stone axes made out of volcanic rocks, coconut shells, calabash carapaces, bamboo arrows, and spears. During this period, woven bamboo baskets and bamboo trunks were used as containers and cooking pans. It is still used by the montagnards tribes in the highland regions. Pottery appeared, but its origins have stirred debate. To some, it "was assumed to be intrusive."[14] However, Nguyen Khac Vien asserts it was discovered as the result of a technical accident. To make their woven bamboo baskets watertight, they covered them with clay and baked them. In the process, the frame burned away, leaving only the shaped clay.[15] Fossils of dogs, buffalo, and deer dating from this period have also been found. And the large variety of skulls unearthed suggests the cohabitation of different groups, including the Austroasians, Austroloids, and Mongoloids. The genetic pool was therefore diversified.

To the South, in the Nghe An Province littoral, man was still hunting and gathering shells. Many graves have been found buried under fifteen-foot-high mounds of shells and indicate existence of burial rituals. The dead were buried in the fetal position, with their knees drawn up to their chests. They were surrounded by implements made out of basaltic rocks, and ornaments made of shells, bones, and baked clay beads. On cave walls in Hoa Binh, southwest of Hanoi, there are drawings of animals with human heads that are horned.

Map 2
Vietnam's Prehistoric Sites

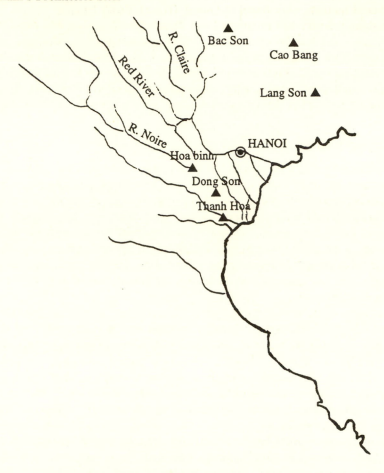

The Bac Son culture dominated the entire south, from the Yang Tse Kiang river valley to Laos, Thailand, Malaysia, Philippines, Borneo, Java, and the Celebes.

Phung Nguyen Culture

Between 3000 and 2000 BC, the Red River delta was settled. Wet rice cultivation was carried out in the region, and thousands of houses were clustered there. They were single-family houses constructed on piles for protection against jungle predators, mostly tigers, for which the descendants of the prehistoric hunters of elephants and rhinoceri seemed to have developed a very healthy fear. There are no traces of collective occupancy. Domesticated animals included poultry, oxen, pigs, dogs, turtles, and frogs. Obviously these animals were raised for food. Blowpipes with stone and clay marbles were used for hunting birds. Shell burial mounds were found in Quang Tri and Thanh Hoa.

The stone industry had progressed and included basalt, silex, and even jade. Axes were small in size—from two to five centimeters in width—and were polished on both sides. Rings and bracelets were of various shapes and colors, and woven bamboo baskets were decorated. Bone loom sticks and spools are indications that a weaving industry had developed. Ceramics of the period bore the "double SS" spiral decoration which later appeared on Dong Son drums.

Dong Son Culture

The second millennium BC was the bronze age in Vietnam, as is evidenced by the quantities of implements such as axes, plowshares, sickles, chisels, vessels, cooking pans, bells, drums, arrowheads, swords, knives, bracelets, and statuettes dating from that time. At this time, the first Vietnamese kingdoms of Van Lang and Au Lac appeared. Slash-and-burn agriculture was practiced in the highlands. In the plains, where water abounded, irrigation systems were developed. The Vietnamese continued to raise fowl, oxen, buffalo, pigs, dogs, turtles, and frogs. The presence of bronze hooks and baked clay sinkers prove the existence of line fishing.

Boats with rudders were carved out of forest trees. They were capable of carrying dozens of passengers. Kilns and potting wheels were used to produce large quantities of jewelry, pans, plates, and pots, some of which were painted. They were generally mass produced, with some specialization and division of labor. Agriculture produced enough of a surplus to feed the labor forces who transferred from the rice fields to the industrial shops. Bartering developed as a result of high productivity. The presence of Chinese daggers and cups indicates the presence of Mongoloids.

Men and women went barefoot and wore long hair coiled on top of their heads. Both men and women lacquered their teeth black, and men tattooed their bodies to deter sea predators. The people were totemist and animist, but unlike the Cambodians, they worshipped the linga as the god of fertility not as an incarnation of the god-king. During annual processions, they carried wooden reproductions of female and male sex organs which they threw to those in the crowd who yearned for children.

In Vietnam, as in China, crocodiles and cranes became the dragons and phoenix of mythology. Vietnamese kings bore on their thigh the tattoo of the Dragon, until King Tran Minh Tong put an end to this practice in 1323. On Dong Son drums, men are shown wearing caps made of crane feathers.

Two elements characterized Dong Son culture: hollow boot-shaped axes and drums. The famous Ngoc Lu drums are sixty-three centimeters high, and their faces are seventy-nine centimeters in diameter. On their faces, there are sixteen tracks, on which there are representations of houses on piles, flocks of birds and stags, and scenes of men hunting, fishing, harvesting, dancing, and playing the khene, a typical Lao flute. Vietnamese experts and their foreign counterparts disagree about the origins of the Dong Son drums. While some think they originated in China, Georges Coedes, a French scholar in the field of southeast Asia, believed that "Tonkin and North Vietnam were probably the center of diffusion of Bronze drums."[16] Le Thanh Khoi, however, cited Barnard's analysis showing that the proportions of the alloy differed. Chinese bronze had a higher copper content and a lower percentage of tin and lead. Moreover, the casting processes were different. The Chinese used molds, and the Vietnamese used the "lost wax" technique, also called "investment casting," which is used nowadays to make instruments of precision.

A central sun shining over human activities on the surface of the drums has been interpreted in various ways. Madeleine Colani, in *Recherches sur le prehistorique indochinois* states that the Dong Son drums are related to a solar cult.[17] Victor Golubew, in *L'age du Bronze au Tonkin et dans le Nord-Annam*, says they were used in funeral rites and symbolized the golden boat carrying the soul of the Dead to the Island of Paradise which rose in the middle of the Ocean of Clouds.[18] This is reminiscent of Khmer architecture in which Mount Maru stands in the middle of the infinite oceans. In present-day Vietnam, the Cao Daists still carry their dead to eternity over the oceans on "Bat Nha" junks. But, for some tribes in the Hauts Plateaux,[19] the sound of a bronze drum is associated with the Voice of the Thunder. Consequently, possession of such a drum is a sign of transcendental power, just as the nine bronze vessels were in China under the Chou dynasty.

THE FIRST RULERS OF CHINA

God Kings and Legendary Emperors

Shen Nung, the Chinese ancestor of Vietnam's Hong Bang, was the second legendary emperor of China and succeeded Fu Hsi, the first legendary emperor. Fu Hsi and Shen Nung marked the transition between the post-Panku era of god kings and the historic period of human emperors.

They came after the last god king, Sui Jong, who deserves mention because he is thought to have brought humanity out of the darkness of prehistoric civilization. He was considered the "inventor of fire," which he produced not through transcendental magic but by systematic observation of the sparks created by a bird pecking a tree. He rubbed wood against wood and created fire. He was also credited with having invented string knots used to make calculations.

Like Fu Hsi, Shen Nung was half man and half beast. Fu Hsi had a human face and the body of a snake tail, while Shen Nung had the head of an ox and a human body. To the Chinese, the ox was symbolic because of its association with agriculture, and it was the proper way to depict Shen Nung, who was the creator of agriculture. Shen Nung was originally from Hupeh and lived in

Ch'on, the imperial capital situated somewhere in Honan Province. For some time, he resided at Ku Fu, the birthplace of Confucius. Later he invented the plowshare and traveled a great deal to teach an early method of planting rice. He also discovered the properties of medicinal plants and established the dual Chinese concept of food and medicine. His book *Shen Nung Pon-tsau King*, the *Classic of Shen Nung Botany*, was to Chinese pharmacology what the later *Huang Ti Nei Ching Su Wen* was to Chinese internal medicine. But Shen Nung's book did not withstand the test of time and faded into the haze of oral tradition. Shen Nung was buried in Ch'ang Sha in 2705 BC and was succeeded by Huang Ti, his longtime associate.

Huang Ti, the first Chinese monarch completely human in appearance, was singled out by Shen Nung for succession because the latter had judged his own offspring completely inept. Although the dynastic concept was not an established tradition at that time, there was contest for the throne which was not settled until Huang Ti succeeded in beheading his opponent, Ch'i Yu, one of Shen Nung's sons. After winning this contest, Huang Ti prudently shared his land with other dignitaries. In doing so, he created a feudal regime. He was also a great inventor. He introduced mud blocks for building houses. This led to a sedentary mode of life for the Chinese, in contrast to the nomadic life of the Hsiung Nu. Huang Ti promoted the use of hieroglyphics, built an observatory to study astronomy, developed the Chinese calendar, and divided time in sixty year cycles. His interest in geology led to the discovery of the mystical properties of jade, which is still considered the most precious gem by Chinese. He probably directed the writing of the celebrated *Huang Ti Nei Ching Su Wen*, the *Yellow Emperor Classic of Internal Medicine*, which even now is used as a reference in Chinese medical schools.

Huang Ti erected the first temple for carrying out religious rituals with animal sacrifices.[20] His knowledge of the time for planting was essential for agriculture. His wife, the Lady of Si Ling, invented the art of raising silkworms, which, centuries later, contributed to the supremacy of Chinese silk on the international market. Not long before, in Fu Hsi's time, people wore animal hides. The weaving industry allowed Huang Ti to provide uniforms to his soldiers. This made them proud enough to overcome the nomadic Hsiung Nu. Under Huang Ti, the empire was significantly expanded. Since he was considered the historical Ancestor of China, there was a tendency to credit him with all sorts of deeds. Before his death in 2595 BC, he was supposed to have discovered a copper mine in the region of Honan. He is thus credited with predicting the coming of the Bronze Age in China.

His son, Shau Hau (2594–2511 BC), gathered no other credit than to have died at Ku Fu, the birth place of Confucius, but his heir, Chuan Hu, who reigned from 2510 through 2433 BC, appeared to have been a good ruler. He regulated the dynastic rites, upgraded the study of astronomy, which was an imperial prerogative since the emperor was the Son of Heaven, reorganized the administration, and extended the boundaries of the state. The court appointed Ti Ku as his successor. Ti Ku (2432–2363 BC) was not of royal origins, but was nevertheless highly praised for his virtues. He promoted music and founded schools, and his rule was a time of peace.

Then came Ti Chi (2362–2358 BC), Ti Ku's degenerate son, who did not last. After six years of corrupt rule, he was deposed by his half brother Yau, with the concurrence of the court. To be fair it must be said that Ti Ku's other siblings were even more successful. One of them, Ch'ong Tang, later founded the Shang dynasty, and another, Hou Tsi, founded the ducal house of Chou.

Yau (2357-2258 BC), along with Shun and Yu who succeeded him, were the three most revered Chinese rulers. In spite of all the catastrophes and calamities which beset China during their time, due to their celebrated virtues, it was nevertheless considered a Golden Age. The three of them were highly praised by Confucius and the great historian Ssu Ma Ch'ien and are still referred to nowadays as role models for monarchs. After seizing power in 2357 BC, Yau endeavored to advance the state of agriculture and to improve knowledge of astronomy, which was useful for the rice cultivation. Yau divided the year into 366 days. Unfortunately, his intimate knowledge of the heavens could not help him in dealing with certain problems on earth, and his efforts to overcome the intemperances of the Yellow River were in vain. By his own account, flooding was "embracing the mountains and overtopping the hills, threatening the Heavens." So in 2258 BC, under the strong advice of his counsellors, he gracefully, and perhaps gratefully, abdicated in favor of Shun, to whom he had once had the wisdom to marry his two daughters.

Although he had been enthroned because of his filial piety, Emperor Shun (2258–2206 BC) showed himself to be an energetic ruler. Since the ravages of the Yellow River were at the top of the government's agenda, he dismissed the officer in charge of the waterworks, the powerful Lord Kun, but he prudently retained Lord Kun's son Yu to serve in the same capacity. When Yau died, Shun observed three years of mourning, but he did not overlook the well-being of his subjects. At his palace, there was a board on which people could write their opinions about the policies of the government. There was also, at the entrance, a drum which people could beat to summon the emperor to hear, in person, their specific complaints.

Emperor Shun chose Yu (2206–2197 BC) to succeed him. His choice of Yu was a wise one, for Yu was not only a flood expert but also a totally dedicated public servant. During the fourteen years he was struggling with dikes and dams, he had not returned home once, even when working in the vicinity, he heard his children cry. In the process, he gained the titles of "Tamer of the Floods" and "Emperor of China."

China's history and heroes, its kings and emperors, served as role models for Vietnamese scholars until they were able to create their own fables. Thus, to celebrate royal virtue, they always referred to Yau, Shun, and Yu. Tran Hung Dao himself, in his call for struggle against the Mongols, also referred to various Chinese heroes of the Spring and Autumn Period.[21]

THE FIRST RULERS OF VIETNAM

As is indicated by Charles Higham, the third millennium BC saw small settlements and weak social organization in central Bac Bo (North Vietnam).[22] This period corresponds to the Phung Nguyen culture.

Traditional Vietnamese history begins with legends and myths that are still illustrated in children's textbooks. The legendary Chinese emperor Shen Nung (2838–2698 BC) had a great grandson, De Minh, who married an immortal in Honan Province. Later, De Minh appointed his youngest son, Loc Tuc, king of Xich Quy, a country that included Kwangsi, Kwangtung, and North Vietnam. Loc Tuc's son, Lac Long Quan, in turn married the daughter of King De Lai, Princess Au Co, who succeeded in giving him one hundred sons. De Lai was the Son of De Nghi, the eldest brother of De Minh. Since Vietnamese society was originally matriarchal, Lac Long Quan continued to live with his own mother, and the hundred sons were under his wife's care. But one day he told his bewildered wife: "I belong to the race of dragons, while you belong to the immortals. We cannot live together. So take fifty boys with you and go to the mountains. As for me, I will take the rest to the south sea." It was the first divorce case in the history of Vietnam and marked a radical transformation in society—the appearance of a patrilineal system.

Vu Quynh, author of the *Linh Nam Trich Quai*, a Chinese compilation of Vietnamese tales cited by Maurice Durand and Nguyen Tran Huan, gave a more detailed account of the separation.[23] Lac Long Quan and Au Co appeared to have been living together. After one year, she delivered a pouch of one hundred eggs, which the couple considered to be a bad omen and therefore decided to leave the pouch in the bush. From the hundred eggs emerged one hundred males who set out to join their parents. Despite the fact that they grew up without suckling, the one hundred male offspring presented a considerable challenge to their parents. Lac Long Quan was probably the first to throw in the towel. He deserted the entire family and went back to his sea palace to lead a more comfortable life. Au Co, who was left with no resources to support her numerous progeny, decided to go back to China, where she had come from. Unfortunately, at the border she encountered the Yellow Emperor, Huang Ti, who opposed the entry of Au Co and her one hundred sons.[24] Although they were intelligent and fearless, the hundred boys knew they would not succeed in fighting against the mighty Huang Ti and his army. They finally called Lac Long Quan for help: "Father, where are you that you leave us, mother and children, widowed and orphaned? We are all stricken with sorrow and distress." When Lac Long Quan arrived, Au Co said to him: "I am from the northern kingdom. I lived with you and brought forth a hundred sons. But you deserted me and went away leaving me with no resources to feed them and bring them up. Now we are without a father and without a husband." Lac Long Quan replied: "I am of the dragon race, and you are of the immortals. Water and fire are opposing elements. Even though the female element (Yin) and the male element (Yang) mate and produce children, they are different breeds and cannot remain together for long." As Au Co was well educated, she refrained from asking him why had he not said so before. Anyway, they parted, each with fifty sons. Lac Long Quan and his group went to the South Sea (Nan Hai). Au Co and her group of sons settled on Mount Phong, in what is nowadays the Bach Hac area of Son Tay Province. Before leaving, Lac Long Quan delivered a lecture to all his sons: "Whether you go up to the mountain or down to the sea, you shall let one another know if you run into difficulties, and you should, by no means, desert one another." It is probable that the hundred sons, who were scattered across the south of China were the Pai Yueh (Hundred Vietnamese).

The Hong Bang Dynasty (2879–258 BC)

Lac Long Quan gave his kingdom to the bravest of his sons, who took the title of Hung Vuong (Brave King). It was bordered by the sea to the East, by Dong Dinh Lake to the North, by the kingdom of Ba Thuc to the West, and by Champa to the South.

The new king, who founded the dynasty of Hong Bang, called it Van Lang. The capital was at Phong Chau, in Vinh Yen Province (Map 3). According to some scholars, the name Van Lang is derived from the ancient word "blang," the name of a bird that was a tribal totem. Today, some tribes still believe that their ancestors were birds—herons or cranes—and dancers adorned with their feathers are often depicted on Dong Son drums.

Social stratification began with the creation of a two-tier aristocracy: the civilian Lac Hau and the military Lac Tuong. The Bo Chinh were low ranking officers in charge of menial administrative work. The system still exists among the Muong tribes, substantiating their common origin with the Vietnamese. The Muong territory included Thanh Hoa, the traditional abode of the Vietnamese kings.

The Hong Bang dynasty lasted from 2879 through 258 BC. Its eighteen kings were all called Hung Vuong, and each one ruled for an average of 145 years. One may be tempted to question these figures and also to challenge Shen Nung's kingship, since he was alleged to have come on the scene in 2737 BC, after the Hung Vuong were in power. However, one must keep in mind that since man is endowed with the knowledge of his inevitable death, he might resort to myth to express his secret aspiration for immortality. As Bronislaw Malinowski explains it: "Myth, warranting the belief in immortality, in eternal youth, in a life beyond the grave, is not an intellectual reaction upon a puzzle, but an explicit act of faith born from the innermost instinctive and emotional reaction to the most formidable and haunting idea."[25] Anyway, the Vietnamese figures are quite modest compared to those of the Sumerians, whose kings Dumuzi and Enmenluanna reigned, respectively, 36,000 and 43,200 years. As for China, each of her thirteen heavenly emperors in the post P'an Ku period reigned 18,000 years.

Map 3
Van Lang

CHINA

Cao Bang

VU DINH

Tan Hung
(Tuyen Quang)

LUC HAI
(Lang Son)

VAN LANG
(Vinh Yen)

Thai Nguyen

PHUC LOC

Phong Chau

CHAU DIEN   VU NINH   NINH HAI
(Son Tay)   (Bac Ninh)   (Quang Yen)

DUONG TUYEN

Ninh Binh   GIAO CHI (Hai Duong)
             Hanoi

Gulf of Tonking

Nam Dinh

CUU CHAN

Thanh Hoa

HOAI HOAN
(Nghe An)

CUU DUC
(Ha Tinh)

VIET THUONG
(Quang Binh)

Quang Tri

The Kingdom of Au Lac (258–207 BC)

One may relate the origin of the Pai Yueh with Au Co's group. Following the family breakup, Au Co probably went over the mountains of northern Vietnam and settled in China's Kwangsi and Kwangtung provinces and founded the kingdom of Xi Ou (Au Viet). Its capital was located in Cao Bang Province (Map 4). The Xi Ou were also part of the Pai Yueh (Hundred Yueh), who expanded into the provinces of Chekiang (Dong Yueh), Fukien (Min Yueh), and Kwangtung (Nan Yueh). In the annals of the Warring States the Chao king Vu Linh refers to them as the "Xi Ou people wearing short hair, having body tattoos and black teeth."[26]

For some time, the Au Viet maintained trade with the kingdom of Van Lang, but it was a love-hate relationship which finally erupted when, in 257 BC, the Au-Viet king, Thuc Phan, marched on Van Lang. The last Hung Vuong was still in bed, sleeping off his wine, when Thuc Phan's troops stormed his palace.

Map 4
Tay Au and Van Lang

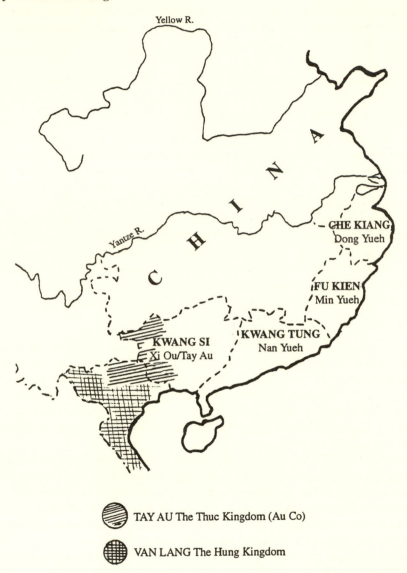

TAY AU The Thuc Kingdom (Au Co)

VAN LANG The Hung Kingdom

When he awakened, he had just enough time to drown himself in a nearby well. Thuc Phan then unified the two kingdoms under the name of Au Lac. He proclaimed himself King An Duong Vuong, and his capital was at Co Loa, near Hanoi. There he erected the famous Co Loa citadel, a formidable fortress with a base nine thousand yards in perimeter. It was surmounted by three spiral ramparts and was capable of warding off attacks by land and by sea. Huge quantities of bronze arrowheads discovered around the fortress suggest that many battles took place at Co Loa. Few details exist on Au Lac society. Some research suggests that the Au Lac economy was based on slavery, which enabled them to build citadels such as Co Loa and maintain a regular army for waging war, which was, in turn, a means for procuring slaves.

CHINA'S HISTORIC DYNASTIES

The Hsia Dynasty

Yu was the first emperor of the Hsia dynasty (1994–1523 BC). His fight against the Yellow River reached Herculean dimensions. He cut canals through mountains and slashed entire forests to give way to branches of the river, of which he had retraced the course. During his time, large regions became inhabited and living conditions greatly improved. He left sixteen successors who, with the exception of the last one, Kieh (1818-1766 BC), do not deserve historians' attention. Kieh's favorite concubine, Mei Hi, was the first on a long list of Chinese femmes fatales. The profligate life-style of Yu's successors reached such a degree of abomination that finally Ch'ong Tang, one of Ti Ku's sons, seized the throne and that marked the beginning of the Shang dynasty.

The Shang Dynasty

The Bronze Age marked the origin of metallurgy in China and the predominance of military weapons over agricultural tools. The Shang resided in the north of China, and An Yang was their capital. In its early years, the Shang dynasty greatly benefited from the faithful service of an excellent counsellor, I Chi. But after he died, things gradually went downhill. Unending conflicts divided the vassal states, and inundations of the Yellow River forced the Shang kings to move their capital.

Chou Sin (1154–1027 BC), the last Shang emperor who was evil beyond redemption, expedited the downfall of the dynasty. One of the reasons for Chou Sin's undoing was the incomparable beauty Ta Ki, whom he entertained in unprecedented fashion. In his palace, naked men and women frolicked around a pond that was filled with wine and was surrounded by trees hung with fresh human flesh. Among the forms of recreation, two were preferred: one was the "heater," a piece of incandescent metal that unlucky people were forced to hold; the other was the "bridge," a metal pillar covered with grease that was installed over a large pit of burning charcoal. The trick was to keep walking on the bridge. Chou Sin also practiced cannibalism on those who angered him: The dignitary Chiu Hou and his wife were chopped and pickled in wine after she resisted the emperor's advances. When Chou Sin's own uncle, the high counsellor Pi Can, dared to remonstrate, the emperor had him opened up alive to see whether his heart really had seven orifices, as it had been rumored to have had.

The murder of Pi Can led three powerful dignitaries, Kwei Kung, I Hou, and Wen Wang, to take action against Ta Ki, whom they held responsible for the emperor's perversions. To supplant Ta Ki, Kwei Kung had his pretty daughter introduced into the imperial harem. But she failed to please the emperor and the ploy ended in typical fashion: Kwei Kung's body was softened with salt and became culinary paste. As for I Hou, he was cut into hundreds of slices that were dried under the sun and became human pemmican. Only Wen Wang escaped death. He was sent, with his eldest son, Po I Kao, into solitary confinement at the Yu Li fortress. There, Po I Kao was cooked in a huge wok and served as soup to his own father. In full knowledge, Wen Wang ate the meal. After three years of captivity, he was released because another of his sons, Wu Wang, offered Chou Sin a rare beauty. Thereafter, father and son staged a coup and defeated Chou Sin in a bloody battle. According to the great historian Ssu Ma Ch'ien, Chou Sin set fire to his palace and perished in the blaze, adorned with all his jewels. He was so hated that Wu Wang shot three arrows into Chou Sin's corpse from his war chariot before getting down to stab it with his Turkish dagger. Only then did he sever Chou Sin's head and hang it on a white banner. So ended the Shang Dynasty.

The Chou Dynasty

Historians refer to Wen Wang as a virtuous and pacific ruler, more interested in improving the famous Fu Hsi trigrams than in governing his territory. These trigrams (Pa kua), which he changed into hexagrams during his imprisonment, are combinations of straight lines, which symbolize the male Yang and broken lines, which symbolize the female Yin (Map 5). Yang and Yin are the two cosmic components that interact constantly to produce all things in the universe. Wen Wang was also the author of the esoteric *I Ching*, the *Book of Changes*. This work, which is based on the esoteric interpretation of sixty-four hexagrams, is universally considered a masterpiece on divination. It actually holds enough moral and social substance to have been accepted by both the individualistic Lao Tse and the socialistic Confucius.

Wen Wang taught his subjects more peaceful methods of advanced agriculture. However, his gentle nature did not prevent him from being involved in the invention of the horse chariot, which was important in warfare. As Wen Wang was quite busy with a variety of interests, his son Wu Wang was the de facto ruler. Wu Wang officially acceded to the throne, as the founder of the Chou house Dynasty, in 1027 BC. He reorganized the system of imperial ancestor worship, and since all the protagonists belonged to the same patrilineage and were descended from Huang Ti, he bestowed on Chou Sin's son Wu Kong the title of King of Corea so he could resume his ancestor worship. This did not induce sincere submission in Wu Kong, for after the death of Wu Wang, he took arms against his heir, Ch'ong Wang.

Actually, the house of Chou owed its prosperity to a man who almost sin-

Map 5
Fu Hsi's Trigrams and King Wan's Hexagrams

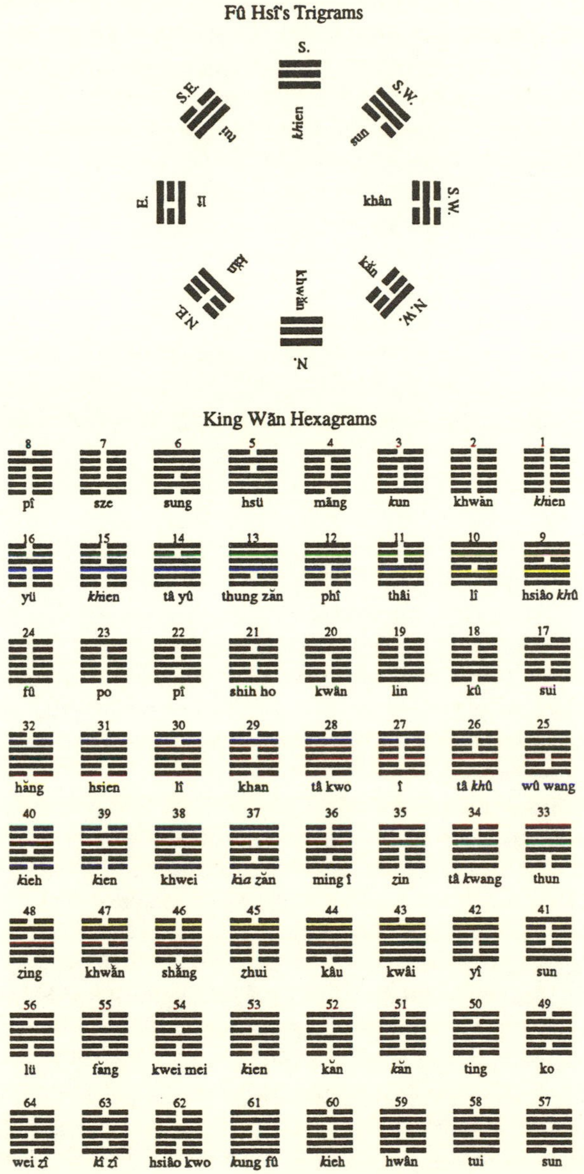

Fû Hsï's Trigrams

S.

S.E. ṭui khien sun S.W.

E. II khân S.W.

N.E. kân khwăn kăn N.W.

N.

King Wăn Hexagrams

8	7	6	5	4	3	2	1
pï	sze	sung	hsü	măng	kun	khwăn	khien

16	15	14	13	12	11	10	9
yü	khien	tâ yü	thung zăn	phî	thâi	lî	hsiâo khû

24	23	22	21	20	19	18	17
fû	po	pî	shih ho	kwăn	lin	kû	sui

32	31	30	29	28	27	26	25
hăng	hsien	lî	khan	tâ kwo	î	tâ khû	wû wang

40	39	38	37	36	35	34	33
kieh	kien	khwei	kia zăn	ming î	zin	tâ kwang	thun

48	47	46	45	44	43	42	41
zing	khwăn	shăng	zhui	kâu	kwâi	yî	sun

56	55	54	53	52	51	50	49
lü	făng	kwei mei	kien	kăn	kăn	ting	ko

64	63	62	61	60	59	58	57
wei zî	kî zî	hsiâo kwo	kung fû	kieh	hwăn	tui	sun

glehandedly built it from scratch: Chou Kung (the Duke of Chou), brother of Wu Wang. Recognizing that only immutability could warrant a viable dynasty, he set out to create a stratified society. He divided the nobility into five ascending hereditary ranks—barons, viscounts, earls, marquis, and dukes—to whom he allocated fiefdoms. Commoners were divided into nine descending categories from producers of grain, at the top, down to gardeners of fruits and vegetables, woodworkers and loggers, cattle and poultry breeders, craftsmen, merchants, housewives who made clothing out of silk, servants, and, at the bottom, unskilled laborers. Under the emperor there was a prime minister, or mandarin of heaven, who controlled the five branches of government administration: the Board of Earth (agriculture), the Board of Spring (rites), the Board of Summer (war), the Board of Autumn (justice), and the Board of Winter (public works). The fact that there was no board for foreign affairs is indicative of the early concept that China was "the world." Therefore there was no need for foreign relations as such.

In his journal, the *Chou Li*, considered a masterpiece on government organization, Chou Kung laid down a detailed blueprint for the life of the emperor as well as all his subjects. The prime minister, besides overseeing the five boards, determined the amount of tax and tributes for the imperial revenues and government expenses, both civil and military. He also organized the imperial household, including the expenses of the emperor, the empress, the crown prince, and the imperial harem. The emperor and, to lesser extent, all his subjects were to observe, in public and in private, certain codes of conduct, and were categorized by their dress, their gestures, their words, and their occupations. Even the emperor's meals were subject to rigid seasonal rules and were served only after being tasted by courageous servants. To preserve the virtue of ladies who might spend their entire lives in the imperial harem without being graced with the emperor's personal favors, eunuchs were introduced to watch over them. The eunuchs might not have succeeded in their moral duty, but their political intrigues brought about the downfall of many dynasties.

As for the common people, they were under the control of the mandarin of the earth, who regulated every aspect of their lives, including their occupations, taxes, religious duties, and marriages. For example, girls had to marry by the age of twenty, and no man could remain single after thirty. All these rules were designed to keep society morally clean. Even the emperor had to submit to the scrutiny of the Pau Shi, the high censor, who was allowed to reprimand him for misconduct.

The Mandarin of the Spring was the most important minister, for he was responsible for the religious life of the nation. At the court, astronomers systematically studied the movements of the sun and the moon in order to set up the calendar, and imperial astrologers speculated on the positions of the stars and planets in order to predict events.

Chou Kung was completely devoted to his brother Wu Wang. When Wu Wang was seriously ill, Chou went to the ancestors' temple and offered his life in return for the emperor's recovery. His appeal saved Wu Wang's life. Later, Wu Wang became suspicious of Chou Kung's popularity. To calm Wu Wang's fears, Chou Kung went into voluntary exile. Wu Wang, realizing his mistake, asked him back. After Wu Wang's death, Chou Kung went on to serve Wu Wang's son.

Wu Wang founded public schools at which students studied for lower-level and higher-level degrees. He sent his own son to study at such a school together with the children of commoners. Promotion to administrative posts was made by examination, without distinction of class or fortune.

The organization of the economy was based on the well-field system. The well-field was a square plot divided into nine equal parts. The eight peripheral squares were allotted to eight farm families who provided free labor for the cultivation of the central square, which belonged to the state.

In 1116 BC, Wu Wang died. The young age of his heir, Ch'ong Wang, was a good pretext for Chou Sin's son Wu Kong to plot and claim back the throne. He was defeated and killed, but his uncle Wei Tzi was granted the title Prince of Sung and carried on the ancestral rites. We shall see, centuries later, the celebrated Sung dynasty, but it was not founded by Wei Tzi descendants.

Ch'ong Wang died in 1079 BC, leaving the throne to his minor son Ch'ong Sang. From then on, the Chou dynasty was in a continual state of decline. A feudal regime can be effective only when the overlord has land to give away. But the Chou, by being too generous in the distribution of fiefdoms, ultimately found themselves only as strong as their vassals, who began to show signs of independence. Actually, most of the vassals had the right to contest central authority because not only did they belong to the same lineage, dating from Huang Ti, but they had also the military power to back their views. In addition, the monarch's rule was based on power and virtue. If he lost his power, virtue was the only thing left to allow him to carry on his mandate as the Son of Heaven. But Yu Wang, another evil monarch (781-771 BC), lacked virtue. He tied his fate with a schizophrenic beauty named Pau Ssi. This lady enjoyed the sound of silk being shredded by hand. So Yu Wang had one hundred bolts of rare silk brought to the palace everyday, and a team of maids specially chosen for their robust hands tore them into pieces. When Pau Ssi had had enough, Yu Wang took her up to the watchtower where a fire was supposed to be lighted only in case of emergency, to notify vassal troops when their help was needed. But Yu Wang started a fire anyway. When the vassal troops arrived and found out the fire was only for the amusement of the imperial concubine, they retired in great confusion. That made Pau Ssi laugh and applaud. Later, in 771 BC, when the Ch'uan Jung barbarians attacked, the vassal troops paid no heed. Yu Wang was killed, the imperial capital was sacked, and the beautiful Pau Ssi was taken to the harem of the Ch'uan Jung chief. The following year, when the Ch'uan Jung were defeated, Pau Ssi committed suicide.

To fend off further invasions, the capital was moved to Lo Yang, on the east side of the Yellow River. What became known as the Eastern Chou dynasty held no real power over its eight vassal states of Ch'in, Ch'i, Ch'u, Chao, Han, Wei, Yueh, and Yen. They were fighting each other for hegemony, if not for the imperial throne. Thus it is written in the *Spring and Autumn Annals*, the Confucian classic in which all actions—either good or bad—were reported in a laconic style, that during the Spring and Autumn Period kings ceased to behave as kings and sons ceased to behave as sons. However, his criticisms failed to restore the values he upheld. During the Spring and Autumn period, thirty-six kings were murdered, and fifty-two states were annihilated. The contenders continued to fight each other for another 260 years, until the Ch'in succeeded in destroying all of them. The unification of China by the Ch'in had a tremendous impact on the fate of Vietnam. General Chao To, who was dispatched by the emperor Shih Huang Ti to conquer Vietnam (Au Lac), decided to keep the country for himself. Hence, Vietnam's annexation was delayed, but its fate was sealed.

THE LONG ECLIPSE (207 BC–AD 939)

Under the Ch'in Dynasty (207 BC–AD 203)

Shih Huang Ti was the First emperor of the Ch'in dynasty. He left an indelible imprint on China. He replaced eight hundred years of Chou feudalism with an imperial system that was to last more than two thousand years—until the Republic was established in 1911 by Sun Yat-sen. The First Emperor, as he liked to be called, transformed hereditary fiefdoms into commissioned commanderies. To prevent any complications from the dethroned rulers of rival states, Shih Huang Ti moved them all to Hsien Yang, his capital, where they lived at his expense, and under his incessant scrutiny.

Shih Huang Ti resorted to oppression and persecution in order to carry out his immense reforms. He had as advisor the remarkable Ly Ssu, an outstanding promotor of the legalist doctrine, according to which people must be guided by law and not by ancient customs and must listen to the emperor rather than Confucius. Legalism led to the infamous destruction of books and records[27] and the ban on Confucian scholars. In 212 BC, more than 460 people were tortured and buried alive. Furthermore, millions of conscripts were sent to build the Great Wall, under the direction of General Mang T'ien, who reported that at least 300,000 died at the site.

In 207 BC, Ch'in troops headed by General Chao To moved to the south and established control over a territory that was later divided into three provinces: Kweilin (Kwangsi), Nan Hai (Kwangtung), and Hsiang (Vietnam). The Thuc put up a fierce resistance. According to legend, at first Chao To was unable to defeat the Thuc. He had to secure possession of a magic bow by sending his aide to woo the Au Lac princess, marry her, and steal the bow. After An Duong Vuong learned of his daughter's treason, he killed her and threw himself into the sea.

Vietnam lost its freedom for the first time. But the Ch'in empire was proceeding toward chaos. According to Ssu Ma Ch'ien, Shih Huang Ti passed away during a trip to Sandy Hill in search of the elixir of longevity. After his death,

the eunuch Chao Kao, tutor of Shih Huang Ti's younger son Hu Hai, in connivance with Ly Ssu, forged an imperial edict placing Hu Hai on the throne and
compelling the legitimate heir, Fu Su, to commit suicide. At that time, Chen
S'e, a private in the Ch'u army, began a mutiny which was to engulf the entire
country and drag in many prominent warlords such as Hsiang Yu and Liu Chi.
Although Chen S'e was poor and unknown, the empire "answered him like an
echo."[28]

In the south, Jen Hsiao, the military governor of Nan Hai, was terminally ill
and transferred power to Chao To. Jen Hsiao recommended that Chao To cut
off the new road to the north in order to prevent an invasion by the rebels. He
also suggested that Chao To proclaim an independent state.[29]

In the second year of Hu Hai's reign (208 BC), Chao Kao succeeded in eliminating his partner and rival Ly Ssu who was sentenced to the full extent of the
law, dismembered, cut in half at the waist, and exposed at the marketplace. As
for Hu Hai, he was nothing but Chao Kao's puppet, and Chao Kao finally forced
him to commit suicide. The throne passed to one of Shih Huang Ti's grandsons,
Tzu Ying, whose only merit was to conspire later in the murder of Chao Kao.

Chao To and Nan Yueh (207–111 BC)

As for Chao To, he wasted no time in acting. To Kweilin and Nan Hai, which
were already under his control, he added Hsiang (Au Lac). He proclaimed himself "Great Chief of the Man Yi" (barbarians) and also "King of Nan Yueh"
(Nam Viet). He moved the capital from Co Loa to Fanyu (Phien Ngu), near
Canton (Map 6). In an attempt to secure full independence, he severed all ties
with China, forsook Chinese culture, and dismissed and even killed all Chinese
employees appointed by the central government. He encouraged local customs
and favored interracial marriages.

Liu Pang (202–195 BC)

During the period that Chao To controlled Nan Yueh (203–111 BC), a shady
bondsman named Liu Pang found himself late in delivering a bunch of convicts
to a government penitentiary. Since the penalty for such a delay was death, Liu
Pang decided to stake everything in joining Chen S'e.

Liu Pang succeeded in taking Hsien Yang, the Ch'in capital, which had been
sacked by Ch'en Se's troops. He captured the young Emperor Tzu Ying, but
deliberately spared his life, leaving the dirty work to his superior, Hsiang Yu.
Hsiang Yu was a military genius, but no political expert. He readily fell into
the trap. He not only had the young emperor summarily executed, but also
burned the capital, destroying thousands of precious books and other cultural
treasures. According to some reports, he did more damage, in this respect, than
Shih Huang Ti himself. This gave Liu Pang a valuable pretext for criticizing
Hsiang Yu and destroying his prestige. The fighting which, in the end, erupted
between the two became an epic tale in which Hsiang Yu, an educated man,
was the hero and Liu Pang, a commoner, was the villain.

Map 6
Nan Yueh (Nam Viet) under Chao To, 203–111 BC

CHINA (Chïn)

\NAN YUEH (NAM VIET)

While Chao To was consolidating his power in Nam Viet, in China Liu Pang finally defeated his longtime rival Hsiang Yu. Liu Pang ascended the throne as Emperor Han Kao Tsu, the founder of the Han dynasty. Because of his humble origins, he was close to the common people and enacted simple laws that they understood, ordered tax exemptions, proclaimed a general amnesty, rehabilitated the victims of land dispossession, prohibited slavery, and demobilized troops. He appointed practical men to the government instead of using fast talking scholars whose erudition he despised, for he was illiterate. According to Ssu Ma Ch'ien, to mark his contempt for the scholars, Liu Pang publicly urinated in their hats. But his common sense was better than any political experience. He established a joint administration that was in part feudal and in part centralized, thus combining both the Chou and Ch'in systems. To secure his grip, he appointed relatives to rule fiefdoms, but he reduced their power by decreasing the size of their territories, which he surrounded by commanderies placed under his personal appointees.

Liu Pang made a vain attempt to subdue the Hsiung Nu in the north. But after one of his senior generals surrendered to the barbarians, he realized that negotiations were preferable. He therefore married a Chinese princess to Mo Tun, the Hsiung Nu chief, and he even consented to pay the barbarian an annual tribute.

In the south, Chao To had become the black sheep of the dynasty. He displayed total contempt for the emperor and did not show up at Liu Pang's coronation ceremony or send gifts or respects. Although the Emperor was not a man of good manners, he could not bear Chao To's insolence. So he decided to send an envoy to Nan Yueh. When the envoy arrived, Chao To was comfortably installed on his couch and did not even rise to greet him. At first, Chao To adamantly refused to listen to the envoy's good advice. He was politely told that unless he proclaimed obedience, the three generations of his family remaining in China would be executed in accordance with tradition. Since this involved a few hundred lives, including those of his own parents, Chao To hastily complied. As for Liu Pang, his imperial ego was satisfied. Thereafter, he turned to more important tasks, and Chao To was left alone.

When Liu Pang acceded the throne in 202 BC, China was in shambles. It had been exhausted by years of warfare. Hence horses had become a rare species. As a matter of fact, Liu Pang could not even find four horses of the same color for his coronation cart. For his troops, he was compelled to purchase horses bred in Mongolia at the price of 300 pounds of gold each and to pay 1 pound of gold for every 120 pounds of rice.[30] To make money, Liu Pang had to sell honorific titles to those who could afford to pay, i.e. rich merchants and speculators in iron and salt. This was the origin of his hatred for the merchant class.

Liu Pang detested profiteers at least as much as he disliked scholars, and probably even more since he forbade merchants to wear silk clothes, ride in carts, and hold office. He also taxed them heavily. Nevertheless, they grew powerful enough to serve as the emperor's economic advisors in later successions.

Liu Pang died in 195 BC leaving a minor son, Hui Ti, to succeed him. His enterprising widow, Empress Lu, who had her eye on the throne since the very beginning, became Empress Dowager. She wasted no time in putting her party in control and in enfeoffing as kings and princesses all members of the Lu family. But she stopped short of taking the imperial throne for herself, fearing the court's opposition. She also sent into confinement those ladies who had been favored by her husband, but for Lady Ch'i, Liu Pang's favorite, she reserved special treatment. According to Ssu Ma Ch'ien, "Empress Lu cut off Lady Chi's hands and feet, plucked out her eyes, burned her ears, gave her a potion to drink which made her dumb and had her thrown into the privy, calling her 'the human pig.'" That prompted Emperor Hui to tell his mother: "No human being could have done such a deed as this! Since I am your son, I will never be fit to rule the Empire.''[31] So shocked, he fell sick for an entire year. Then he disregarded the affairs of the Empire and spent the rest of his life drinking.

Despite these crudities, Empress Lu was a good administrator and was able to secure internal peace. But when she tried to control China's natural resources by prohibiting the trade of iron and gold products with Nan Yueh, Chao To's reaction was swift. He proclaimed himself emperor of Nan Yueh and invaded Ch'ang Sha, in what is now Honan Province. A punitive expedition sent by Empress Lu could not withstand the rigors of the tropical climate and had to withdraw from Nan Yueh. Chao To was not the only man to show disrespect to her majesty. When her husband, Liu Pang, died, Mo Tun, the impudent chief of the Hsiung Nu, sent her a fresh letter suggesting she forgo mourning and come to live with him. According to Ssu Ma Ch'ien, she died of a bite from a blue dog that was the reincarnation of Liu Ju-i, the king of Chao.

After her death, Emperor Wen Ti sent an envoy to Nan Yueh to demand that Chao To relinquish his title of emperor. Chao To, who had mellowed in his old age, humbly complied in the hope that his renewed allegiance could save his dynasty after he departed. Chao To's submission removed a weight from Wen Ti's chest for he would not be able to wage a war in the south against Chao To. At that time, the Han treasury was in serious difficulty. Wen Ti had to allow merchants to mint money, which was a disaster. Wen Ti was not able to control production, and minting money soon became a household activity throughout the empire. Ching Ti, who succeeded Wen Ti, continued the lucrative but dangerous sale of titles, which allowed the bourgeoisie to rise steadily at the expense of the decadent aristocrats. Then came Wu Ti, the Star Emperor.

In 141 BC, Han Wu Ti acceded to the throne and began his expansionist policy. First, the Hsiung Nu were subdued—however, only for a while. Then the conquest of the southwest, with roads built through the mountains, consumed more lives and money. The new province of Lak Lang in Korea was populated, at a high cost, with mass migration from China. A famine in Shensi Province also caused the migration of a large number of people to better lands. An enormous amount of money was spent to repair the Yellow River dikes and to dig new canals. When the Hsiung Nu rose again, the emperor had to reduce the expenses of his own table to pay for their submission. But the imperial treasury was soon depleted, and Wu Ti had to resort to various measures. He had his favorite white deer in Ch'ang Sha park killed. Their hides were cut into one-foot-square pieces and embroidered along the edges with silk thread. The hide squares served as currency, and each was valued at 400,000 copper coins.[32] Unfortunately there were not enough stags to keep the government budget balanced. All kinds of coins were fabricated, one after the other, until they were no longer marketable.

As a last resort, Wu Ti had to call for the cooperation of the merchant class. One salt broker, one iron speculator, and one merchant investor were appointed economic advisers. Magicians were also hired to set things straight with heaven.

But private minting remained a basic problem until the government withdrew the privilege and replaced it with a state monopoly. Moreover, each minister had his own reform plan, for matters from sheep trading to horse breeding. Price controls came last, with all goods from the provinces stored in the capital and sold by the government itself. Some ministers had sale stalls in the market. For those who silently disagreed with the government's policy, a new law was enacted to punish those who bore "disapproval at heart."[33] As a result, to stay alive, everybody heartily supported the government. Fortunately, China got out of economic difficulty soon enough to allow Wu Ti to complete his extraordinary expansion, putting the Han in control of Central Asia, including Bactria and Fergana.

Chao To's successors in Nan Yueh were pale reproductions of their forebear. Ever since Chao To resumed his allegiance, the Chaos relied more and more on Chinese protection. A family intrigue marked the end of the Chao dynasty. One of the later kings, Chao Hu (Trieu Van Vuong), sent his eldest son, Ying Ch'i (Anh Te), to Ch'ang An (Trang An) to be held hostage as a part of his tribute. To assuage his solitude on foreign soil, the young prince married Cu Ch'i, a Han woman of certain beauty but doubtful virtue, who allegedly gave him a son, Chao Hsing (Trieu Hung). Later, Anh Te went back to Nan Yueh to succeed his father. In the process, Cu Ch'i became queen of Nan Yueh, and Chao Hsing became heir to the throne. For the Vietnamese court, that was a bad move, for Ying Chi had originally had a Vietnamese wife and a son named Kien.

When Ying Ch'i died, Chao Hsing took over as Trieu Ai Vuong. The Han court sent an envoy with imperial compliments to the new king. But it so happened that the Chinese ambassador, An-Kuo Shao-Chi, had been Cu Ch'i's lover in the good old days. The king, the queen mother, and the ambassador felt so happy to be together that they decided to go back to China and give Nan Yueh as a present to the emperor. The plot was discovered by the Vietnamese chief minister, Lu Chia, and all three were promptly executed. Kien ascended the throne under the name of Chao Yang (Trieu Duong Vuong). He could last only if he did not have to deal with Han Wu Ti, the greatest ruler of the Han dynasty.

Using the murder of his ambassador as a pretext, Emperor Han Wu Ti invaded Nan Yueh in 111 BC. At that time, China had reached her apogee. Wu Ti has reverted to Confucianism in order to secure social peace. Confucian scholars flocked back en masse to staff the National University and the civil service. As for the people, they began to respond to the appeal of esoteric Taoism. Land taxes were reduced, but more state control was put on salt, iron, liquor, and coinage. The Great Wall was extended to protect new commanderies. The emperor finally subdued the northern barbarians, but only for a while. He conquered Korea in the northeast, and eastern Turkestan in the northwest. His next move would be for Szechwan and Kweichau in the west and Nan Yueh in the south. Foreign trade was developed with Central Asia via the famous Silk Road and reached as far as Greece and Rome. Actually, Wu Ti was also looking for allies against the Hsiung Nu. In this respect, he did not hesitate to use troops to force the loyalty of the kingdom of Ta Yuan (Fergana).

In 111 BC, after having installed new commanderies in Yunnan and Szechwan, the Chinese forces pushed further down and swooped over Nan Yueh. Trieu Duong Vuong lost his life in the attack.

Under the Early Han Dynasty (111 BC–AD 39)

Chiao Chou (Giao Chi Bo)

For the second time, Nan Yueh was under the control of China. It was now called the commanderie of Chiao Chou and was divided into nine counties, three of which were in what was formerly Hsiang: Chiao Chih (Giao Chi or Tonking); Chiu Chao (Cuu Chan or Thanh Hoa), and Jen Nan (Nhat Nam or Annam) (Map 7).

Han Wu Ti died in 87 BC. The allegiance of the Hsiung Nu provided relative peace, and Han Wu Ti's six successors relaxed their grip over the barbarians. The Silk Road lost momentum, external trade declined, and economic conditions worsened. Palace intrigues resumed among the consort families, in spite of the precautions that Wu Ti himself had taken. After he chose his heir, he immediately put the chosen heir's mother to death lest she should become like Empress Dowager Lu.

P'ing Ti ruled from 1 BC to AD 6 and left a one-year-old son, Liu Ying. This prompted Wang Mang, a nephew of the Empress Dowager Wang Chen Ching, to appoint himself regent. He then seized the imperial seal, the symbol of power, from the young boy and proclaimed himself emperor in AD 9. He founded the Hsin dynasty, which did not last because of violent opposition from a collateral branch of the Han, which thwarted his socioeconomic reforms. And yet he was sympathetic to the plight of the peasantry, and for them he promoted land revision. First he debased the currency, forcing the nobility to exchange their gold for copper coins. Then he set a standard land allotment, and those with land surplus had to give it away to their poor relatives or neighbors. Sale of land was forbidden.

In foreign policy, he succeeded in creating division among the Hsiung Nu tribes, and his efforts to establish peaceful relations with other non-Chinese peoples were quite effective. Unfortunately, unremitting floods from the Yellow River destroyed crops, causing famine and mass migration. The peasants, possibly encouraged by the Han contenders, burst out, looting and killing. It was the period of the Red Eyebrows, so called because they painted their foreheads red.

Finally, Wang Mang was defeated in 25 AD by Kuang Wu Ti, who was enthroned as the first emperor of the Eastern Han dynasty—so called because the capital was moved to the east, to Lo Yang. China was then in such terrible

Map 7
Chiao Chou under the Han, 111 BC

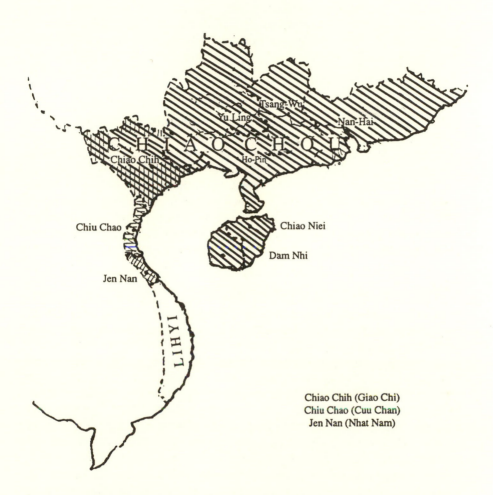

HAN EMPIRE

CHIAO CHOU

Yu Ling   Tsang-Wu   Nan-Hai
Chiao Chih   Ho-Pin

Chiu Chao   Chiao Niei

Dam Nhi

Jen Nan

LIHYI

Chiao Chih (Giao Chi)
Chiu Chao (Cuu Chan)
Jen Nan (Nhat Nam)

shape that the new emperor did not want to hear about it. But for the Vietnamese, the Wang Mang period was the origin of the first revolt.

The Trung Sisters (AD 40–43)

So far Chiao Chih had enjoyed relative independence under the Chao dynasty. But with the Han enforcing direct administration, the ruling power of the local aristocracy was threatened. The first Han governors were moderate, but when Wang Mang usurped the throne, thousands of his opponents fled to Chiao Chih.

They were mostly scholars who had to be employed in the Chinese administration and thus competed, on the job, with the local intelligentsia. The tax on salt
and iron had to be increased to pay for additional administrative expenses, and
land was seized from Vietnamese landowners to be distributed to the new immigrants. Moreover, the Han started an acceleration of sinicizing the common
people, forcing them to follow Han customs. Men had to grow hair, and women
had to wear pants instead of skirts. Shoes, wooden clogs, and caps were also
forcibly imposed on the population. Confucian morality was enforced, and marriages were arranged by parents, whereas they had once been decided upon by
the young couple. Worship of tribal spirits was replaced by veneration of Chinese deities. The Vietnamese people were exasperated.

In AD 40, the tyrannical governor Su Ting (To Dinh), attempting to quell
discontent, ordered the execution of a Vietnamese notable named Thi Sach. The
event triggered a vast uprising led by Thi Sach's wife, Trung Trac, and her
sister, Trung Nhi. In less than one year, they seized sixty-five Chinese citadels,
forcing Su Ting to take refuge in neighboring Nan Hai (Kwangtung). The two
sisters proclaimed themselves queens and established their capital at Me Linh
in the province of Vinh Yen. China appointed the fearsome Ma Yuan to deal
with the two women which did not enhance the Han's prestige. At Cam Khe,
the two sisters refused to surrender and chose to drown themselves in the nearby
Hat Giang River.

Under the Later Han Dynasty (AD 43–544)

Ma Yuan undertook the division of Chiao Chih into smaller sections, which
he placed under direct Han administration. Sinicizing started with the teaching
of Chinese agricultural methods—the use of plowshares drawn by cattle and the
practice of irrigation to improve land fertility. As for the local aristocracy who
were held responsible for past troubles, new legislation kept them away from
all economic and social decisions, which now were made by Chinese officials
only. To make sure Chiao Chih would not forget the lesson, Ma Yuan erected
a bronze column with the inscription "If this column collapse so will Chiao
Chih!" The popular reaction was clear—each passerby threw a stone at the
monument, which soon disappeared under a mound of stones. The first to oppose
Han rule were the minority tribes, the Muong, T'ai, and Man, who rejected
cooperation with the invaders and went to settle in the mountainous regions. As
for those who remained on the littoral, they adapted to Han culture one hundred
years later. As archeological finds show, the original Vietnamese bronze drums,
axes, swords, and jewelry disappeared, leaving room for Chinese artifacts, pottery and coins.[34]

Under Emperor Ling Ti (AD 168–189), the assimilation was deemed completed and Vietnamese were allowed to hold various posts in the Han administration. At that time, because of the appearance of the Yellow Turbans, there
was a need for more government officials. Many Vietnamese were therefore

appointed chiefs of Chinese prefectures, and a Vietnamese was even promoted to general in the Imperial Guard. But not all were collaborators. In 157, Chu Dat led a revolt of 5000 men in Cuu Chan, followed in 178 by Luong Long, who led a revolt of 10,000 men in Chiao Chou.

Shi Hsieh (Si Nhiep) (187–226)

While most governors acted as vicious despots, forcing peasants to go underwater to retrieve precious stones or up to the mountains in search of rare wood, some like Shi Hsieh (Si Nhiep) (187–226) found themselves the object of popular veneration. Shi Hsieh was an exceptional ruler, pacifist and tolerant, able to secure peace in a period dominated by the Yellow Turbans. He was also remembered for having introduced the study of classics in Chiao Chou.

The Chinese court was in turmoil because of imperial succession. Young consorts who bore no sons took recourse in black magic in order to subdue the emperor. Empresses dowagers, contrary to the tradition of primogeniture, chose only minors to accede to the throne. The intrigues resulted in many executions, injuries, and demotions for the defeated parties. Those still alive after such purges were exiled to Chiao Chou. Since the deportees were usually high ranking officials, this may explain, in part, the success of the Han assimilation in the south.

The last years of the Han dynasty were not happy ones. The economic situation, despite many reforms, failed to respond to the needs of the people. At the court, the power of the eunuch caused discontent among the high officials. In AD 126, a group of nineteen eunuchs were made nobles by Emperor Shun Ti for having helped him ascend the throne. The following rulers did the same for similar political reasons. But Ling Ti, besides having ennobled forty-two eunchs, set a dangerous precedent by naming one of them commander in chief of his army. All government offices were placed under the eunuchs, who were even responsible for the emperor's health care. So much power within a small group could only generate jealousy and conflicts, thus adding to the confusion in the empire.

The Chinese people saw all the troubles as signs marking the end of the mandate of heaven for the Han dynasty. Therefore, those who dared either proclaimed themselves emperors or supported others. The Hsiung Nu, who remained quiet for a while, joined the Yellow Turbans led by Chang Chueh, whose public exhortations had converted even the imperial palace guards. Soon, uprisings spread to the west, the north, and the east, with the Tibetan Ch'iang, who twice threatened the capital at Ch'ang An, the barbarian Wu Huan and Hsien Pi, and lastly the Man tribes from the south.

Ling Ti died in 189. His wife and his mother started fighting over who would succeed him. His eldest son, Liu Pien, helped by the eunuchs, ascended the throne, and the empress mother became Empress Dowager. The anti-eunuch party staged a coup. After fierce fighting inside the palace, all the eunuchs were exterminated. As for the emperor himself, he escaped from Ch'ang An and took refuge in Lo Yang. From then on, he was no more than a figurehead. In AD 203, overwhelmed by economic and political problems, Emperor Hsien Ti (190-220) relinquished the government of Chiao Chih to Shih Hsieh. Chiao Chih became the autonomous Chiao Chou.

But the Chinese empire was an immense battlefield for all kinds of warlords who, after putting away the Yellow Turbans, managed to exterminate each other. Finally the Han empire disappeared and was replaced by the states of Shu Han, Wei, and Wu. This was the celebrated period of the Three Kingdoms of war epics and romantic tales.

Under the Sui and the T'ang Dynasties (603–939)

During the Three Kingdoms Period, Chiao Chou was under Wu (Map 8), one of the three contending states. The skillful governor, Shih Hsieh, had easily obtained from the Wu king recognition of Chiao Chou. But in AD 226, Shih Hsieh died, and Emperor Wu Kuan (Ngo Quyen) refused to extend the same privileges to his son Shih Yu. Instead, he arbitrarily divided Chiao Chou into Kwang Chao (Quang Chau) and Chiao Chao (Giao Chau). Shih Yu started a rebellion and was defeated by Wu troops. Afterward, Kwang Chao and Chiao Chao were reunited as Chinese territory. For the third time, Vietnam was under direct Chinese rule.

Trieu Au

In 248, Emperor Wu Kuan appointed Luc Dan as governor of Chiao Chao. To uproot Shi Hsieh partisans and subdue the population, Luc Dan used barbarian methods that led to Trieu Thi Trinh's revolt. This twenty-three-year-old lady, had a long history of violence.[35] She had killed her mean sister-in-law, but had managed to remain on excellent terms with her sister-in-law's husband, who was her. brother With his help and under the name of Trieu Au, she built a retinue of one thousand soldiers. Despite her glittering golden armor and her massive elephant, she was defeated and gallantly committed suicide at My Hoa.

The Wu were of barbarian stock and were ruthless and rapacious. Their behavior, far beneath that of the civilized Han, finally led to another revolt. This time the Vietnamese killed their Wu governor and gave their submission to the Wei, who in turn lost it to the Tsin (Tan). Under the Tsin, conditions did not improve for the Vietnamese. The new dynasty had its own problems, including continual warfare between the north and south. In 317, after the Hsiung Nu invaded the entire north, the Chin moved to the east and became the Eastern Tsin Dynasty under Emperor Yuan Ti.

In 589, the Sui Dynasty was established. The unification of China was achieved, but the Sui emperor, Yang Ti, had grandiose visions. More than one million persons were coerced into building the Yun Ho, the Grand Canal,[36] which nowadays covers eight hundred miles, the distance between the Great Lakes and the Gulf of Mexico.[37] At colossal expense, the emperor changed his

Map 8
Chiao Chou under Wu (Nhat Nam under Champa)

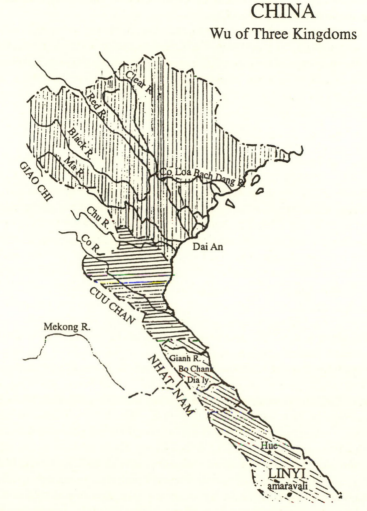

CHINA
Wu of Three Kingdoms

capital three times during his twenty-eight-year reign. From the original Yang Chou, he moved to Lo Yang, and ultimately to Ch'ang An. These extravagances and the ensuing popular discontent prompted the T'ang to overthrow the Sui.

The T'ang Dynasty

In 618, Li Yuan, the powerful governor of a northern province, and his son Li Shih Min, a reputed warrior, defeated the Sui emperor, Yang Ti, and founded the T'ang dynasty. In 626, Li Yuan died and Li Shih Min succeeded him as

Emperor T'ai Sung. Under him, China surged again as a puissant empire. The T'ang, unlike the Han, were a highly respected family of aristocrats whose access to the throne was unchallenged. Because of his personality, Li Shih Min exerted an extraordinary influence over friends and foes alike.

When he died in 649, Li Shih Min left the throne to his son Kao Tsung, aware that the latter was involved in a romance with Li Shin Min's favorite concubine, Wu Chao. Wu Chao had entered the imperial harem at the age of twelve and soon became the imperial favorite. Hence, to punish Wu Chao for her infidelity, Li Shih Min ordered in his will that she be sent to live out the remainder of her life in a Buddhist monastery. But the new emperor, Kao Tsung, took her back and bestowed on her the rank of empress. Since the young monarch was rather wet behind the ears, he was quite happy to have his wife carry out imperial tasks for him. Under the previous emperor, she had acquired much experience in the affairs of state. This arrangement contributed so much to Kao Tsung's health that he died relatively late, in 683.

Wu Chao succeeded Kao Tsung as "Emperor Wu." At first she was criticized by the court for her incestuous relations with father and son, but her reign was relatively calm and prosperous after she skillfully replaced high dignitaries with lower class officials loyal to her. In 705, at the age of eighty-one, she abdicated in favor of her son Chung Tsung and then passed away in the same year. Chung Tsung did not remain on the throne for long. His wife, who was anxious to emulate her mother-in-law, poisoned his breakfast. But she was outwitted by Li Lung Chi, one of Wu Chao's nephews, who seized the throne in order to install his own father. Later, Li Lung Chi reigned as the Emperor Ming Huang (712-756), a noted artist and lover.

Under Ming Huang, China experienced a Golden Age. Art and literature flourished with such great poets as Li Po, who was to become, by God's unfathomable design, the permanent pope of the Cao Dai religion in Vietnam, and Po Chu-i, who would cry in sorrow over the fate of an imperial favorite. She was the emperor's daughter-in-law, the ravishing beauty Yang Kuei Fei. Minh Huang fell under her spell. So he forced his son, Prince Chou, to divorce his wife and to let her settle in a convent as an unmarried lady. She was therefore eligible to enter the imperial harem. There she wasted no time in dominating the monarch, who was in his mid-sixties. In addition to placing her own relatives in key posts, she granted many imperial favors to an ugly Turkish general, An Lu Shan, whom she made governor of Liao Tung Province.

An Lu Shan, who had immense military power in his hands, revolted. He captured the capital, Ch'ang An, and forced the imperial couple to take refuge in Shensi Province. There the imperial guards mutinied. They accused Yang Kuei Fei of being responsible for the empire's predicament and asked for her head. Minh Huang had a difficult decision to make. He could either let Yang Kuei Fei go alone, or he could go with her. At the time, he was seventy-two years old and had amassed a mountain of wisdom. Thus, he opted to stay alive, even with a broken heart. The eunuchs took Yang Kuei Fei to a nearby temple where they strangled her with all due respect.

This sad event was the inspiration for Po Chu-i's immortal poem "Everlasting Wrong," and centuries later, popular tales continued to celebrate the two lovers. Even now, the plight of Yang Kuei Fei still troubles the Chinese soul. To be fair, it must be said that one of her greatest merits was to have set obesity as a canon of beauty, and probably during her lifetime, all the ladies of the court desperately tried to cling to the fashion.[38] Whether her tragic end inspired them or not, they all went back to the tradition of oriental frailty, "pale skin, moon face and boyishly slim figure."[39]

PATTERN OF RESISTANCE

To the Vietnamese peasant, Chinese domination brought nothing but trouble. After the Ch'in, the Han, and then the Wu, during the Three Kingdoms period, they were again under the Wei, the Chin, the Sung, the Ch'i, and the Liang. Each of those dynasties had its own dictates but the common denominator, except in a few instances, was despotic exploitation, which was carried out at different levels depending on the dynasty.

Vietnamese historians claim that the T'ang rule was the worst. A series of endless revolts seems to confirm their view. First of all, in 679 the T'ang arbitrarily divided Chiao Chao into twelve commanderies with fifty-nine districts, while Jen Nan (Nhat Nam) became a Chinese protectorate. To the north, to keep the Vietnamese in check, they installed the new commanderie of Man Chau, inhabited by the Muong, who were not so friendly to the Vietnamese although they were of the same stock.

Thus, a pattern of resistance toward China developed. The revolt of the Trung Sisters and of Trieu Au had shown that Vietnam had the will and the capability to fight for freedom. From then on, the Vietnamese would take advantage of any Chinese weakness to get rid of their domination. The political disintegration of the empire after the Han and the bureaucratic errors of each following dynasty served their purposes.

At the end of the Eastern Chin Dynasty, a Vietnamese named Lo Tuan revolted in the Red River delta. He had to kill himself after his junks were burned to ashes by the Chinese. In 468, Ly Truong Nhan slaughtered several Chinese officers and proclaimed himself governor of Chiao Chao. He died the following year, and the Chinese had to confirm his cousin, Ly Thuc Hien, in his office. But they defeated Ly Thuc Hien a few years later.

Ly Nam De (548–549)

Since the time the Vietnamese first lost to the Chinese, in 207 BC under the Ch'in, 750 years had passed. Thanks to Chao To, Chinese culture was forsaken and the Chinese immigrants adopted local customs and became more and more Vietnamese. But later, when the Han and the T'ang sinicized the local people, the Vietnamese aristocracy became more and more Chinese. This explains, in part, the case of Ly Bon, a Vietnamese subject who was Chinese by birth and became first king of Nam Viet.

At the end of the Wang Mang period, Ly Bon's ancestors fled to Nan Yueh (Nam Viet) where they remained for seven generations. In 502 AD, the Liang emperor Wu Ti appointed Tieu Tu governor of Chiao Chih. Tieu Tu introduced higher taxes, conscription, and mobilization. In 541, Ly Bon revolted, and in 544, he proclaimed himself Ly Nam De, Emperor of Nam Viet. He called Vietnam "Van Xuan" ("Ten Thousand Springs") and built up an administration and a court. His kingdom covered the entire delta of the Red River from Langson down to the Hoanh Son border with Lin Yi (Champa). On that land, the future Dai Viet would emerge. Three years later, Ly Nam De was defeated by the Liang general Chen Pa Sieu. Ly Nam De retreated to Laos where he was murdered by Lao barbarians, who sent his head to Chen Pa Sieu. After Ly Nam De's death, his cousin Ly Thien Bao, who had fled with him, took over as King Dao Lang Vuong. In 555, Dao Lang Vuong died, and Ly Phat Tu, another one of Ly Nam De's aides, took power as Hau Ly Nam De (Later Ly Nam De).

Trieu Viet Vuong (549–571)

In Nam Viet, one of Ly Nam De's lieutenants, Trieu Quang Phuc, to whom Ly had relinquished the power before he retreated, continued to fight against Chen Pa Sieu until the latter was called back to China to deal with another rebellion. That gave Trieu Quang Phuc the opportunity to crush Pa Sieu's lieutenant, Duong San. Trieu Quang Phuc retook Long Bien citadel and proclaimed himself Trieu Viet Vuong. Now Nam Viet had two kings: Hau Ly Nam De and Trieu Viet Vuong.

Hau Ly Nam De (571–602)

After several encounters, the two parties agreed to share the land. Emperor Hau Ly Nam De agreed to settle at O-dien in the province of Hadong, while King Trieu Viet Vuong remained at historic Long Bien. To reinforce the alliance, Trieu Viet Vuong married his daughter to Ly Nam De, whose gratitude would be to lead a surprise attack against his father-in-law. Trieu Viet Vuong was defeated and drowned himself in the Dai Nha River, in the province of Nam Dinh. As he had been a good monarch, a temple was erected in his honor.

At that time, China was beginning to show signs of upheaval. The Sui emperor Yang Ti had exhausted the patience of his subjects. The construction of the Grand Canal had cost an enormous amount in both money and lives. Furthermore, Yang Ti's Korean war was a monumental failure.

Ly Nam De, who was well informed about the situation in China but misjudged the weakness of the Sui, revolted in 602. He was defeated and died in captivity in China.

Ly Tu Tien (687)

In addition to being forced to pay taxes on salt and iron and on products such as ivory, rhinocerous horns, and pearls, peasants also had to provide from twenty to fifty days of corvée per year. Minority tribes often had to exchange an ox or a horse for a measure of salt. As a result, a T'ai chief, Ly Tu Tien, led a revolt in 687, but it was in vain. Rebellions that followed it, however, picked up momentum and led to the dawn of independence.

Mai Hac De (722)

During the T'ang period, Vietnamese uprisings grew in number. In 722, Mai Thuc Loan, a native of the province of Ha Tinh, revolted and took over the district of Nam Duong in Nghe An Province. There he built many fortresses and, because of his dark complexion, proclaimed himself Mai Hac De (Black Emperor). He was defeated by the Chinese and took refuge in the mountains, where he died.

Phung Hung (791)

In 791, the T'ang emperor Te Tsung's governor, Cao Chinh Binh, because of his abusive tax increases, triggered an insurrection. It was led by Phung Hung, a man from the province of Son Tay. Cao Chinh Binh probably succumbed to a cardiac arrest when the Vietnamese population stormed his palace. The emergence of Phung Hung was short-lived, for he soon passed away. His son Phung An surrendered because of the numerical superiority of the Chinese.

Khuc Thua Du (906–923)

The Chinese empire then returned to a state of confusion. 907 through 960 was an incredible period in which it seemed as if China had invented the revolving door, through which each past dynasty made a comeback, tried its luck, and left. It was the time of the Five Dynasties: the Later Liang came first and were followed by the Later T'ang, Later Chin, Later Han and Later Chou.

In 906, a serious movement in Chiao Chao took advantage of the turmoil in China. It had the basic ingredient for success: a general consensus. In Hai Duong Province, Khuc Thua Du, who was renowned for his wealth and his benevolence, was chosen by the Vietnamese people to replace the Chinese governor, who graciously relinquished his powers, for his emperor was of no help to him.

But after the fall of the T'ang Dynasty the Later Liang resumed Chinese domination by appointing Liu An as pacificator of the south and governor of

Kwang Chao and Chiao Chao. At that crucial moment, Khuc Thua Du died, leaving power to his son Khuc Hao.

Khuc Hao (907–917) was a wise ruler. He reorganized the administration, built roads, and sent his son, Khuc Thua My, as ambassador to Kwangsi in order to secure an alliance against the Chinese. Soon after the death of Liu An, a discord with the Later Liang gave his successor, Liu Kung, a pretext for proclaiming his independence as emperor of Nam Han (Southern Han). Later, Liu An compelled Khuc Thua My to pay him tribute. But Khuc Thua My preferred to give his allegiance to the Liang. In 923, Liu An retaliated by attacking Chiao Chau where he captured Khuc Thua My and replaced him with his own governor.

In 931, one of Khuc Hao's former officers, Duong Dien Nghe, overthrew the Nam Han domination and ruled as governor of Chiao Chau until he was assassinated by his lieutenant, Kieu Cong Tien, in 937. The Khuc Thua Du period was the prelude to Vietnamese independence.

NOTES

1. So called, for animal bones are part of Chinese pharmacopeia.

2. Cheng Te K'un, *Archeology in China* (Cambridge, Eng.: W. Heffer, 1989), pp. 17, 18.

3. Chong Key Ray, *Cannibalism in China* (Wakefield, NH: Longwood 1990), p. viii.

4. Gordon T. Bowles, *The People of Asia* (New York: Charles Scribner's Sons, 1977), p. 51.

5. Cheng Te K'un, *Archeology in China*, p. 15.

6. Bowles, *The People of Asia*, p. 48.

7. Cheng Te K'un, *Archeology in China*, p. 15.

8. Ibid., p. 37.

9. A methodology based on phylogenetic classification promoted by Willi Henning and Izaak Walton.

10. Andrew Kramer, *American Journal of Anthropology* 91: 1 (1993): 163.

11. Brian Harrison, *Southeast Asia: A Short History*, 3rd ed. (New York: St. Martin's Press, 1966), p. 4.

12. Bowles, *The People of Asia*, p. 189.

13. Ibid., p. 194.

14. Ibid., p. 205.

15. Nguyen Khac Vien, *Histoire du Vietnam* (Paris: Editions Sociales, 1974), p. 14.

16. Georges Coedes, *The Indianized States of Southeast Asia* (Honolulu: East West Center Press, 1964), p. 7.

17. Madeline Colani, *Recherches sur le prehistorique indochinois* (Hanoi: BEFEO, 30, 1939), pp. 299–422.

18. Victor Golubew, *L'age de Bronze au Tonkin et dans le Nord-Annam* (Hanoi: BEFEO, 1929), pp. 1-46.

19. Mountainous regions of Indochina populated by minorities tribes.

20. Since his Classic of Internal Medicine (*Huang Ti Nei Ching Su Wen*) shows a thorough knowledge of human anatomy, he was probably involved in human sacrifices.

21. *Binh Thu Yeu Luoc* (*Essential of Military Arts*) proclamation.

22. Charles Higham, *The Archeology of Mainland Southeast Asia* (Cambridge: Cambridge University Press, 1989), chronological table, p. xvi.

23. Maurice Durand and Nguyen Tien Huan, *An Introduction to Vietnamese Literature* (New York: Columbia University Press, 1985), p. 2.

24. Lac Long Quan was Au Co's cousin. Obviously incest taboos existed at that prehistoric time and Huang Ti's act symbolized the opposition of the society to incest.

25. Bronislaw Malinowski, *Magic, Science and Religion* (Prospect Heights, Ill. Waveland Press Inc, 1992), p. 110.

26. Gian Chi and Nguyen Hien Le, trans., *Chien Quoc Sach* (Los Angeles: Dai Nam, n.d.), p. 458.

27. Except works on medicine, agriculture, and divination.

28. C.P. Fitzgerald, *China: A Short Cultural History*, 3rd ed. (New York: Praeger, 1950), p. 150.

29. Burton Watson, *Records of the Grand Historian* (New York: Columbia University Press, 1961), vol. 2, pp. 239, 240.

30. Fitzgerald, *China*, p. 161.

31. Watson, *Records*, vol.1, p. 323.

32. Fitzgerald, *China*, p. 166.

33. Watson, *Records*, vol. 2, p. 96.

34. Pham Van Son, *Viet Su Tan Bien* (Los Angeles: Dai Nam, n.d.), B–I, p. 196.

35. Trieu Au was reputed to have had "three meter long" breasts that she carried on her back, over her shoulder. Ngo Si Lien, *Dai Viet Su Ky Toan Thu* (Los Angeles: Dai Nam, n.d.), p. 173.

36. The Grand Canal connects the Yellow River to the Yangse River.

37. Karl A. Wittfogel, *Oriental Despotism* (New Haven: Yale University Press, 1957), pp. 33, 40.

38. C. P. Fitzgerald, *History of China* (New York: American Heritage Publishing Co., 1969), p. 103.

39. Ibid.

2

THE INDIANIZED
NEIGHBORS

In the third century BC, Vietnam, under the name of Au Lac, emerged as an independent state. It was probably the first such state in the Indo-Chinese peninsula. Although the entire region was at one time or another under China's domination, only two countries, Vietnam and Yunnan, adopted Chinese culture. But while Yunnan became completely absorbed by China, Vietnam followed a long, arduous journey toward independence. The other Indo-Chinese kingdoms were under the influence of Indian religions before splitting between Buddhism and Islam. The various Indianized states were incapable of living together in harmony and fought among themselves and against others. This was the cause of their eclipse, but the world is indeed grateful for their contributions to the culture of Southeast Asia.

LIN YI (CHAMPA)

According to Cham tradition, Lady Po Nagar was the builder of the Cham nation. She was born into a farmer family in the Dai An Mountains of Khanh Hoa Province. With the assistance of spirits, she hid in a piece of sandalwood which drifted across the sea toward China. There, she married a royal heir and bore two children. Later she went back to Champa, and there she founded the Cham nation, of which she was the first queen.

At the beginning of the first century, a Javanese named Houen Houei, who brought with him the cult of Vishnu, married the queen of Lieou Ye, who may have been Lady Po Nagar, and founded the kingdom of Lin Yi (Lam Ap), later called Champa (Chiem Thanh), around Chau Doc (South Vietnam). Soon pressure from the neighboring Chen La, whose citizens worshipped Siva, drove the kingdom of Lin Yi to the north where it bordered on the Vietnamese district of Nhat Nam. At that time, Lin Yi was known to the Chinese as the district of Tuong Lam (Forest of Elephants). In 102, during the Eastern Han

Dynasty, the Chinese had to install an administration in Tuong Lam to protect Nhat Nam against incursions from Lin Yi.

At the end of the Han Dynasty, in AD 192, Khu Lien, a native of Tuong Lam, slew the Chinese prefect and proclaimed himself king of Lin Yi. His territory extended from south of modern Hue down to Cam Ranh Bay. Later, in the ninth century, it was expanded westward over the Annamite Chain and bordered on southern Laos and northern Chen La.

The Cham people had dark complexions, protruding noses, deep eye sockets, and curly hair. They were extremely clean, and they washed and perfumed their bodies many times a day with camphor and musk. They wrapped a single cotton cloth around their bodies and walked barefoot, save the wealthy and the aristocracy who wore shoes. They wore necklaces and earrings of metal loops. They were irascible and had the fearful reputation for practicing both homeopathic and contagious magic.[1] In earlier times, they dwelled in trees and lived by fishing. Later, they built houses and grew rice, red peppers, bananas, coconuts, sugarcane, and betel nuts. From the fiber of various plants, they produced excellent ropes, mats, and baskets. As fish was the main part of their diet, they became hardy seamen—they excelled at trading, fishing, and pirating. They were animist, and had no specific ancestor cult. Their dead were burned at the river's edge, and the ashes and bones were thrown into the water. Mourning consisted of a onetime haircut. Widows who decided not to remarry would neither cut nor comb their hair. Cham society was matriarchal, and women had the right of inheritance. But such rights were immaterial, at least for the aristocracy, since widows had to follow their dead husbands onto the pyre, in accordance with Indian traditions.

The scarcity and barrenness of their land drove the Cham toward expansion at the expense of their neighbors. Their long struggle with the Vietnamese proved to be particularly fatal. After fifteen centuries of striving for wealth and supremacy, they disappeared, leaving behind a culture that is now part of Vietnam's heritage.

In 270, during the period of the Northern and Southern Dynasties in China, T'ao Huang, the Chinese governor of Chiao Chou, reported that the king of Lin Yi, Fan Hsiung (Pham Hung), kept raiding his domain with the assistance of Funan. In 284, King Fan Tat (Pham Dat) sent the first Cham embassy to the Eastern Chin emperor. In 336, at Fan Tat's death, his commander in chief, Fan Wen, seized the throne. The Cham capital was then Amaravati, which was probably in the region of Hue. In 340, Fan Wen dispatched an envoy to China to ask for the fiefdom of Chiao Chou. Because his request was denied, he seized Jen Nan in 347. He perished two years later during another expedition. In 353, his successor, Fan Fat (Pham Phat), was severely defeated by the Chinese governor of Chiao Chou, who succeeded in taking back Jen Nan after having destroyed fifty Cham forts. In 380, Fan Fat's successor, Fan Hu Ta (Pham Ho Dat), took the reign name of Bhadravarman I[2] and moved the capital to Indrapura (Tra Kieu) in Quang Nam. He built temples and palaces, all oriented to

Map 9
Champa and Chen La

the north, on high ground at Mi Son and Tra Kieu. The material, which consisted of fresh clay bricks joined with molasses, was fired until total hardness was achieved. Stones were not used for construction and were only used in decorations by the Cham, who were outstanding sculptors. Only a few sites that serve as evidence of the Indian style of Cham culture remain in Vietnam. They include Po Nagar (Nha Trang), Panduranga (Phan Rang), and Indrapura (Quang Nam) (Map 9). Under Fan Hu Ta, Champa became an important state. In 399, as the pattern of driving north had become a Cham tradition, Fan Hu Ta went up to seize the Vietnamese provinces of Nhat Nam and Cuu Chan. He built Cham towers along the coast from Phan Rang to Da Nang. From 405 through 413, Fan Hu Ta continued to fight against the Chinese governor Do Tue. At their last encounter, Fan Hu Ta disappeared without a trace, after having lost his general, Fan Kin (Pham Kien), and one hundred men.

His successor, Fan Yang Mah (Pham Duong Mai), resumed destruction along the coast of Vietnam. In 425, for the first time, Chiao Chou, under Do Tue, took the initiative and invaded Linyi. Do Tue's troops caused enormous destruction. They took prisoners and forced Fan Yang Mah and the people of Linyi to pay an annual tribute. Yet in 433, the irrepressible Fan Yang Mah took no shame in asking China for the territory of Chiao Chou. Brutally rebuked, Fan Yang Mah and the Chams then turned against their protectors, the Khmer, and in the mid-fourth century annexed the Khmer district of Panduranga (Phan Rang). Later they cast desolation over Angkor, which caused an irreversible split and turned friendly Funan (Cambodia) into an implacable foe.

In 446, annoyed by the Chams' bellicosity, Sung troops moved down on Linyi. This punitive expedition, under Governor T'ang Ho Chih, brought about unexpected results. The Chinese discovered a 50-ton Buddha statue made of solid gold and took it away. The Cham king died of a broken heart for having lost it and was succeeded by a few rulers whose reigns were not significant. In 529, Rudravarman I was on the throne. He was the lineal descendant of a king who had abdicated decades before in order to enter a Buddhist monastery. In 543, Rudravarman invaded Nam Viet, but was beaten off by Ly Bon. One of Rudravarman's successors, Indravarman II, chose Indrapura as his capital. Since he was not related to Vikrantavarman, he proclaimed that "he assumed the sovereignty of Champa solely by means of destiny and thanks to the merits he acquired in numerous previous existences."[3] His rule was a peaceful one and was devoted to the erection of numerous monasteries and temples. His successors seemed to have maintained the status quo until 950, when Indravarman III defeated a Khmer invasion in the vicinity of Kauthara (Nha Trang).

In 979, taking advantage of the demise of the Vietnamese king Dinh Tien Hoang and his son, who were assassinated by their palace officer, the Champa king Paramesvaravarman sent a naval expedition against Dai Co Viet (Viet Nam). A storm prevented him from landing, but when the new king, Le Dai Hanh, dispatched an envoy to Champa, Paramesvaravarman put the messenger in prison. In 982, Le Hoan retaliated by killing the Cham king and destroying Indrapura. Indravarman IV, who succeeded to the Cham throne, left Indrapura (Quang nam) for the safety of Vijaya (Qui Nhon), in the south. Champa was forced to resume paying tribute to Dai Co Viet.

After the passing of Indravarman IV, a Vietnamese named Luu Ke Tong (Lieou Ki Tsong) seized power and proclaimed himself king of Champa. The accession of this alien ruler caused a mass migration of the Cham population to South China.

In 988, in Vijaya, when Luu Ke Tong died, the Cham enthroned one of their own as King Harivarman II. Harivarman II came back and settled in Indrapura. He began his reign under peaceful auspices. He built temples, paid his tributes, and exchanged prisoners with Dai Co Viet (Map 10). But later on Cham raids resumed, putting an end to the ephemeral peace. In 1000, his successor, Harivarman III, moved back to the more secure Vijaya (Qui Nhon). Harivarman III left no significant trace during his ten-year rule. In 1021, he was succeeded by Paramesvaravarman II. At that time, relations with Dai Co Viet were so bad that Crown Prince Ly Phat Ma, the future Ly Thai Tong, led an invasion of Champa. In 1042, the new Cham king, Jaya Simhavarman II, resumed raids

Map 10
Dai Co Viet and Champa (Champa under Harivarman II)

against Dai Co Viet. In 1044, King Ly Thai Tong returned to Champa at the head of a sea expedition. After capturing Vijaya, he put Simhavarman II to death and took back to Dai Co Viet Simhavarman's entire harem. His successor, Jaya Paramesveravarman I, who was more congenial, learned a good lesson from his predecessor's death. He kept sending regular tributes to Dai Co Viet and China.

In 1061, Rudravarman III (Che Cu) took the throne and established a good relationship with Dai Viet.[4] But in 1068, he unleashed his troops against the Vietnamese. Ly Thanh Tong's riposte was devastating. The Cham forces were destroyed, and Vijaya was set on fire. Rudravarman fled into Angkorian territory, where he was followed and captured. He was taken to Dai Viet as a prisoner and later obtained his release against the transfer of the three provinces of Ma Linh, Bo Chinh, and Dia Ly (now the provinces of Quang Binh and Quang Tri) (Map 11). This event marked the first step in Vietnam's official "March to the South" policy.

There are no records of the return of Rudravarman III to his throne, but in 1074, there was a Prince Thang, king of Champa, who took the name of Harivarman IV. Although he had some success in fighting the Vietnamese and the Khmers, he ended up paying tribute to the former. As he had done his share on the military field, he spent the rest of his life "restoring Champa to its ancient

Map 11
Dai Viet with the Ly, First Conquest of Champa, 1069

splendor''[5] by supporting old temples with generous donations. One year before he died, he enthroned his nine-year-old son, who was later forced out by his own uncle. In 1086, the young boy came back as King Jaya Indravarman II (Che Ma Na). He later followed the bad advice of a Vietnamese renegade named Ly Giac and attempted to recover the three provinces once yielded to Dai Viet by Che Cu. He was able to keep them for only a few months and was finally defeated by the seventy-year-old Marshall Ly Thuong Kiet. Since that time the three territories have belonged to Vietnam.

Jaya Indravarman II died in 1113. He was followed by his nephew Harivarman V. After Harivarman V, the Jaya Indravarman II's adoptive son, Jaya Indravarman III, tried to live in peace with his neighbors, but the Khmer invaded Champa in 1145. Jaya Indravarman III disappeared during the invasion, and his heir, Rudravarman IV, fled to Panduranga. Champa fell into the hands of the Khmer.

The succeeding Cham rulers had their share of vicissitudes until the time of Jaya Indravarman IV, who made a name for himself because of his Angkor onslaught. In 1177, after having secured Vietnamese neutrality, he swooped down on the Khmer capital and put the king of Chen La to death without further ado. Angkor was destroyed.

In 1252, according to Tran Trong Kim, endless territorial claims from Champa induced the Vietnamese king Tran Thai Tong to retaliate again.[6] In the process, he captured the king of Champa's concubine, Bo La Gia, along with many other prisoners.

The Cham then set out to defy the Mongols. In 1265, the new king, Indravarman V, refused to pay homage in person to Kublai Khan. Indravarman V died before experiencing the Mongol leader's wrath, but his son Che Man, known as King Jaya Simhavarman III, had to face the challenge. In 1282, pretending to need to settle a rift with Java, Kublai Khan applied for passage through Champa. Jaya Simhavarman III's denial infuriated the Khan, who decided to punish Champa. Hence he asked Annam for passage to Champa. He was given the same refusal, and therefore he decided to teach everybody a good lesson. Actually, he was seeking an excuse for conquest of the south. In 1285, Kublai Khan sent down 500,000 troops under Toghani and Sogetu. The latter was killed in combat and the ensuing defeat of the Mongols put an end to the Mongol invasion of Annam and Champa.

The struggle against the Mongols brought together the Vietnamese and the Cham, and a honeymoon period ensued, during which the Annam King Tran Anh Tong married his sister Princess Huyen Tran to the Cham king Jaya Simhavarman II, although not without tough bargaining. But Princess Huyen Tran's unwillingness to die with her husband was considered a national disgrace. In retaliation, Jaya Simhavarman II's son Che Chi set out to recapture two districts once ceded by his infatuated father. He was defeated and taken as a prisoner to Annam, where he died of shame and anger. His brother Che Da A Ba was assigned to govern Champa for the Dai Viet, as a vassal prince of the second rank. Two years later, when Tran Minh Tong succeeded his father Tran Anh Tong, who retired as Highest King, the new Cham ruler, Che Nang, again attempted to reconquer the lost territories. In 1318, Tran Minh Tong dispatched generals Tran Quoc Chan and Pham Ngu Lao against him. Che Nang was defeated and escaped to Java. He was replaced on the throne by a Annam protege, general Che A-nan. In 1342, after Che A-nan died, his son-in-law Tra Hoa Bo De seized the throne, thus prompting the legitimate heir, Che Mo, to call for help from Annam.

After Tra Hoa Bo De, the awesome warrior Che Bong Nga took power. His origins are not clear, but under his rule, Champa reached its apogee and extended from Kampot in the west to Binh Thuan (Phanthiet) in the east, and from Binh Thuan to the Gate of An Nam in the north. He took the name of Binasuor, and because of his military victories, an aura of legend surrounded him. From 1361 through 1390, Binasuor defeated Annam at Da Li, Indrapura, Vijaya, Nghe An, and Thanh Hoa. In 1367, he captured the commander in chief of the Dai Viet expedition. In 1371, he overran Thang Long, the Annam capital. In 1377, he

killed the Annam king, Tran Due Tong, in battle. The following year, he came
back to sack Thang Long, forcing the new king, Tran Phe De, and his father,
Tran Nghe Tong, to abandon the capital. Ultimately, in 1390, Che Bong Nga
met with death—he was a victim of treason. His successor, Jaya Simhavarman
V (La Khai), abandoned the territory Che Bong Nga had reconquered. In 1400,
Jaya Simhavarman V died and was succeeded by his son Indravarman VI (Ba
Dich Lai), who turned against the Khmers. To obtain Dai Viet neutrality, Indravarman VI yielded the critical province of Indrapura, the traditional abode
of the Cham rulers.

Thus having secured his back, Indravarman VI succeeded in defeating the
Khmer king, Ponhea Yat, causing the final abandon of Angkor. A period of
peace followed, allowing the introduction of Islam from Java. The new religion
contributed to the division of the Cham conscience and Champa converted to a
different culture, which alienated its traditionally Hindu and Buddhist neighbors.
When hostilities resumed against Annam, the Chams faced them alone.

In 1471, in response to a Cham raid against Hoa Chou, King Le Thanh Tong
invaded Champa. At that time, the Cham called for help from Cambodia, but
the Khmers had not forgotten the destruction of Angkor. So they kept their
hands off and allowed the Vietnamese to level the Cham capital of Vijaya,
killing 60,000 and taking 30,000 prisoners. This was the end of a great kingdom.
Champa was reduced to a minor Viet province which became utterly assimilated
under the modern Nguyen Dynasty. Nowadays, 60,000 Cham dwell mainly in
the provinces of Ninh Thuan and Binh Thuan.[7]

Until the end, Champa showed an assertiveness and a resilience deserving of
a better fate. Its disappearance marked the decline of the Hindu states, which
had not realized the important role Champa played in their common defense.
Champa had been the buffer between Vietnam and Cambodia. After the disappearance of Champa, Cambodia found itself between Thailand and Vietnam,
between the hammer and the anvil.

CAMBODIA: FUNAN AND CHEN LA

The history of this Khmer nation is so rich that there are many versions of
its origins. Around the first century AD, the ancestors of the Khmer and Cham,
who were of the same Indonesian stock, dwelled around the great lake Tonle
Sap. Then the Brahman Kaundinya (Hun T'ien) arrived from India. He was a
Siva worshipper. He met the naked Princess Soma and dressed her in precious
silk. After having taught her his religion, he married her. They founded the
Kingdom of Funan. Its capital was at Banam, south of modern Phnom Penh.
Their descendants were the builders of the fabulous Angkor.

In addition to the story of the Brahman Kaundinya and his naked princess,
there is also the tale of the fabulous Naga, a nine-headed giant snake, which
was the protector of the Khmer nation. He dwelled in the forest near the Tonle
Sap and used to rest on the shores of the lake. One day, while he was dozing

near the water, a daughter of Indra stopped by to observe a flock of graceful egrets dancing under the sun. Sensing her magnetic presence, the snake-deity awoke and immediately fell under the spell of her divine radiance. They married and founded the Angkor Dynasty. There are many other myths and legends associated with the historical origins of Cambodia.

Anyway, in the second century, the extremely aggressive Funanese (or Funanites) spread forth from their original capital of Banam to cover the entire region of Cochin China and the Menam (Char Phraya) River valley. At that time, the capital of Funan was at Vyadhapura. Oc Eo was the main port through which Hinduism was carried into the peninsula. The first king, the great warrior Fan Shih Man, led a series of conquests to the west, which ended with his death when he attacked Chen Lin, somewhere near the modern border between Burma and Malaysia. During the following twenty-five years, his succession evolved in a series of vendettas which became a monarchic tradition. His legitimate heir, Chin Cheng, was assassinated by his nephew Fan Chan, who then ruled for twenty years before being murdered in turn by Ch'ang, a vengeful brother of Chin Cheng. Ch'ang did not have much time to enjoy his feat since he was soon killed by Fan Hsun, a general who wanted to be king. According to Chinese records, in the middle of the Three Kingdoms period, Fan Chan sent embassies to India and to China.[8]

At the end of the fourth century, a second Indian migration came to Funan, probably with the second Brahman Kaundinya (Tien Chu Chan T'an) who set out to rule the country.

After the Brahman departed, Sri Indravarman, a high dignitary succeeded him to the throne. In 480, Kaundinya Jayavarman, a Chiao Chen Ju, ascended to the throne.[9] Kaundinya Jayavarman sent merchants to Canton and by offering numerous presents obtained recognition from the Chinese emperor. But as one of his sons usurped the Lin Yi throne, Kaundinya Jayavarman asked the Chinese to help punish him. The emperor accepted his gifts, but failed to understand his paternal concern. Against Jayavarman's expectations, the emperor went on to invest his son, Fan Tang Ken Ch'un, as the king of Lin Yi. Probably, he did not have much trust in the people of Funan who, according to the Southern Ch'i and Liang annals were "malicious and cunning."[10] Later, Chou Ta Kuan, an envoy of the emperor of China, gave a more vivid description of the Funanese.

After having reached its apogee, Funan slid into decay. With prosperity, morals declined, and debauchery spread from the court to the street. Administrative posts were for sale, and the critical waterworks were neglected.

The death of Kaundinya Jayavarman in 514 was the prelude to the end. His son and heir, Gunavarman, was assassinated by his half brother Rudravarman, and the queen mother, Kulaprabhavati, was compelled to retire to a distant palace near an artificial lake. And yet Rudravarman was a fervent Buddhist, who even sent Buddhist teachers to China. Since the people were opposed to his usurpation, it was a good opportunity for Chen La to throw off the Funanese yoke.

Originally, Chen La was created by the union of a hermit named Kambu Svayambhuva and a nymph named Mera—thus the word Kampuja. Located southwest of Nan Yueh (Nam Viet), Chen La's capital was at Vat Phu. On the top of nearby Ling Kia Po Po Mountain, the Chen La king built a temple to the god Bhadresvara, to whom he offered human sacrifices. The first rulers of Chen La were Srutavarman and Sreshthavarman, about whom not much is known. Their descendant, King Bhavavarman, was the son-in-law of the Khmer Kaundinya Jayavarman. He entrusted his brother Chisatrena with the task of overthrowing the usurper. In 549, taking advantage of a flood that destroyed the region and caused a furor, Chisatrena moved to conquer Funan. The campaign lasted ten years. However his success troubled the Chinese emperor, who decided to stop him. In the end, Bhavavarman also began to experience stubborn resistance from many regions of Funan and readily complied with the Chinese. He recalled Chisatrena, explaining that they needed to consolidate their gains before going further.

When Bhavavarman died in 600, Chitrasena succeeded him as king Mahendravarman, and the second phase of the Funan conquest took place. On the one hand, Mahendravarman secured Champa's neutrality; on the other, he courted the Chinese emperor with multiple demonstrations of obedience. After annexing a few more territories, Mahendravarman died, probably in 635. He was succeeded by Isanavarman.

Besides sending regular embassies to China, Isanavarman consolidated his relations with Champa by marrying a Cham princess and using Cham officers in his army. He set his own dynastic rules. Only sons of the queen could accede the throne. To protect the succession, once a new heir was proclaimed, all his brothers had to have either a nose or a finger amputated. They were permanently forbidden to hold office, and they had to reside in separate locations to prevent any collusion.

Isanavarman conquered Aninditapura and settled in his new capital Isanapura. At the time of his death, in 635, Chen La had succeeded in annexing the Mon kingdom of Dvarati. Isanavarman was succeeded by Indravarman, with whom he seemed to have no family link. There are no records on Indravarman's reign, except that he had a son who succeeded him in 657 as Jayavarman I.

After a rather peaceful reign during which he built a few monuments in the vicinity of Vyadhapura and Vat Phu, Jayavarman I died leaving no heir. The country was then divided under three rulers: Queen Jayadevi, Bhavavarman's daughter; Prince Pushkara of Aninditapura, who became king of Sambhupura (north of modern Kratie); and Baladitya, who claimed descendance from Gaundinya and Princess Soma and governed the region south of Aninditapura. In 706, the breakup was complete. In the north, there was the unified Land Chen La with Bhavapura as its capital, and in the south, there was a politically divided Water Chen La with Angkor (Borei) as its capital.

In the seventh or eighth century, an incident brought Water Chen La under the domination of Java. At that time, Sumatra Malaysia, and Java were under the rule of the powerful Sailendras. One day, the Sailendra Maharaja of Zabag overheard that the young king of Chen La had several times declared that he would be glad to see the Maharaja's head on a plate. With one thousand armed junks, the Maharaja of Zabag sailed up to Chen La, captured the Khmer king, and asked, "What have we done to Chen La that you should wish to see the king of Java dead? . . . I am going to treat you, therefore, as you threatened to treat me, after which I will return to Zabag without the spoils of war to which I am entitled, but let my clemency serve as a lesson to others."[11] Then he had the king of Chen La beheaded and took his head back to Java. From that time on, so went the legend, the kings of Chen La bowed to the south in deference to the kings of Java.

In 802, Jayavarman II, who was in exile in Java, was sent back to Chen La to serve as a puppet of Java. It was a miscalculation for Jayavarman was no puppet. He brought back from Java the concept of Devaraja—the cult of the god-king. As the god-king had, by definition, no other king above him, he simply rejected the domination of Java. The concept of Devaraja, which was conspicuously supported by the Khmer priest class, held the nation together for six centuries. To make sure that Java was thwarted forever, the Khmer priests led by the powerful Brahman Hiranyadama, took recourse to homeopathic magic. Since Chen La had been lost because of the beheading of its king, its freedom would be regained by beheading—at least in effigy—the leader of the Sailendras. Hiranyadama trained and ordained the Brahman Sivakaivalya, who became the first high priest of Devaraja. Inside all Khmer temples was displayed the Royal Linga, symbol of both Siva, the god of creation and destruction, and his human reincarnation as the Khmer king. As they died, the Khmer kings reclaimed their divinity. Therefore, all Khmer monarchs devoted themselves to building sanctuaries not only to worship the Hindu deities, but also to serve as their burial monuments.

Jayavarman II set his capital at Indrapura, east of modern Kompong Cham. This marked the start of the 600-year Angkor dynasty, during which fabulous temples and a no less fabulous irrigation system were built. Haunted by the humiliation inflicted upon the Khmers by the Maharaja of Zabag, Jayavarman II decided that his capital would be built at a strategic location, protected by natural defenses and rich enough in natural resources to provide building material and to feed an army of slaves. Consequently he left Indrapura in search of a new capital. His first choice was Hariharalaya, southeast of Siem Reap, near Phnom Kulen, where he could find huge sandstone quarries. Afterwards, he moved to Amarendrapura, and then to Mahendrapura, thirty miles southeast of Angkor. Finally, he came back to Hariharalaya to stay. He died in 850 and was deified under the name of Paramesvara. His death marked the first consecration of the Devaraja cult.

In 850, his son Jayavarman III ascended to the throne. He was interested in big game hunting and was credited with having created the famous Royal Regiment of Elephants, with more than 10,000 enormous beasts. He reinforced the status of the priestly class and multiplied the aristocracy's privileges. In 877, he met his fate under the stomping feet of a mad elephant.

His cousin and successor, Indravarman I, devoted his reign to agriculture and economy. In the religious realm, he was probably the first to adopt a syncretistic cult. Temples built on the tops of five graded terraces served as residences for the trinity of Siva, Vishnu, and Rama. The architecture was based on Indian cosmology. Inside the universe, the earth was an enormous square surrounded by mountains, and beyond the mountains were the infinite oceans. In the center was Mount Maru, the core of cosmic energy, where the gods resided. Indravarman I's religious views were rather Buddhist. He believed that human existence was the wheel of Karma, moved by desire and passion in an endless cycle of creation, destruction, and reincarnation. If desire and passion were extinguished, they would no longer provide the energy needed to move the wheel. And so the life cycle would end, liberating man from matter. Having reached that state of nonexistence, man would become a divine spirit and enter the state of nirvana.

Indravarman I might not have entered nirvana through the door of orthodox teaching. In fact, he might never have been enlightened, for his passion to work for man surpassed his devotion to the gods. Furthermore, by trying to achieve mastery over the environment, he tried to thwart their designs. Since the monsoon rains caused floods and destroyed crops, as did dry season droughts the rest of the time, with the help of Funanite experts and thousands of slaves, he set out to build at Indratataka, near the Tonle Sap, a system of "barays" (reservoirs) for water preservation and distribution. His example was followed by many of his successors. Probably nowhere on earth did Georges Groslier's phrase "agriculture hydraulique" bear more significance than in Cambodia.[12] An immense irrigation network, intricate in layout, ingenious in conception, was settled over an area of some 12.5 million acres with barays of 30 million cubic meters each.[13] According to John Audric, the barays were not dug in the ground. They were built on the surface by walls erected so that the level of the barays was always above that of the plain. They received rains and overflow water. "In the dry season, the sluices were opened and the water streamed through the irrigation channels by the force of gravity."[14] Water machines moved by wind completed the system, which provided multiple benefits. It prevented soil erosion; it enabled three or four rice harvests per year; it transformed Cambodia into an inexhaustible storehouse of fish, and it provided the country with a vital network for transportation and even included the city moats, which allowed delivery of supplies directly to the gates of the cities. Besides, the hauling of heavy stones for the construction of temples would not have been possible otherwise. Later the resulting wealth helped Suryavarman II pay for the colossal expenses of the construction of the temple of Angkor Wat. In 879, Indravarman I built the six towers of the Preah Ko and in 881, the pyramid of Bakong. He died in 899 with the posthumous name of Isvaratoka and was succeeded by his son Yasovarman I.

Yasovarman I was to last only eleven years. He had for an advisor the Brahman Vamasiva, who belonged to the Sivakaivalya family, head of the Devaraja cult. Yasovarman might not have been the greatest Khmer king, but he was certainly the first to use modern propaganda. Temples, palaces, and public places were constructed to show the magnificence and grandeur of the king. Artists, poets, and sculptors were hired to glorify him as a god or as a super giant who could destroy elephants and kill tigers with his bare hands. Some inscriptions showed the measure of his megalomania—for example, "In observing him (Yasovarman), the Creator was amazed and appeared to be saying to himself 'Why did I create a rival for myself in this King?' "[15] Under his reign, the new capital at Yasodharapura (Angkor) was constructed with a moat of 200 yards wide surrounding the entire city. The Preah Viharn was erected and towered 1600 feet above the plain. In 893, Yasovarman I erected the Lo Lei Sanctuary over the great lake Indratataka that had been constructed by his father Indravarman I. As Harihalaya had become overcrowded, Yasovarman I chose to build his masterpiece at Phnom Bakheng. But he did not neglect irrigation work. His reservoir at Yasodharatataka measured seven kilometers by 1.8 kilometers. He died in 900.

His two sons, Harshavarman I and Isanavarman II, were not interested in construction, although they contributed greatly to renovations. Then, Isanavarman II was forced out by his brother-in-law, who became Jayavarman IV and did not fare any better. His son Harshavarman II had a short stay on the throne, and in 944 was followed by Rajendravarman II.

Rajendravarman II was by his mother a nephew of Yasovarman and by his father Mahendravarman, a lineal descendant of the ancient Chen La dynasty. He decided to move back to Yasodharapura, his ancestral abode. He also promoted construction of numerous sanctuaries. In 950, an expedition against Champa allowed his troops to steal a gold statue from the Po Nagar Temple. From then on, until the reign of Jayavarman V, the Khmer kingdom had a century of calm and creativity. But in accordance with the concept of retribution, centuries later the Khmer emerald buddha was seized by the Thai, and at present, it remains a subject of dispute between Cambodia and Thailand. In 952, Rajendravarman II erected the Eastern Mebon in the center of Yasodharatataka. Banteai Srei followed.

In 968, Rajendravarman II died and was named Sivaloka. His son Jayavarman V protected the Brahmans, who expanded their properties and accumulated enormous wealth. But high dignitaries still practiced Buddhism. In 1001, Jayavarman V died and was named Paramaviraloka. He was succeeded by his inept nephew Udayadityavarman, who lasted only a few months. Udayadityavarman was unable to cope with the rivalry that had developed between Jayaviravarman, who ruled Angkor, and Suryavarman, who held the East. For 9 years, they fought each other, until Suryavarman won the Angkor throne in 1010. Perhaps because he claimed to be descended from both Indravarman and Yasovarman, and surely because he was victorious, he had no problem in being anointed by the high priest as Suryavarman I. During his reign, Buddhism was brought back, and the

Preah Viharn was erected and Cambodia expanded to the west. At his death in 1050, Suryavarman I received the coveted Buddhist title of Nirvanapada.

His son Udayadityavarman II was a prolific king who chose to be praised for his sexual prowess. But his everlasting credit was to have built the Baphuon, part of Angkor Thom, where he proudly displayed a linga made of pure gold. The Baphuon was certainly the most perfect specimen of Khmer art. Another achievement was the huge reservoir he built. It was 8 kilometers by 2.2 kilometers and was the largest ever built so far. Despite his artistic feats, the king had many troubles with his subjects. In 1051, the famous warrior Aravindahrada led a revolt, was defeated, and fled to Champa. In 1065, one of the king's favorite generals, Kamvau, rebelled and lost his life. Peace finally came back and allowed Udayatiyavarman II to die in his bed in 1065.

In 1066, his young brother succeeded him as Harshavarman III and started to rebuild the country, which had been damaged by the insurrections. Then, in 1074 and for six years thereafter, he had to settle a score with the Cham King Harivarman IV, who had defeated the Khmer before at Somesvara and captured their general. During that campaign, Sambhupura (Sambu) was destroyed. In 1076, under the instigation of the Chinese, the Cham and Khmer attacked Nghe An (Dai Viet). Both were defeated.

After the death of Harshavarman III in 1080, the Mahidharapura Dynasty began. There is little to say about the two first kings, Jayavarman VI and Dharanindravarman I, until Suryavarman II appeared. He defeated Dharanindravarman I in a single day's battle and was crowned king by the Brahman Divakara in 1113. Among the fabulous Khmer builders, Suryavarman II was the greatest. He took forty years to build Angkor Wat, which was "bigger than the Vatican city."[16] Under his influence, the Khmer state reached its cultural apogee. Although he considered himself the reincarnation of Vishnu, he persisted in showing a very poor military record. After declaring allegiance to China, he created havoc among his Viet and Cham neighbors. In 1128, with 20,000 men, he assailed Ba Dau in the province of Nghe An. He was beaten off by Ly Cong Binh, and lost his commander in chief and 169 men as prisoners. He came back in the fall with 700 junks and raided Nghe An again. Again he was defeated by Nguyen Ha Viem. In 1132, he forced the Cham to join him. Together they were mauled by Duong Anh Nhi. In March 1132, Cambodia and Champa offered tribute to Dai Viet. But two years later, in 1134, the Khmers alone invaded Nghe An and were crushed by Ly Cong Binh.

Unable to beat the Vietnamese, Suryavarman II turned against his ex-allies in reprisal for their defection. In 1145, Suryavarman II seized the north of Champa and its capital, Vijaya. There he installed Harideva, the brother of his wife, as king of Champa. And when later Jaya Harivarman I ascended to the Cham throne, he came back with General Sankara to mark his disapproval. The Khmer army was smashed by the Cham at Rajapura and Virapura. In 1149, Jaya Harivarman I recaptured Vijaya and slaughtered all the Khmer occupation forces, including Harideva. In the fall of 1150, the Khmers staged a revenge campaign, but the entire operation was swept by torrential rains. This put an end to Khmer claims over Champa. To the west, Suryavarman II's efforts to expand the Khmer borders met with no better luck.

Leaving the world to marvel at his Angkor Wat masterpiece, Suryavarman II passed away unnoticed around 1150 and was succeeded by his cousin Dharanindravarman II. But he had left the Khmer state in economic and political disarray. Suryavarman II had been absorbed by his huge constructions and had neglected the welfare of his subjects. The elite were jobless, and the common people were impoverished. Discontent spread throughout the entire kingdom.

His successor, Dharanindravarman II, stopped spending money on building Hindu temples. But, as he was a fervent Buddhist, he erected more and more Buddhist sanctuaries. Economic problems worsened. Under Yasovarman II, who followed, peasants and slaves revolted. This triggered massive repressions which threatened to deprive the kingdom of its labor force. The revolt's leaders were buried alive, and the hands, fingers, toes, and noses of their followers were amputated. At that point, Tribhuvanandityavarman, with the support of the aristocracy, seized the power. Yasovarman II was killed. As for his brother Jayavarman VII, he fled to refuge in Vijaya.

The Cham, who were waiting to take their revenge, wasted no time in taking advantage of the Khmer internal turmoil. Having secured the neutrality of the Thai, they invaded the Khmer state in 1170, but were repulsed with heavy losses caused by a regiment of elephants. There was horrible carnage. Cham soldiers were stomped by the mad beasts and turned into bloody pulp on which the crocodiles in the moats voraciously feasted.

Undeterred, the Chams went home and rehearsed for the next invasion. In 1177, they came back by sea, sailing up the Mekong to Angkor. They totally surprised the Khmers. The Khmer king, Tribhuvanandityavarman, lost his life in battle. Angkor was totally sacked. Temples were desecrated, palaces burned, and treasures ripped from their caches. Women were raped and killed, including the ladies of the court, who were valued for their light complexion as well as for their priceless jewels. Thousands of prisoners were taken back to Champa. After the huge orgy was over, the Cham sailed back "red-eyed and exhausted after their sexual excesses."[17] This was the first of a long series of humiliations for Angkor before it was finally abandoned.

The Cham then made a mistake. They allowed Jayavarman VII, who had taken refuge in Champa after the usurpation of Tribhuvanandityavarman, to return to the Khmer state, where they expected he would be their docile puppet. But Jayavarman was not a puppet. He was the descendant of the two most respected lines of ancient kings—he was not only the cousin of Suryavarman II, but was also related to Hashavarman III on his mother's side. After having witnessed the destruction caused by the Cham, Jayavarman vowed to take revenge.

Following his coronation as Jayavarman VII in 1181, he sent the famous Royal Regiment of Elephants to overrun Champa. He destroyed the kingdom and took back to the Khmer state the Cham population, whom he used as slaves to rebuild his capital, Angkor. He placed a Khmer prince on the throne of Champa and left occupation troops there. For twenty years, from 1223 to 1243, Champa remained a province of the Khmer, until a Thai invasion finally compelled the Khmer to withdraw.

To the west, the Thai also challenged Khmer suzerainty. In 1218, Jayavarman VII, who had mellowed with age and preferred building temples to waging war, died at the age of ninety. He had been an excellent monarch—energetic but patient, ambitious but realistic. Although a fervent Theravada Buddhist, he respected Brahmanism. He built Angkor Thom, with its superb Bayon. He built numerous other edifices of lesser importance around Angkor. Some were sanctuaries, and some were rest areas for kings. He also built 102 hospitals scattered throughout the country.

After Jayavarman VII, the Khmer state began to decline. The protection Jayavarman VII gave to Buddhism was one of the sources of the decay. Because Buddhism calls for tolerance and compassion, the Khmer gradually lost their fighting spirit. His successor, Jayavarman VIII, realized that the cult of the god-king was better served by the frowning trinity of Siva, Vishnu, and Rama than by the smiling Buddha.

Beginning in 1238, there were a series of events that portended the future of Angkor. First was the appearance of the kingdom of Sukotai and its king Rama Kamheung. He sent a hit man to Sukotai in search of Phra Ruang, the Thai chief. Unfortunately, against his expectation, the hunter got killed by the hunted. Then, in fear of reprisal, Phra Ruang threw his lot in with a widespread revolt involving the Thais of Ayudhya and those of Laos. In 1238, they chased away the Khmer governor and invaded the Khmer kingdom. Phra Ruang became the awesome king Rama Kamheung. By the end of the thirteenth century, the Khmer had lost the Menam valley to him. But in 1250, the Khmer kingdom still spread over one million square kilometers and controlled twenty tributary states. In 1296, the Thais reached Pegu, Nergui, and Tenasserim to the west, the Malay peninsula to the south, and Laos and Vientiane to the north. But in 1313, when they invaded Vijaya (Champa), the intervention of Viet King Tran Anh Tong reversed their fortunes.[18] Obviously, the incident was not worthy of mention in the annals of Vietnam.

The second event relates to the end of King Jayavarman VIII. According to some, in 1295 Jayavarman VIII was too old to be of any use and abdicated in favor of his son-in-law Srindavarman. But according to Manich Jumsai, there was another version of the story. In 1290, a man named Ta Chey was made royal gardener for having produced the best cucumbers in the Khmer kingdom. Jayavarman VIII allocated a large plot on which he was to cultivate his cucumbers. The king also gave him a spear to keep intruders away. One night, a sudden craving for sweet and juicy cucumbers led the king to venture into the garden. It was dark but Ta Chey could see the king, whom he stabbed to death with the spear. Thereafter, the court dignitaries gave him the king's daughter in marriage, and as dowry, they gave him the throne.[19]

So Ta Chey became King Suryophon, or Indravarman III. Under him, Buddhism became the state religion. He died in 1346 and was succeeded by his son Nipean Bat, or Srindrajayavarman, father of the famous Lampong who generously supported his son-in-law Fa Ngum in regaining the throne of Laos. The Suryophon dynasty ended up by abandoning Angkor. Indravarman III changed the religious fabric of the Khmers from Hinduism to strong Theravada Buddhism. His rule also marked the prelude to modern Cambodia by the abandoning of mythical Angkor for contemporary Phnom Penh. Chou Ta Kuan gives yet another version of the circumstances of Jayavarman VIII's tumultuous succession. His daughter stole his golden sword and gave it to her husband, Srindavarman who acceded to the throne. Her brother, the heir apparent, led a coup, but was captured, had all his toes cut off, and spent the rest of his life in a nasty dungeon. In 1307, Srindravarman abdicated to Yuvaraja, his son and heir, and became a serene hermit living in the luxuriant Cambodian forests.

The third event will be described later. It has to do with the creation of the kingdom of Ayudhya by King U Thong who, under the reign name of Ramatibodi I, would lead Angkor to its demise.

Chou Ta Kuan's Report

The Sukotai success against the Khmers was not without external help. The cunning Mongols were working behind the scenes. So, in 1283, after helping the Thais overthrow the Cambodians, Kublai Khan encouraged Annam to fight both Cham and the Cambodians. Then, in 1295, he sent a special embassy to Cambodia to offer Chinese protection if the Khmers would pay to him a regular tribute. The protracted negotiations gave enough time for his envoy, Chou Ta Kuan, to observe Khmer culture and make startling revelations to his nosy emperor. His account was the most comprehensive study of Khmer culture at that time. In addition to the fabulous wealth displayed in their golden temples and palaces, the *Khmer* aroused the curiosity of the Chinese because of other aspects of their customs. According to Chou Ta Kuan, the Khmers raised enormous crocodiles for protection as well as for food. The bellies of those beasts, which were bigger than boats, were used in a dish that was in great demand. Like the Cham, the Khmer people went bare chested and bare footed. They adorned themselves with a profusion of gold rings and bracelets. Only kings and queens had the soles of their feet painted red. Homosexuality was widespread, and compared with the Chinese, Khmer women had no sexual morality. They were very carnal, and left their husbands if they were not satisfied. Their reason was that they were not spirit and cannot sleep alone.[20] The rite of passage focused on girls and consisted of a ceremony of deflowering called Chen-t'an in Chinese. In the fourth month of the Chinese calendar, by notice from the Khmer Minister of Rites, each family hired a Buddhist or Taoist priest, whom they paid with silk, wine, rice, areca nuts, and articles made of silver. A banquet, with blaring music, song, and dance was held for the family and neighbors, while the priest and the girl waited, in their respective pavilions, for the time indicated by a mark on a burning candle. Then the monk came into the girl's pavilion and performed the operation with his bare fingers which he washed later in wine. Relatives and friends marked their forehead with the mixture. Some preferred to sip it, as a matter of taste. Until she found a husband, the girl remained the property of the monk. This initiated rumors that some priests had not performed only with their hands.[21]

Another singular custom consisted of the collection of human galls, which were kept in jars for the king's consumption, as was also practiced in Champa. In many cultures, the human gall is considered the symbol of courage, and the collection of gall would not have made Chou Ta Kuan frown, even if they had been picked out from dead bodies. But the tradition in Cambodia, as well as in Champa, required that galls be taken from living human beings, at night with a special knife. As a result, the Khmers avoided going out after dark, thus making the job of collection more and more difficult to carry out. One day, because they had not reached their quota, the gall collectors tried their hands on some Chinese residents. Later they claimed that "the gall of a Chinese had been placed in the jar with the others, causing the contents to rot."[22] Since such rumors cast doubt on the courage of the Chinese, Chou Ta Kuan's pride might have been badly hurt. But he was pragmatic, as the Chinese are, and was gratified that his countrymen were subsequently spared.

King Lampong (Lampang Paramaraja) (1346–1352)

After having lost to the Sukotai, the Khmers, under King Lampong (1346–1352), had to face the mighty Ayudhya. At first, Ramesuen, Ramatibodi's son, was defeated, and Sisavath, Ramatibodi's grandson was killed. In December 1351, a Thai army under Pangua, Ramatibodi's brother-in-law, came back with a vengeance and laid a seven-month siege to Angkor, during which King Lampong died. His two sons Barom Racha and Thommo Soccarach escaped with their uncle Soryotey. After a bloody onslaught, 100,000 Khmers were taken prisoner. Ramatibodi put his son Basath on the Khmer throne and gave him a 10,000-man garrison. When Basath died of disease in 1355, his uncle Baat succeeded him. But he succumbed to cholera three months later. Another uncle, Pisey, took over. This was the first time Angkor fell to the Thai.

In 1357, King Lampong's brother Soryotey, who had taken refuge in Laos, recaptured Angkor by surprise and became king Suryavamsa Rajadhiraja (1357-1363). During the melee, Pisey disappeared. In 1369, Ramatibodi I died, and his throne was usurped by Pangua (Boromaraja I), the conqueror of Angkor. After Boromaraja I's passing, Ramesuen retook the throne and put his son to death. In 1370, Suryotey bid allegiance to the Ming and reigned without further problems. Until Thommo Soccarach took the throne in 1380, as King Dharmasoka, the line of succession was not clear. There are also serious discrepancies on the dates of accession.

Then in 1388, the Khmers attacked the two provinces of Chantaburi and Cholburi, hauling away 8,000 Thai families. This gave Ramesuen a good pretext to come back to Cambodia in 1393. This time, he easily found supporters among the aristocrats, who readily conspired against their king. For the second time, after seven months of siege, Angkor fell to the enemy, with the help of many Khmer princes and generals. King Dharmasoka was killed. The habitual looting, burning, raping, and killings occurred again. The sacred sword was taken to Ayudhya.

In 1430, Soryotey's son Ponhea Yat resumed hostilities to regain the throne, but court disputes sparked mass desertion to Ayudhya. As was usual with decaying societies, natural catastrophes—floods and malaria—alternated with violent incursions from outside. The Chams and the Thais were attracted by the Khmer women's reputed lust and wealth. Indeed, the conspicuous eroticism of the apsaras, temple dancers dressed in rubies and gold, inflamed the imagination of the mercenaries. Boromaraja II sent his troops back to Angkor. The city was pillaged again. Among the priceless spoils was the famous emerald Buddha, which the Thais took to Ayudhya, thus starting a controversy that continues today. The Thai Prince Intaburi, son of Boromaraja II, was left behind on the Khmer throne. Soon he was killed by Ponhea Yat, who recaptured Angkor and proclaimed himself King Soryopor.

Soryopor, as a descendant of the Cucumber King Suryophon (Indravarman III), had probably not much love for Angkor, which had been the achievement of the previous dynasties. Also, the capital was in shambles after so many raids. In 1431, he left Angkor to its fate to become a ghost city and moved to Phnom Penh, thus starting the post-Angkorian episode of Cambodian history.

After the abandon of Angkor, the Devaraja cult waned. The god-kings who had been the masters of the fabulous culture also died. Only poor human kings, preoccupied with their successions and their sexual desires, remained. There was an effort to revive Angkor, but it came to no avail. There was no attempt to build another Angkor elsewhere either. The state of decadence was well on its way and was affected by the converging pressures of Cambodia's Thai and Vietnamese neighbors. Without the French presence, Cambodia would have ended up annexed by Thailand and Vietnam, as Champa had been annexed by Vietnam.

Soryopor's succession was a source of trouble. Soryopor died in 1467 and was succeeded by his son, King Noreay. But when Noreay died in 1473, his son Chau Ba Soryotei and his brother Phra Srei fought over the succession. The Thai King Trailokanart sent his troops to take both of them to Ayudhya as prisoners. Then Thommo Reachea, another one of Soryopor's sons, began a three-year war and was victorious. In 1478, he proclaimed himself King Dharmaraja. He made peace with the Thais and left his son Prince Ong in Ayudhya as hostage. Later he married a very beautiful commoner and bestowed on her family the highest honors. In return, he was murdered by his wife's uncle, Neai Kan, who seized the throne and forced his brother Ang Chan to take refuge in

Ayudhya. Eight years later, Ang Chan came back and killed Neai Kan. Then, he proclaimed himself King Ang Chan.

In 1549, when the Thais were having succession problems that led to the accession of monk Maha Chakrapat, Ang Chan attacked Prachin and took its inhabitants to Cambodia as slaves. Maha Chakrapat demanded that Ang Chan send a white elephant as tribute. Upon his denial, the Machiavellian Thai king designed a scheme so that the two Khmer brothers would kill each other. He sent Prince Ong against Ang Chan. Prince Ong was shot to death on the back of his elephant, and the Thais lost 10,000 troops. Maha Chakrapat came back with 50,000 men to force the issue. Ang Chan had to submit and deliver the white elephant as a symbol of his allegiance. But when the Thais had to deal with Burma, Ang Chan resumed his raids and even reached the suburbs of Ayudhya in 1564.

In 1566, Ang Chan died and was succeeded by his son Borom Reachea, who, with various fortunes, engaged in large-scale wars. He ended up by being tossed out of Thailand and turned against Larnchang (Laos), whose King Setthatirat was Maha Chakrapat's son-in-law. In 1576, Borom Reachea passed away and was succeeded by his son Sattha, who preferred to live in peace with the Thais. Maha Dhammaraja, the king of Thailand, agreed because he was quite preoccupied with the Burmese. So, for the first time in history, a Cambodian prince, Soryopor, fought side by side with a Thai prince, Ramesuen, against the Burmese. But soon a question of etiquette made the two princes oppose each other. During the victory celebration, Soryopor refused to bow to the young commander in chief, Ramesuen. In response, Ramesuen had the head of a prisoner hung on Soryopor's boat. Soryopor became quite upset and retired with his troops at once. King Maha Dhammaraja was not aware of the quarrel and at another battle against the Burmese, was extremely surprised to see Soryopor raiding Prachin, a Thai territory.

In 1590, Ramesuen finally took his revenge against Soryopor. His father King Maha Dhammaraja, died, and Ramesuen succeeded him on the throne. In 1591, he forced the Phra Charuk passage and laid siege to Lovec. After three months, lack of provisions forced him to withdraw. But he came back in 1593 with an enormous force, to which the Khmer mounted an equal defense. In 1594, Lovec fell to the Thais after heavy bombing and charges by Thai elephants equipped with armor and ironclad feet. Sattha fled to Vientiane with his son. The Thais took Soryopor and his family to Ayudhya together with 90,000 Khmers. Ramesuen left a Thai general in command, with 20,000 occupation troops. Cambodia was no longer a power in the region. It became a tributary of the Thais, who from Ayudhya appointed and controlled the Khmer kings.

In 1613, a Cambodian prince, Chung Prey, led a secret army and killed the Thai governor general. The Khmer situation became so chaotic that Ramesuen had to reestablish Soryopor on the Khmer throne, with all the royal apparatus. Soryopor kept Lovec as his capital. Curiously enough, he forced his court to adopt Thai etiquette and finally, in 1618, was deposed by his own son, Chettiah

II, who opposed the Thai influence. In retaliation, Bangkok dispatched three armies, which Chettiah II quickly defeated. He then moved his capital to Ou-dong. In 1623, to improve his alliance with Vietnam, he married Ngoc Van, a daughter of Lord Thuong (Nguyen Phuc Lan), the ruler of Cochin China. This was the beginning of massive Viet immigrations into Preykor (Saigon). Actually, Preykor was not the first Viet colony in Cambodia, since the Viet had settled in Bienhoa and Baria long ago. But it legitimized the Viet presence in Cambodia.

Chettiah II died in 1626. Afterward, the succession became a chain of palace tragedies. First, as the heir, Ponhea To, was only fifteen years old, his uncle Outey was named regent. But the young monarch was fatally attracted to one of Outey's beautiful wives, and he ended up being chopped to death together with the adulterous princess. His brother Ponhea Nu succeeded him in 1630, under the same regent, and died ten years later. As there was no other heir, Outey enthroned his own son Ang Non I (Nac Ong Non). His other son, Ang Chan, with a retinue of Cham and Malay mercenaries proceeded to slaughter everyone in the palace, including Outey himself. But at the time of the coup, two members of the Outey family were away on a hunting trip. Later, in 1658, when both came back with a gang of Cham and Malay killers, Ang Chan fled to Hue, where he pleaded allegiance to Chua Hien (Nguyen Phuc Tan). Nguyen Phuc Tan placed him back on the throne of Cambodia. When he died in 1664, his son Ang Non succeeded him. In 1674, the legitimate heir, Ang Chei (Nac Ong Dai), with Thai help overthrew Ang Non. Viet troops had to go to Phnom Penh to look for the troublemaker. Ang Chei fled into the jungle, where he died. But his son Ang Sor (Nac Ong Thu) surrendered to Nguyen Phuc Tan, who found out he had bet on the wrong horse. Since Ang Sor was the son of the legitimate heir, he was appointed first king at Phnom Penh, while Ang Non was relegated to the rank of second king at Saigon. It goes without saying that both had to pay separate tributes.

It seems that Ang Sor moved to Angkor for a while, but, unable to revive the capital to its ancient splendor, he went back to Phnom Penh in 1672. There he was assassinated by his nephew-in-law, who not only had his niece, but also wanted his wife. Obviously the widow did not approve of the scheme, although it had become the palace tradition. She therefore hired a team of Chams and Malays to dispose of the double usurper. The killers were perhaps the same ones who had been employed before by other members of the royal family under similar circumstances.

Ang Em, Ang Sor's brother, succeeded him with the agreement of the Viet, after he yielded to them the entire littoral of West Cambodia. But the two sons of Ang Sor, Ang Thom (Thommo Reachea) and Ang Ton fled to Thailand.

In the meantime, Ang Non, the second king, started to have problems. This came from the fact that in 1679, a Chinese renegade general Duong Ngan Dich, who had fled China, was authorized by Nguyen Phuc Tan to settle in Cambodian territory. Soon, he was murdered by his assistant, Hoang Tien, who persuaded Ang Non to join him in a coup against Ang Sor, the first king. In 1688, both were defeated at Phnom Penh and put to death. Ang Em, the son of Ang Non, pleaded allegiance to Nguyen Phuc Tan and was allowed to succeed to Ang Non as the second king.

In 1714, Ang Thom came back from Thailand with 15,000 Thais and attacked Ang Em in Battambang. He was defeated, but he persisted and laid siege to Oudong, where Ang Em hurried to rally the Thais. Of course, the Viet did not like his turncoat comportment and scornfully called him the "King of Thailand." Indeed, as regicide had become a palace tradition, opportunism was his only way of staying alive. He "abdicated four times and was crowned five."[23] But in 1736, he definitively abdicated to his son Sotha II, and the situation became even more confused. Sotha's uncles, Ang Thom (Thommo Reachea) and Ang Ton, with Thai troops took Phnom Penh and even pushed down to Hatien, where they were beaten off by Mac Cuu's son, Mac Thien Tu, who was consequently promoted to the rank of admiral by Lord Nguyen Phuc Khoat.

Ang Thom reigned as Thommo Reachea from 1738 to 1747. He was succeeded by Ang Ton's son, Outey II, who created havoc at the Viet border. As a result, he had to yield Go Cong and Tan An provinces as payment for his depredations. This was not the end of his troubles, for Taksin, the new king of Siam, demanded allegiance which Outey II rejected on the grounds that Taksin was only a commoner. This prompted Taksin to dispatch an army under Phya Chakkri. The Viet were also poised for the defense of Cambodia. What was expected to be a bloody confrontation turned out to be a friendly arrangement allowing Phya Chakkri to go back to Bangkok and replace Taksin, who had become hopelessly mad. Finally, in 1757, Outey II had to abdicate in favor of Ang Non II. As Ang Non II was a minor, his uncle, Ang Nhuan, gave South Bassac to the Nguyen rulers in exchange for being named regent. Later, when Ang Non II was enthroned, the Viet investiture cost him North Bassac.

Now almost the entire area of Water Chen La was in the hands of the Nguyen as the price the Cambodian kings had to pay for Viet protection. In 1698, because a census indicated the presence of only 200,000 inhabitants in the region, the Nguyen decided to send in Viets from Quang Ngai.

The rivalry between Siam and Cochin China contributed a great deal to the disruption of the Cambodian monarchy. There was a calm period when the Nguyen waged war against Tay Son, leaving Cambodia at the mercy of the Thais. But afterward, coups and contrecoups resumed, until Ang Eng arrived in 1799 to inaugurate the modern dynasty.

SIAM (THAILAND)

The Thais came from the Altai Mountains in Mongolia and moved east into central China. Citing Professor W. Eberhard, Manich Jumsai writes that "as far back as 1450 BC, the Thai people had lived in the valley of the Yellow River before the Chinese. At this period, there were no indications of Chinese civilization.[24] During their long migration to the south, the Thais settled first in Yunnan, where they grew rice and pigs. But various Thai groups speaking Thai-Lue were found in South China, Tonking, the Shan states, Assam, and Hainan.

In the seventh century, they founded the powerful kingdom of Nan Chao in Yunnan. At the beginning of the reign of T'ang Hsuan Tsung, Yunnan existed as a confederation of six Chaos. The southern one, Nan Chao, was ruled by King P'i Lo Ko, whose dream was to unite the six kingdoms under his aegis. In 931, he celebrated the founding of his new capital, Ta Li, with a banquet to which the five other Yunnan kings were invited. When he had all of them well intoxicated, he set fire to the building and then proclaimed himself king of Yunnan without any opposition, the potential contestants having been permanently silenced. Seven years later, he invaded Tibet, where he installed a new capital. The T'ang who were having some disagreements with Tibet, were pleased enough to confirm P'i Lo Ko in his title of king of Yunnan. His son, Prince Feng Chia Yi (Ko Lo Feng), married a T'ang princess. But after P'i Lo Ko's death in 742, Ko Lo Feng rebelled against Yang Kuei Fei's brother and invaded Kweichow. In 751, he defeated the T'ang troops at Hsia Kuan, killing 60,000 Chinese soldiers together with their general Li Ming. An Lu Shan's rebellion gave Ko Lo Feng free hand to invade Burma and seize the Irrawaddy valley. He wrested control of Szechwan, Kweichou, and Hunan. Then, in 860, he proclaimed himself emperor of Ta Li.

In 863, Nan Chao swept Chiao Chao (Vietnam) with 50,000 troops, killing the Chinese governor and slaying 15,000 Viet. But they had to retreat under the T'ang forces. In the thirteenth century, Yunnan fell to the Yuan and became a Chinese province. The exodus further south gave the Thais other colonies in the southeast, among which was Thailand. In the thirteenth century, the first kingdom of Sukothai emerged under Rama Kamheung. Later, in the fourteenth century, Ramatibodi I founded the kingdom of Ayudhya.

Sukhotai

The first Thai territory was a Khmer tributary in the north of the Indochinese peninsula, and the Thai were compelled periodically to carry sacred water from Thale Chubsorn to Louvo for the anointment ceremony of the Khmer kings. The containers, which consisted of earthen jars, could barely withstand transport in bullock carts through the jungles. Thus, the Thais had to invent woven bamboo vessels which they made waterproof with wood oil. In 1238, they had had enough of the Cambodian kings and their sacred water. So they staged a rebellion, led by Phra Ruang, a Thai chieftain who was married to one of Jayavarman VII's daughters. Phra Ruang seized the upper Menam valley and, as King Rama Kamheung, founded the kingdom of Sukhotai. He then dispatched an embassy to Kublai Khan to secure Chinese neutrality in his forthcoming war with Cambodia. Kublai Khan, who had not forgotten Khmer Jayavarman VIII's insolence,[25] gave his blessing, and Rama Kamheung invaded Angkor. In spite of a general mobilization in which women and children had to fight, the Khmers were defeated. In 1296, the Thai captured Angkor Thom.

Ayudhya

In 1350, the Thai Prince U Thong, renowned for his lightning attacks, seized a large island in the Chao Phya River. Under the name of Ramatibodi I, he founded the prestigious kingdom of Ayudhya which would last for 400 years. To secure his borders, he captured Louvo, the last Khmer defense in the Menam valley. To the south, he extended his territory to the Malay peninsula and to the west, to the coast of Martaban.

In 1351, as is described above, Ramatibodi I dispatched his son Prince Ramesuen to invade Cambodia, but he was beaten off by the Khmer Prince Soryotey. In the battle, Sisavath, the Thai king's grandson, was killed, and the Thai retreated. But in the winter, Ramesuen, under his uncle Pangua, the powerful governor of Suparnbury, returned, for a seven-month siege. King Lampong was killed, the Khmer capital was again looted, and the Thais went home taking with them quantities of slaves, both male and female. A son of King Ramatibodi, Prince Basath, was left behind to rule Angkor. Three years later, he died of disease and was replaced by his uncle Baat who, three months later, succumbed to cholera. Prince Pisey then ascended to the throne. In 1357, Soryotey, who had previously escaped, took Angkor by surprise and regained the Khmer throne. As for the Thai Prince Pisey, he disappeared mysteriously, leaving not a trace. Ramatibodi put an end to the war, but until his death in 1369, there were sporadic incursions between the Thais and Khmers.

In 1420, with the help of Khmer conspirators, Ramesuen invaded Angkor for the second time, and the Khmer King Dharmasoka was executed. The Khmer regalia and sacred sword were taken away to Ayudhya. Again, thousands of Khmers were carried back to Thailand as slaves for the construction of the Thai capital.

In 1430, Ayudhya King Boromaraja II sent a third expedition against Angkor. It came back with an enormous booty, including the famous emerald buddha. At that time, Boromaraja II set his son Intaburi on the Khmer throne, but he was assassinated by Ponhea Yat's mercenaries. After a bloody massacre of the Thais, Ponhea Yat ascended the Angkor throne as King Soryopor. Since Angkor was so close to the Thai border, Soryopor prudently moved the capital to Phnom Penh. But, the Khmer had not changed. They resumed their palace intrigues after the death of Soryopor. His brother Phra Srei fought against his heir Soryotey. Annoyed by this perpetual state of confusion, the Thai King Trailokanart arrested the two contenders and took them back to Ayudhya. He gave the throne to Thommo Reachea, son of Soryopor, who had pledged allegiance and given his son Prince Ong as hostage to the Ayudhya court.

Then, the Thai themselves had their own palace predicaments. In 1548, Queen Sri Sudachan poisoned her husband King Prajai and placed her lover Khun

Worawongsa, a commoner, on the throne. To avenge the unfortunate Prajai, Thai dignitaries lured both the queen and the usurper into a journey to view a white elephant. On the way, the couple was killed together with their newly born daughter. In 1549, Prince Tieraja, a monk, was enthroned as King Maha Chakrapat. Once in power, Chakrapat had to forsake Buddhist chastity and married a very beautiful princess. He resumed hostilities with the Khmers. After having invoked their refusal to deliver a white elephant, he ordered the invasion of Cambodia. He sent as hostage Prince Ong, against his relative Ang Chan. In the ensuing battle at Siem Reap, the Khmer King Ang Chan killed Prince Ong and captured more than 10,000 Thai troops. Maha Chakrapat finally succeeded in subduing Cambodia, but that white elephant caused nothing but trouble. The Thais took it from the Khmers, and then lost it to the Burmese who could not keep it either. Finally, that strange animal fell in to the hands of the famous Portuguese adventurer Captain de Brito.

But that was not the only problem for the Thais. Burma had become a nuisance. Burma had invaded Thailand many times, seizing the Shan states and Larncharng and even attacking Ayudhya. A Burmese was placed on the throne of Chiang Mai. In 1555, King Chakrapat was defeated, and the Burmese took away his beautiful wife. In 1569, the Burmese finally seized Ayudhya and took the entire royal family and 70,000 Thais back to Burma. They left their man, Thai Prince Dhammaraja, on the Thai throne. Prince Dhammaraja was a wise politician. He asked the Burmese to appoint his own son Ramesuen as military commander of Ayudhya. At the age of seventeen, Ramesuen enjoyed the prestige of a great warrior. He was also an outstanding politician. In 1584, he proclaimed independence from Burma and concluded an alliance with Cambodia. In retaliation, the Chiang Mai army under Burmese command marched on Ayudhya. Cambodia's King Satha dispatched Prince Sri Soryopor with 20,000 Khmers to help Ramesuen.

Soon, as reported in the previous section, a personal conflict placed the two commanders at loggerheads. The dispute was to have fatal consequences for the Khmers. Back home, while Ramesuen kept the incident to himself, Soryopor's report infuriated Sattha. To the Khmer king, the Thais deserved a lesson of "savoir vivre," and at the first opportunity, he stabbed them in the back.

In 1587, the Burmese invaded Thailand again. As the Thai were preoccupied with their enemy in the north, King Sattha attacked the two Thai provinces of Prachin and Nakorn Nayok in the south. Ramesuen threw the Khmers back to the border. In 1590, the Thai King Dhammaraja died, leaving the throne to Ramesuen (1590–1605). To overthrow Ramesuen, the Burmese invaded Ayudhya with 200,000 troops, under their crown prince. Ramesuen killed the prince in hand to hand combat, and the Burmese retreated. Now he was ready to take care of Cambodia.

Ramesuen made his first foray against Cambodia in 1591 to evaluate the Khmer forces. Two years later, in 1593, he launched his biggest campaign with four combined land and sea armies. The Cambodians put up a formidable defense, displaying 10,000 men at Battambang, 20,000 at Pursat, 30,000 at Bori-bun, and 10,000 at Phnom Penh, which was also protected by 150 gunboats. Despite the help of Spanish and Portuguese mercenaries, who were manning their heavy artillery, the Khmers lost.

During the campaign, King Sattha asked for rescue from the Spanish in the Philippines. But Ramesuen and his troops did not waste time in surrounding Lovec. After having delivered an ultimatum to Sattha, giving him three days to surrender, the Thais began very heavy bombing, then hurled their elephants against Lovec, forcing Sattha to flee to Vientiane. Ninety thousand Khmers were taken to Ayudhya as slaves. As for Prince Soryopor, he was sent into confinement in Thailand with his entire family. He was released later to assume the Cambodian throne.

Then Thailand had to deal with Burma again. In 1767, the Burmese invaded Thailand and captured Cambodian Phala, known as the Leper King, whose family fled and took refuge in Ha Tien and Cambodia. At that time, Taksin Phya of Mang Tak, son of a Chinese named Yen from Sow Chow (Kwangtung), revolted and seized the Thai throne. As he demanded allegiance from the Cambodian King Outey, the Khmers rebuked him, citing his lowly origins. This prompted Taksin to dispatch a punitive expedition under Phya Chakkri.

Taksin went mad under strange circumstances. Among his numerous wives, two of the most seductive were women of the traditional dynasty of Ayudhya, Princesses Chim and Ubol. One day, the king's bedroom curtains were found to have been gnawed by rats. Taksin imprudently ordered his two Portuguese pages to hunt down the predators. Soon, news spread that the two handsome lads had spent their time with the two princesses. The furious king had a showdown with his two wives, who felt deeply offended by his suspicion. Instead of displaying restraint in their language, they managed to add insult to injury. They not only refused to answer their husband's questions, but also challenged him to send them back to their illustrious families. Taksin lost his temper and had them submitted to the most horrible tortures. Both were flogged, and salt was put on their bloody wounds. Their delicate hands and feet were hacked off. Finally, they were cut through the breasts. One of them, Princess Ubol, was two months pregnant.

When that insanity was over, Taksin wanted to kill himself, and the queen mother, Songkardan, had to send for high priests to restrain him. From that time, Taksin sank into profound meditations which led him to believe he could fly in space. So he compelled the high priests to pay him respect as a living deity. Those who refused were defrocked, then flogged and directed to clean latrines. He also thought he had powers of divination and sent for housewives found in the marketplace, whose fortunes he would tell. If a housewife agreed he was right, he rewarded her with gifts. Otherwise, she was brutally caned and tossed out.

Gradually, this madness led to serious problems. During the wars with Burma, many people buried their riches. Now to dig them up, they needed government licenses. Only high officers who believed in Taksin's divine powers were allowed to deliver such licenses, for exorbitant fees. Among them was the governor of Ayudhya himself, who pressured people for more and more pay off. A rebellion ensued, led by Khun Sra, Bunnag, and Khun Keo, who burned the governor's palace, killing his wife and children. Taksin was aware that one of the rebels, Khun Keo, was the brother of Phya Sanka, an army officer stationed at the Dhonbury garrison. He therefore dispatched Phya Sanka to quell the revolt, but Phya Sanka instead joined his brother and marched on the royal palace. Taksin asked the high priests to mediate. The rebels demanded that the king be removed and retired as a monk. Then Phya Sanka appointed himself regent. At his instigation, a group opposed Phya Chakkri's return to the country. They were defeated, Phya Sanka was put to death, and Phya Chakkri proclaimed himself king. Taksin was brought to a high court presided over by Phya Chakkri. Because they had been comrades in arms, Phya Chakkri was reluctant to impose the death penalty on Taksin. But the ex-king was dragged out of his sight and summarily executed.

In Vietnam, Taksin was well known by Nguyen Anh, who had a relative at the Bangkok court. One day Taksin, who said that in a trance he had seen the Viet stealing his pearls, demanded that he return the jewels. As the Viet prince could not comply, and for a good reason, Taksin put him to death.

THE LAO KINGDOM

Laos, located to the west of Vietnam, played a sporadic role in Vietnam's life, a role that was not always laudable. Preoccupied with its survival in the Asian world of ruthless competition, Laos often resorted to treacherous policies. But an alliance with the Lao had contributed to Nguyen Anh's final victory over the Tay Son.

The Lao kingdom appeared late, in the fourteenth century, as a settlement of Thai-Lao in the valley of Dien Bien Phu, while the other Thai group, the Thai-Syam, moved to the lower Menam to form the kingdom of Ayudhya. Another group of Thai-Lao settled in Luang Prabang and replaced the native Khas tribes. Subsequent vicissitudes led the early Lao princes to accept Khmer domination and share Indianized Khmer culture. At one point, the Lao Prince Fa Ngum had to take refuge in Angkor after his throne was seized by his own grandfather. He married a Cambodian princess, and in 1353, with the help of King Lampong, his father-in-law, he regained the throne and founded the Thai kingdom of Larncharng, which was ultimately shared by Sukhotai and Ayudhya.

Under Prince Fa Ngum, Laos rose to be a significant power in the region. Its territory extended over the upper Mekong, the Black River, and Xieng Khouang. It bordered Vietnam to the east and Cambodia to the south. The Lao even extended their protection to Chiang Mai and Ayudhya. In 1421, when Annam revolted against China, Luang Prabang offered to help. But when the Lao troops arrived in Annam, they sided with the Chinese Ming and attacked the Viet at night by surprise, killing one general. In 1478, after having defeated both Chinese and Chams, the Viet turned against Laos with a vengeance. First they demanded from the Lao a white elephant as a symbol of submission, which of course the Lao rejected. Then three Viet armies converged over Luang Prabang from which the Lao King Setthathirat fled.

In 1558, when the Burmese warrior, King Bayinnaung, invaded Chiang Mai, further threatening Luang Prabang, King Setthathirat moved his capital to Vientiane to put a distance between himself and the Burmese. This did not stop King Bayinnaung from pursuing the Thais and taking Ayudhya four years later. Despite Setthathirat's help, Ayudhya was totally sacked. As the Burmese ruler set out to punish the Lao for their alliance with the Thais, the ruler of Chiang Mai also fled to Vientiane. In 1571, Setthathirat mysteriously disappeared during a raid against Cambodia.

During the period 1641–1647, under King Souligna Vongsa, who was married to a Le princess, Vientiane reached its apogee. An agreement was reached with Nam Ha (Cochin China) regarding border definition. Land on which houses were built on piles was to be considered Lao territory.[26] But soon Laos was divided into three kingdoms. To the north of Vientiane, there was Luang Prabang under King Sisarath, and to the south, there was Champassak (Bassac) under King Sisarath's brother Nokasat. This was not precisely a quiet environment for King Souligna Vongsa. The Trinh found themselves trapped in the protection of their Vientiane ally. At the end of his life, Souligna Vongsa experienced a family drama. His only son seduced the wife of the chief of the palace guard. This was a capital offense for which Souligna Vongsa had to sentence his son to death. But when he passed away in 1700, there was no heir to succeed him, except for two baby grandsons. The Trinh put his nephew Sai Ong Hue (Trieu Phuc) on the throne. He married into a Trinh family. The grandsons escaped to Luang Prabang where they proclaimed their independence. In 1778, the Thai occupied Vientiane, putting an end to Trinh control.

In 1806, under King Anou, Laos became a "bird with two heads." In other words, it was a dual tributary of both Thailand and Cochin China. But King Anou, whose ancestors had been invested kings of Laos by the Thai, managed to secretly train his troops against his benefactor. In 1827, when he learned of an imminent British attack on Siam, he revolted and marched on Bangkok. He was defeated and fled to the Viet. But the Nguyen did not wish to confront their Thai allies, so they confined themselves to a symbolic gesture. They sent two companies of soldiers to reinstall Anou on the throne. In 1829, Anou was again defeated by the Siamese near Vientiane and fled to China, knowing he could not count on the Viet any longer. On his way to safety, he was captured by Prince Noi of Xieng Khouang who delivered him to the Thais. Anou died in Bangkok while Vientiane underwent total devastation. Thereafter, all inhabitants were forcibly relocated to the Thai side of the Mekong River.

As for the Nguyen king, to demonstrate his authority, he had Prince Noi arrested and charged for having betrayed an ally. He was put to death and his territory, Xieng Khouang, was conveniently annexed to the Viet kingdom.

NOTES

1. Homeopathic magic, which is based on the principle of "like produces like," makes use of dolls and effigies. Contagious magic, which is based on the principle that anything that comes in contact with the body still affects it even when removed, makes use of nails, hair, teeth, saliva, and so forth.

2. Like the Khmer, the Cham adopted the South Indian Pallava style and called themselves Varman (King).

3. Georges Coedes, *The Indianized States of Southeast Asia* (Honolulu: East West Center Press, 1964), p. 123.

4. In 1054, under King Ly Thanh Tong, Dai Co Viet became known as Dai Viet.

5. Coedes, *The Indianized States*, p. 154.

6. Tran Trong Kim, *Viet Nam Su Luoc* (reprint ed., Los Angeles: Dai Nam, n.d.), B.I, p. 125.

7. Nguyen Khac Ngu, *Mau He Cham* (Montreal: Nghien Cuu Su Dia, 1986), p. 17.

8. Coedes, *The Indianized States*, p. 41.

9. A Chiao Chen Ju is a descendant of Kaundinya.

10. Coedes, *The Indianized States*, pp. 58-59.

11. John Audric, *Angkor and the Khmer Empire* (London: R. Hale, 1972), p. 39.

12. Hydraulic agriculture does not have the same connotation for Wittfogel.

13. D.G.E. Hall, *A History of Southeast Asia* (New York: St. Martin's Press, 1964), p. 124.

14. Audric, *Angkor and the Khmer Empire*, p. 46.

15. Ibid., p. 49.

16. Ibid., p. 55.

17. Ibid., p. 67.

18. Manich Jumsai, *History of Thailand and Cambodia* (Bangkok: Chalermit, 1970), p. 20.

19. Ibid., p. 21.

20. Audric, *Angkor and the Khmer Empire*, p. 89.

21. Ibid., p. 87–88.

22. Ibid., p. 94.

23. Ibid., p. 134.

24. Manich Jumsai, *History of Thailand and Cambodia*, p. 1.

25. In 1283, the Mongols sent troops, under Sulayman, to invade Cambodia. They were captured by Jayavarman VIII, who refused to return them to China.

26. Hugh Toye, *Laos: Buffer State or Battleground* (London: Oxford University Press, 1968), p. 16.

3

VIETNAM'S DYNASTIES

If, in her struggle for independence from China, Vietnam had to rely solely on Confucian ethics and Taoist *Wu-Wei* (nonaction), no pattern of resistance could have successfully developed. But the people of Vietnam found in Mencius a staunch supporter, since he opposed the concept of divine right. According to Mencius, a ruler's only right consisted of the proper exercise of his rule. If he failed, he was supposed to retire. If he used force to remain in power, he would face the opposition of the people. To King Hsuan of Ch'i, Mencius gave a warning "When you [King] make the water more deep and the fire more fierce, they [the people] will in like manner make another revolution."[1]

As for the Viet kings themselves, at the onset of independence, they ruled over a stratified Confucian society, but whether or not it was a feudal society is indeed open to question. First, scarcity of land was a negative factor for classical feudalism let alone an Oriental despotism, which was distinguished by huge irrigation networks, institutionalized corvee, and organized terror for social control. Second, it is possible that, after a long period of enslavement, the first Viet rulers developed the conservative mentality of civil servants and simply considered themselves managers "responsible for the preservation of land, waters, roads."[2] Thus, for them, waterworks were a matter of public utility, not a feature of Asiatic production. Indeed, some lands were allocated, with or without hereditary privileges, to members of the royal family, various dignitaries, and the Buddhist church. Later, under the Tran, the concept of usufruct was formally introduced, and Le Thanh Tong adopted a wage system consisting of payment both in kind and in cash. In the sixteenth century, King Le The Tong himself became salaried at the service of his prime minister, Lord Trinh Tung.

Traditionally the first dynasties were not considered legitimate because either they did not have the moral qualifications to receive the mandate of heaven, they had not inherited such a mandate from royal ancestors, or they did not last long enough to deserve historical classification.

THE NGO DYNASTY

Ngo Quyen (939–965)

The era of dynastic kingdoms began with Ngo Quyen. Ngo Quyen came from Son Tay Province. He was Duong Dien Nghe's son-in-law and chief of Thanh Hoa Province. To avenge Duong Dien Nghe's murder, Ngo Quyen attacked Kieu Cong Tien, who asked the Nam Han to come to his rescue. A Yunnanese expedition under Hoang Thao came down the Bach Dang River to meet Ngo Quyen. The Viet general, who was an outstanding strategist, installed a bed of iron stakes at the bottom of the river and chose to start fighting at high tide. When the tide went down, all the Nam Han junks were impaled on the iron stakes. Hoang Thao was taken prisoner and executed. Although Ngo Quyen's action was initiated as a family affair, his victory had far reaching political implications. It established a monarchic regime that was the first manifestation of Vietnam's national identity.

In 939, Ngo Quyen proclaimed himself King Ngo Vuong and chose the ancient Co Loa as his capital. He began to set up dynastic rule, administrative structures, and courts. Unfortunately, like the Chinese, the Viet kings had succession problems.

Binh Vuong (945–950)

When Ngo Quyen died in 944, his brother-in-law Duong Tam Kha could not resist the temptation of shoving aside Ngo Quyen's son and heir, Ngo Xuong Ngap, and seizing the power as Binh Vuong (King Pacificator) (945–950). Ngo Xuong Ngap fled to the mountains. His young brother Ngo Xuong Van was then adopted by Binh Vuong. One day, Binh Vuong sent Ngo Xuong Van to crush a revolt in Son Tay Province. But after going halfway there, Ngo Xuong Van came back and forced Binh Vuong down to the rank of duke.

Hau Ngo Vuong (950–965)

Ngo Xuong Van was a good, prudent man. To secure his position, he first established himself as King Nam Tan Vuong. Then he sent for his elder brother Ngo Xuong Ngap with whom he offered to share the throne. Ngo Xuong Ngap could only concede. He took the title of Thien Sach Vuong. Both became known as the Hau Ngo Vuong (later Ngo kings) (950–965). In 954, Thien Sach Vuong died amid numerous revolts leaving to his young sibling the task of dealing with them alone.

Ngo Xuong Xi (965–967)

In 965, Nam Tan Vuong was killed in combat. At that time, Vietnam was sinking into total anarchy. Twelve self-appointed governors were fighting among themselves, and the Ngo successor, Ngo Xuong Xi (965–967), was unable to impose peace. With him, the Ngo dynasty faded away.

CHINA'S NORTHERN SUNG DYNASTY

In China, power had passed into the hands of the Later Chou. In 960, the last emperor of the Later Chou named his youngest son as heir, under his mother's regency, but the military disagreed. Hence the senior officers staged a coup d'etat. They awoke their commander in chief, Chao Kuan Yin, at dawn and, by acclamation, compelled him to don the imperial yellow gown. Chao Kuan Yin, who came from a distinguished northern family, had served the T'ang faithfully and then the Chou. He refused to do his officers' bidding unless all of them took a vow of absolute obedience to him, which they did without realizing they had fallen into his trap. Only when he was on the throne did he unveil his rare wisdom. To prevent any other disturbances, he decided to send into permanent retirement those who had engineered the coup. During a celebration party, he complained that he could not sleep at night because his generals were coveting his throne. Of course, the generals emphatically denied ever having had any such intent, and some even offered to resign to show their good faith. He agreed that life was short and that they should enjoy it with all the wealth he was going to bestow on them. "Be happy," he further threatened. They took the hint, and the following day all tendered their resignations for reasons of health.

As Emperor T'ai Tsu, Chao Kuan Yin inaugurated his reign with clemency toward the deposed dynasty. In the domestic realm, he rallied all conflicting parties. In the area of foreign policy, independent states were subdued without much bloodshed. For instance, in 970, the news of an impending invasion of Nam Han served as a warning for Dinh Tien Hoang, who hastily declared his obedience to the Chinese Emperor. T'ai Tsu generously confirmed him with the title of king of Chiao Chih, and his son Nam Viet Vuong was named protector of Annam. T'ai Tsu (960–976) was the founder of the Sung dynasty. His idea of unifying China did not derive from any expansionist view, but rather from a sincere desire to have "only one empire under heaven." His conviction was so deeply rooted that to one warlord who begged for independence, he showed genuine surprise by asking him what his people had done wrong to be excluded from the empire. In 976, T'ai Tsu abdicated in favor of his brother, who became Emperor T'ai Tsung.

THE DINH DYNASTY

Dinh Tien Hoang (968–979)

At the end of the Ngo dynasty, among the twelve self-appointed governors ruling chaotic Annam, Tran Minh Cong of Thai Binh Province was lucky enough to have secured the services of Dinh Bo Linh. Dinh Bo Linh was a distinguished officer whose military prestige dated far back to his childhood, when he repeatedly won tournaments against neighboring youths. After Tran Minh Chau's death, Dinh Bo Linh moved to the district of Hoa Lu, where he proceeded to recruit troops for his own account. Later, after his victories over the Hau Ngo kings, all the governors agreed to enthrone him as King Van Thang Vuong (King of Ten Thousand Victories).

In 968, Dinh Bo Linh took the title of Emperor Tien Hoang De and established his capital at Hoa Lu. He renamed the country Dai Co Viet. He built many palaces and had five empresses. He appointed his relatives to key posts and made his son, Dinh Lieu, King Nam Viet Vuong.

Dinh Tien Hoang parallels China's Shih Huang Ti. He not only unified the country but also resorted to barbaric methods to hold it together. In front of his palace, he had huge woks full of boiling oil in which he made minor lawbreakers swim. In his gardens, he kept starving tigers for the more serious offenders. He boasted having reorganized his army into ten divisions of 100,000 men each.[3] If this seems far removed from the reality of the time, it was a sufficient deterrent for any ambitious contender. Nevertheless, even though his reign was relatively peaceful, when the end came, he did not die in peace. His succession problems were probably the worst in Vietnam's history, probably because he was the only Viet monarch who practiced polygyny. Each of his five wives was a full-fledged empress. When he nominated as heir his youngest son, Hang Lang, he met with opposition. In addition to the remaining four empresses, his eldest son, King Nam Viet Vuong, who had been instrumental in helping his father's career, felt so cruelly betrayed that he had his young brother put to death at once.

Dinh Ve Vuong (979–980)

In 979, a minor palace officer named Do Thich dreamed one night that he had swallowed a mighty dragon, which, according to his fortune-teller, was a revelation of his imperial destiny. Taking his imperial destiny for granted, the foolhardy man killed both Dinh Tien Hoang and Nam Viet Vuong, the emperor and the king. But he was caught by the palace guards, like a petty thief, and was promptly executed. Another one of Dinh Tien Hoang's sons, Dinh Tue, succeeded him as Dinh Ve Vuong.

THE EARLY LE DYNASTY

When he acceded the throne, Dinh Ve Vuong was only six years old and the commander in chief, Le Hoan, a man from the province of Ha Nam, assumed the regency. Besides his military attributes, Le Hoan was also the empress dowager's lover. That incited two loyal dignitaries, Dinh Dien and Nguyen Bac, to revolt. Both were killed. In China, Emperor T'ai Tsung decided to take advantage of this confusion to resume Chinese domination. That news prompted the Viet generals to enthrone Le Hoan, in order to have a military leader conduct the war. Of course, the empress dowager was more than happy to give her consent. So her son, King Dinh Ve Vuong, was demoted and was thereafter called Phe De (Dethroned King).

Le Dai Hanh (980–1005)

In 980, Le Hoan became Emperor Le Dai Hanh. The Sung emperor opposed his promotion. The Chinese were aware of his liaison with the empress dowager, and to embarrass both, they demanded that she and her son, the young Dinh Tue, come to the Chinese court to pay homage. Even if Le Hoan was ready to get rid of the young king, he was in no way willing to lose the boy's gorgeous mother. So he refused to comply and instead prepared for war. In 981, a combined Chinese sea and land force arrived in the Red River delta. At that time, the Sung maintained maritime supremacy in the Eastern world. Le Hoan lost a naval battle on the Bach Dang River, but somehow managed to kidnap and kill the Chinese commander in chief, Hou Yen Pao (Hau Nhon Bao), thus causing the retreat of the entire Chinese force. Since he had taken two senior generals prisoner, Le Hoan offered to return them in exchange for formal recognition. The Sung emperor, preoccupied with the Hsiung Nu who were again attacking the north, had to agree. He granted Le Hoan the title of governor. In the following years, he promoted him to duke and finally named him Nam Binh Vuong, king of Chiao Chih. Then, as the Sung waned, Le Hoan displayed more and more signs of his independence.

Le Dai Hanh was a good ruler. He wiped out the recalcitrant Muong tribes in Thanh Hoa Province and put down other revolts in the kingdom. He improved road conditions and transportation. He replaced Chinese currency with Vietnamese money. He invaded Champa, razed its capital of Indrapura, and took their royal ballet troop to Vietnam. Although they did not learn the Cham dance style, the Viet did, at least, share many characteristics of their music. Champa was reduced to the state of being a Viet vassal. It had to pay an annual tribute to Vietnam, which had become a big power. As such Vietnam would later show its imperialistic nature by carrying out the total extermination of Champa.

Le Trung Tong (1005)

Le Dai Hanh died in 1005, leaving the throne to his third son Long Viet, who took the title of Le Trung Tong after a few months of fighting with his siblings. But three days after his coronation, he was murdered by his young brother Le Long Dinh.

Le Long Dinh (1005–1009)

Le Long Dinh was to be a perfect copy of the infamous Chou Sin of China's Shang dynasty. He was equally ingenious in his choice of vicious amusements.

According to some historians, Le Long Dinh used to wrap people with oiled straw, to which he set fire, or he sent people to the tops of giant trees which he then felled. He also put them in cages which he immersed in the sea. But what he enjoyed most was cutting sugarcane with a sharp, heavy knife, using the shaved head of a monk as a chopping block. The worst was when he missed, and he missed more often than not. As for the court, Le Long Dinh had his buffons mock the ministers during cabinet meetings. Finally, his sexual excess kept him in bed for the rest of his life. His death marked the end of the Early Le dynasty.

THE EARLY LY DYNASTY

Ly Thai To (1010–1028)

With the help of an influential monk, Van Hanh, a senior official named Ly Cong Uan succeeded Le Long Dinh. Ly Cong Uan was from the province of Bac Ninh and had strong Buddhist support since he was the adopted son of another influential monk named Ly Khanh Van. After his enthronement as Emperor Ly Thai To in 1010, he moved the capital from Hoa Lu to Thang Long (Hanoi). Ly Thai To built pagodas and provided state help to the Buddhist church. He imported copies of the Buddhist book Tripitaka from China. He also changed Le law, reorganized territorial administration, built dykes, and constructed the canals of Dau Nai and Lam. He improved the economy to such an extent that he could impose taxes on agricultural products, mulberry trees, mineral resources, precious woods, rhinoceros horns, elephant tusks, and salt. He engaged close relatives to monitor tax collection. In foreign politics, he won recognition from the Sung, asserted his suzerainty over Champa, and successfully kept turbulent Cambodia at bay.

Ly Thai Tong (1028–1054)

When Ly Thai To died in 1028, his sons started fighting for the crown. Prince Phat Tu came out victorious and became Emperor Ly Thai Tong. Although he pardoned his brothers, he set a new rule to force all officials to come to Thang Long every year to renew their allegiance to the throne. Those who failed to attend the ceremony were subjected to fifty strokes of the cane. It must have been lethal punishment, for history does not record any absenteeism. Ly Thai Tong appears to have been a good warrior-king. He spent his time repressing many revolts. Power was decentralized and each region was under a local chief—a situation that invited nothing but troubles, mostly among the barbarian Muong and Nung tribes who dwelt in the mountainous areas. Champa and Laos also maintained pressure on Vietnam.

In 1038, the chief of the Nung tribe, Nung Ton Phuc, called himself Emperor Chieu Thanh Hoang De, his wife Queen Ninh Duc Hoang Hau, and their region the kingdom of Trang Sinh Quoc. The following year, he was put to death by Ly Thai Tong. But one of his sons, Nung Tri Cao, escaped with his mother. In 1041, Nung Tri Cao came back to seize a district in Quang Nguyen Province. He then proclaimed it the state of Dai Lich. He was captured, but was pardoned because he was the only survivor of a family that had been exterminated by the Viet. Feeling somewhat guilty, Ly Thai Tong decided to preserve his lineage by appointing him prince of Quang Nguyen Province. In 1048, the recalcitrant Nung Tri Cao revolted again, this time calling himself Emperor Nhan Hue of Dai Nam. Having petitioned in vain for recognition from the Sung, he set out with a vengeance to invade China and succeeded in seizing eight districts. Unable to dislodge him, the Sung emperor was prepared to ask Vietnam for help, but was dissuaded from doing so by his general, Dich Thanh, who, as a matter of national pride, preferred to send in his own troops. Nung Tri Cao was finally defeated, and took refuge in Ta Li (Yunnan), where he was murdered by the natives. Actually, the action of the Nung was not a claim to independence but a claim to the throne. They believed they shared a common ancestor with the Vietnamese and therefore Vietnam also belonged to them.

As for Champa, not only had it ceased to pay annual tribute but also it had resumed its murderous raids. Ly Thai Tong retaliated with a sweeping operation, taking 5,000 men prisoner and capturing thirty elephants. The Champa commander surrendered by offering the head of his king. But the Viet repression was so brutal that Ly Thai Tong himself had to stop it by proclaiming martial law. The Viet had stormed the Cham capital of Phat Te in Thua Thien Province and captured the Champa royal consort Mi E. On the way back to Vietnam, Mi E drowned herself in the river, refusing to serve another man. Besides winning wars, Ly Thai Tong is also credited for having created the postal service. He gave tax breaks to veterans and the poor. He forbade the sale of minor slaves and humanized the penal code by regulating arrest and interrogation procedures. Penalties had to match the nature and magnitude of the crimes committed. And although oriental monarchs had harems, he limited the number of concubines and consorts to thirteen, attendants to eighteen, and musicians and dancers to one hundred. Furthermore, to make sure the ladies had no time to devote to palace intrigues, he ordered them to keep busy practicing the art of silk weaving. He died peacefully in 1054, having given Vietnam a period of relative prosperity. Thanks to his military skill, he succeeded in gaining the respect of the Sung emperor. All in all, Ly Thai Tong was a good king.

Ly Thanh Tong (1054–1072)

Prince Nhat Ton succeeded Ly Thai Tong as Ly Thanh Tong, and Vietnam was renamed Dai Viet. Ly Thai Tong was venerated for his benevolence and his culture. In winter, he made sure that prisoners had enough to eat and to keep warm. One day, during a court audience, he pointed to his daughter and said "I love my people as I love my daughter. Because they are not educated, they have committed offenses against the Law. From now on, please do not be too harsh on them.''[4] He was a superior scholar and was credited for having built the famous Confucian Temple of Literature. In addition, he was responsible for the reorganization of the army. He equipped special units with catapults. In 1069, he subdued the raucous Champa and this time captured their king, Che Cu. For his ransom, Che Cu had to give away the three Chaus of Dia Ly, Bo Chinh, and Ma Linh, which are now the provinces of Quang Binh and Quang Tri (Map 11). This was the first time Dai Viet had annexed a Cham territory, and marked the beginning of the March to the South.

Ly Nhan Tong (1072–1127)

Ly Thanh Tong died in 1072. Can Duc, the seven-year-old son of his favorite lady, Y Lan, was named to succeed him and was to be assisted by a relative, the high counselor Ly Dao Thanh. Fearing the empress dowager's influence over the young emperor, Lady Y Lan advised Can Duc to suppress the empress together with seventy-two of her attendants. This mass murder triggered a tremendous reaction from the court. Only the prestige of Ly Dao Thanh could prevent further catastrophe. Can Duc took the title of Ly Nhan Tong. Thanks to the loyalty of his high counselor, Ly Nhan Tong was able to rule his country successfully. His contribution to national education was exceptional. In 1075, he created the first mandarin examination. The next year, he founded the National Institute for the Recruitment of Superior Teachers. In 1086, he opened the National Academy with a national examination. The entire administration was then staffed with scholars who had graduated from these institutions or with the laureates of government-run competitive examinations. In the field of public works, Ly Nhan Tong began construction of the famous Co Xa Dike to protect the capital against flooding. In the military field, those subject to the draft could pay for deferments and allow the government to hire peasants as their replacements. This led to the development of peasant-soldiers in villages and districts.

Ly Nhan Tong's economic policy was inspired by the Wang Mang reforms of the end of the early Han. Ly Nhan Tong reorganized finances by promoting the concept of government loans with interest. The government lent to peasants who would pay back their loans with their rice at harvest time. For merchants, he had a special office in the capital which not only lent them money but also bought back unsaleable products. These protectionist measures hurt the Chinese merchants, and in protest, they stopped all trade with Vietnam. In retaliation, and for the first time in history, a Viet army invaded China under the pretense of protecting the Chinese from their own emperor. In 1075, the Viet general Ly Thuong Kiet attacked Kwangtung, where he killed more than 8,000 people. Another general, Ton Dan, assailed the district of Ung Chau whose chief, To Dam, committed suicide after having forced thirty-six members of his family to kill themselves. The entire citadel refused to surrender to the Viet army. According to some reports, the Viet troops massacred some 100,000 Chinese, including the Kwangsi governor, Truong Thu Tiet.

CHINA'S SOUTHERN SUNG DYNASTY

The Sung emperor's response was unequivocal. In 1076, for the first time, a Sino-Cham-Lao coalition invaded Annam, but it was stopped by Marshall Ly Thuong Kiet. In that protracted campaign, the Chinese lost 400,000 men. Thus when the Viet offered a cease-fire, the Sung emperor readily accepted, leaving only a few troops as garrison in the provinces of Cao Bang and Langson. He renounced the occupation two years later, when he had to face the Kin invasion.

The loss of North China to the Kin barbarians marked the decline of the Northern Sung, and in 1126 they moved their capital from K'ai-feng to Hangchou. This was the beginning of the Southern Sung dynasty. Massive migration to the south propelled China into a second Golden Age. It was during the Southern Sung dynasty that many discoveries occurred, including the application of gun powder to warfare, printing with movable type, which helped produce books for the education of the illiterate masses, the improvement of porcelain technology, the development of water power from the spoon and tilt hammer, the water clock for time keeping, and the sundial. In the maritime sector, the proliferation of seagoing junks under the Chinese flag was made possible by the invention of the magnetic compass, new boat-building technology, and the introduction of multiple masts, the sculling oar, and treadmill wheels for propulsion. These marine inventions also allowed the Southern Sung to maintain the most sophisticated war fleet, armed with catapults and explosive bombs and capable of carrying hundreds of sailors. Unfortunately, Emperor Kao Tsung never followed his generals' advice to cross the Yangtze and expel the Kins from North China.

On the cultural side, the Southern Sung dynasty was an age of poetry and landscape painting. Women's fashion included foot binding, which was supposed to indicate an aristocratic lineage.[5] Confucianism was at its zenith. The social order that had been severely impeded by earlier upheavals in the north was reestablished. Taoism, with its cosmology and esoteric alchemy, also played an important role as did the Wu-Hsing, or five elements, theory of transformation (wood, fire, earth, metal, and water) and the concept of Ch'i (vital energy). By that time, the I Ching was the "livre de chevet" of every fortune teller, and the philosophy of li (principle) became the major subject of Chu Hsi's teaching.

Back in Annam, the ruling dynasty was not free of troubles with Champa. It had become a pattern for Annam to periodically enforce authority over that impossible neighbor, and in 1075, Nhan Tong decided to colonize the three provinces once yielded by Che Cu. But later, helped by a former renegade Viet, the Cham again revolted and took back the provinces. In 1104, seventy-year-old Marshall Ly Thuong Kiet was sent to crush the Champa King Che Ma Na. Until he died in 1127, Ly Nhan Tong enjoyed peace, having secured his position as the overlord of the south without any opposition from the Northern Sung, who were still preoccupied with the invasion of the northern barbarians.

Ly Than Tong (1128–1138)

Ly Nhan Tong had no male heir and was followed by his nephew Ly Than Tong, who was fortunate enough to inherit a quiet succession. He had excellent advisors. But aside from declaring a general amnesty and restituting land to those who had been unjustly deprived, he was not credited with any outstanding achievements. The six-month rotation for soldiers was certainly a good idea since it released manpower for farming, but it failed to have a major impact on the economy. Ly Than Tong died at the age of twenty-three. His short life put an early end to his ambitions if he ever had any.

Ly Anh Tong (1138–1175)

Ly Than Tong's three-year-old son Thien To took the title of Ly Anh Tong. In 1140, a man named Than Loi, who claimed to be the natural son of Ly Nhan Tong, claimed the throne. With a retinue of 1000, he managed to seize a few districts and proclaim himself king. But in 1164, the Southern Sung recognized Ly Anh Tong as king of Annam. Aided by his army chief, To Hien Thanh, Ly Anh Tong reorganized the army. Under Ly Anh Tong the first map of Annam was drawn. He also built a Confucian temple in the capital, Thang Long.

Ly Cao Tong (1176–1210)

Ly Anh Tong died in 1175, leaving a three-year-old heir, Long Can, under To Hien Thanh's regency. The queen dowager, Chieu Linh, preferred to have her eldest son in power, but failed to obtain the concurrence of To Hien Thanh. Long Can acceded the throne as Ly Cao Tong (1176–1210). His rule was the prelude to the end of the dynasty. Leaving the administration of the kingdom to his mother's relatives, he spent time in trivial pleasures, building palaces and going hunting. Under false accusations, he executed his chief palace guard, Pham Binh Di. That prompted Quach Boc, one of Pham Binh Di's lieutenants, to storm the palace, forcing the king and his heir, Prince Sam, to take refuge in Nam Dinh Province. There Prince Sam married the daughter of Tran Ly, a rich fisherman who succeeded in helping Ly Cao Tong regain the throne. When, a year later, in 1210, Ly Cao Tong died, Prince Sam succeeded him as King Ly Hue Tong.

Ly Hue Tong (1211–1225)

Ly Hue Tong named his wife, Tran Thi, first consort and her brother, Tran Tu Khanh, duke. Later, suspecting Tran Tu Khanh of treason, Ly Hue Tong demoted Tran Thi to the rank of royal maid. The queen dowager would have liked to have seen her daughter-in-law dead, but she met with the resistance of Ly Hue Tong, who was still fond of his wife. To protect her against a possible poisoning, he shared with her his personal meals. Finally, unable to endure the queen mother's pressure, Ly Hue Tong and Tran Thi sought protection from Tran Tu Khanh.

After Tran Tu Khanh had overpowered the opposition, Ly Hue Tong reestablished Tran Thi and Tran Tu Khanh in their positions. Later, at Tran Tu Khanh's death, Ly Hue Tong appointed Tran Tu Khanh's cousin Tran Thu Do to replace him. Ly Hue Tong's succession was a serious problem, for he had no male heir. He did have two daughters, the eldest of whom was married to Tran Lieu who was Ly Hue Tong's brother.

Ly Chieu Hoang (1224–1225)

In 1224, Ly Hue Tong who had become mentally ill, named his younger daughter, the seven-year-old Princess Chieu Thanh, his heir, before retiring to a nearby pagoda as a Buddhist monk. The court would have been opposed to the enthronement of a woman if it had not been for Tran Thu Do's idea. He had probably dictated the king's decision. According to French historians, Tran Thu Do was the Mazarin of the Tran regime. Although of humble origins and without much education, he was able to place Annam on firm ground economically and militarily, allowing it to resist the Mongol invasion later on.

Princess Chieu Thanh succeeded her father as Ly Chieu Hoang ("King" Chieu Hoang). By then, Tran Thu Do had become the lover of the queen mother, Tran Thi. Since he was also her cousin, Tran Thu Do found himself in total control. He placed all the Tran family in key positions and in a turn of his Machiavellian mind, assigned his nephew Tran Canh as the Ly Chieu Hoang's escort. Six months later, as he had planned, the king-princess married Tran Canh to whom she yielded the throne. So ended the Ly dynasty, after 215 years of rule.

THE EARLY TRAN DYNASTY

Tran Thai Tong (1225–1258)

Tran Canh was only eight years old when he became the first king of the Tran dynasty and took the title of Tran Thai Tong. Actually, by tradition the title of Thai To designates the founder of a dynasty, and the fact that Tran Canh was assigned the second rank, Thai Tong, implies that Tran Thu Do was the founder of the Tran dynasty. Anyway, Tran Thu Do wasted no time in appointing himself grand chancellor with full civil and military powers. Tran Thu Do was shrewd and cruel. He had no scruples about eliminating whomever he suspected of being a threat to the Tran house. Ly Hue Tong, although now retired as a harmless monk, was still considered a serious menace. So Tran Thu Do decided to get rid of him at the first opportunity. He went to his pagoda residence and found him busy weeding his garden. He said: "When one removes bad grass, one must also remove all the roots!" Ly Hue Tong took the hint and replied: "I know what you mean!" Then he went into his house and hanged himself. After Ly Hue Tong's suicide, Tran Thu Do demoted his widow, Queen Tran Thi, to the rank of princess so that he could marry her.

As for Queen Chieu Tong, since she bore no child to Tran Thai Tong, she was, by Tran Thu Do's order, lowered to the rank of princess and forced to marry the king's brother Tran Lieu. As for Tran Lieu's wife, who was Chieu Tong's sister, she was given to the king, her brother-in-law. Since she was pregnant, by the double swap, the succession problem was resolved. But by moral standards, the swap was considered double incest. So the two brothers reacted. Prince Tran Lieu rebelled, and King Tran Thai Tong ran away from the palace. A stalemate ensued which Tran Thu Do turned into a peaceful arrangement between all parties. Prince Tran Lieu was the father of Marshall Tran Hung Dao by his first wife, Nguyet, and although he had to accept that dishonorable arrangement, he deeply resented it. In his last moment, he asked Tran Hung Dao to avenge his honor.

As for Tran Thu Do, he remained obsessed by the idea of having the Ly dynasty suppressed. As a consequence, he had the Ly dynastic temple erected over a large pit. When the entire Ly house came to pay their annual respects to their ancestors, the building collapsed and all attendants were buried alive. Those who survived went into hiding and changed their name from Ly to Nguyen.

Despite the familial strifes, Tran Thai Tong was wise enough to finally accept Tran Thu Do's political dictates. After the turbulent Muong and other minority tribes were subdued, Vietnam was reorganized into twelve provinces, each with their own administration. All kinds of taxes were introduced including a new personal tax. Those who owned up to two hectares of land cultivated with rice would have to pay one quan (ligature) annually, those who owned up to four hectares two quans, and those with over five hectares three quans. In addition to the personal tax, rice farmers had to pay a land tax based on land classification. The land taxes were paid in measures of rice, while other taxes were paid with government coins. Taxpayers were divided into three categories by age. Minors were from eighteen to twenty years old; adults were from twenty to sixty years old; and seniors were over sixty. Everything was taxed, including areca nuts, betel leaves, and edibles. The penal code was reinforced: petty thieves had their hands cut off; tougher criminals were crushed by elephants.

The numerous taxes helped the government offset expenses for public works, such as the Red River dikes, and create a special administration in charge of dikes. The armed forces were built up through a draft, and royal relatives were allowed to raise their own troops. The administration was reorganized into separate civil and military bodies. Promotions every ten and fifteen years were instituted, respectively, for mandarins and officers. Regarding education, the first doctoral degree examination took place in 1232. In 1247, doctoral degrees were set in three ranks and covered studies of the three religions: Buddhism, Taoism, and Confucianism. In 1253, the National Institute and the Military Academy were created for civilians and the military. All the innovations paid off, for besides having very few troubles, the country was in relative peace and was able to resist the Mongol invasion later on.

Like all his predecessors, Tran Thai Tong had perennial problems with Champa. In 1252, he invaded the southern kingdom and took thousands of prisoners, including the royal concubine.

At that time, the Southern Sung dynasty was bending under the Mongols, who had extended their control over all of North China. After the death of Genghis Khan, Kublai Khan took over as the founder of the Yuan dynasty. In 1257, after the conquest of Yunnan, Kublai Khan sent an envoy to force Tran Thai Tong's allegiance. The Annam king reacted strongly. Not only did he put the Yuan envoy in jail, but he also dispatched the illustrious Marshall Tran Hung Dao to defend the northern border. Despite his military ability, Tran Hung Dao was submerged under the Mongol wave and had to take refuge in Son Tay Province. The Mongol commander Wu Leango Tai pushed down to the capital, Thang Long, prompting Tran Thai Tong to flee to the province of Hung Yen. To the desperate king, Tran Thu Do said "As long as my head has not fallen down, please do not worry."[6] Fortunately, the Mongols, who were used to the cold northern steppes, could not endure the tropical climate and had to withdraw. Tran Thu Do succeeded in having the Mongols accept a Viet triennial tribute. In 1258, Tran Thai Tong abdicated in favor of his son Tran Hoang. The Court elevated him as Thai Thuong Hoang (Highest King) to co-rule with Tran Thai Tong. It would become the custom of Vietnamese rulers to abdicate in favor of their designated heirs. Such a policy had two purposes. First, the abdicated rulers could give their successors on-the-job training, and second, their presence was a deterrent to any attempt by their other children to seize power.

Tran Thanh Tong (1258–1278)

Prince Tran Hoang was enthroned as King Tran Thanh Tong. He was credited for carrying out social reform. All the royal family members were ordered to hire the poor to cultivate their lands. This set a good example for the rich bourgeoisie as well. Tran Thanh Tong did not face internal troubles, but he did have problems with the Yuan, the Mongol dynasty ruling China. First, he was told to pay the triennial tribute and to provide, among other things, the Yuan with best scholars, fortune-tellers, craftsmen, and culinary experts. Tran Thanh Tong also had to accept the presence of a high censor who did not rule Annam, but was there to spy in view of a further Chinese invasion. Aware of the Yuan dynasty's designs, Tran Thanh Tong increased his defense by quietly mobilizing youth for military training. In the realm of education, he gave his brother Prince

Tran Ich Tac, an outstanding scholar, the privilege of opening new academies, one of which was run by the famous poet Mac Dinh Chi.[7] At the same time, a national examination winner, Le Van Huu, completed the first history of Vietnam, from the Chao dynasty through the last of the Ly. The work was commissioned in 1247 and took twenty-five years to complete.

Despite his apparent submission, Tran Thanh Tong never faithfully carried out his tribute to the Yuan. Finally, in 1266 he asked that no more scholars, fortune–tellers, and craftsmen be included in the tribute. Kublai Khan accepted under the condition that Tran Thanh Tong consent to come and show respect in Peking, send his brother or son as hostage, provide a census of the Viet population, pay taxes, and submit to Chinese military service. Furthermore, the high censor was to be maintained. In response, Tran Thanh Tong used a dilatory approach, claiming that his physical condition prohibited a long trip to Peking. Kublai Khan reacted by asking for the delivery of the infamous Ma Yuan column. The Chinese envoy came back with the word that the monument had been lost. Finally, in 1275, Tran Thanh Tong let the Yuan know that he would no longer accept a ''High Censor'' because Vietnam was not a barbarian state and therefore needed no supervisor. He wanted the title changed to ''High Advisor.''

Tran Thanh Tong was ready for armed confrontation since his request amounted to a rejection of Chinese authority. Kublai Khan threatened to prepare for an offensive against Vietnam. The Viet king replied by reinforcing his defense. In 1277, the Highest King Tran Thai Tong died, prompting the monarch Tran Thanh Tong to abdicate in favor of his son Prince Tran Kham. Tran Thanh Tong became the Highest King, and, as was now the tradition, continued to share government responsibility.

Tran Nhan Tong (1279–1293)

Tran Kham began his rule as King Tran Nhan Tong in 1279. He inherited a difficult situation. Tensions with the Yuan, who were now in complete control of China, resulted in a new series of diplomatic and political skirmishes. First, the new Chinese ambassador Sai Thong scolded him for assuming the throne without the Yuan emperor's approval. Against court etiquette, Sai Thong boycotted all banquets arranged in the ambassador's honor and insisted that Tran Nhan Tong come with him to Peking. Tran Nhan Tong replied that he was raised in Vietnam and was not accustomed to the Chinese climate. In 1282, another Mongol envoy raised the tribute issue. Tran Nhan Tong agreed to send his uncle, Prince Tran Di Ai, to pay homage in his place. The angry Yuan emperor, in an attempt to topple Tran Nhan Tong, sent Tran Di Ai back to Thang Long with the title of king of Annam. He was escorted by Sai Thong. Tran Nhan Tong's troops were waiting for them at the Nam Quan frontier. After a short clash, Tran Di Ai was captured and Sai Thong fled back to China with a Viet arrow in his eye. It was more humiliation than any commoner, let alone the Mongolian emperor, could tolerate. War broke out between the Viets and the Mongols. It was to last for four long years—from 1284 through 1288.

Tran Hung Dao and the Mongols

In 1284, under the command of a son of Kublai Khan, Toghan (That Hoang), who was assisted by two senior generals, Sogetu (Toa Do) and Omar (O Ma Nhi), 500,000 troops arrived at Nam Quan. They asked for passage through Annam, on the pretense of attacking Champa. In response to Tran Nhan Tong's refusal, Sogetu set out for Champa by sea, planning to attack Annam from the south. Tran Nhan Tong appointed Tran Hung Dao commander in chief of his forces, but he had only 200,000 troops at his command.

Because of the ominous imbalance of forces, Tran Nhan Tong wanted to negotiate but it was too late. He then sought popular consensus and held a referendum at Dien Hong Palace. There, the determination of the elders convinced him to accept the Mongol challenge.

When the request for passage was denied, Toghan threw off his mask and stormed Langson, forcing Tran Hung Dao to retreat to Chi Lang and Van Kiep. At that moment, Tran Nhan Tong suggested surrendering, but Tran Hung Dao refused and instead issued a long proclamation in which he entreated his army to follow the example of past Chinese heroes, going back to the time of the Hsia.[8] Aroused by this appeal, all Viet soldiers had the words "Death to the Mongols" tattooed on their arms. When the Viet lost Van Kiep, Toghan, at the sight of those tattoos, retaliated with a general massacre. On their advance to the Red River delta, the Mongols used artillery to sweep away the Viets and entered Thang Long without resistance. Tran Nhan Tong, Tran Thanh Tong, and Tran Hung Dao had already left for the region of Thanh Hoa. Inside the capital, the Mongols massacred the entire population.

At his end, Sogetu failed to subdue Champa and moved to join his forces with Toghan's. Under their combined pressure, the governor of Nghe An, Tran Kien, surrendered, causing the retreat of General Tran Quang Khai. Tran Kien headed for China as a defector, but he was murdered on the way by some unruly tribes. His relative Le Tac succeeded in escaping and spent the rest of his life in China, where he wrote the famous Annam Chi Luoc, the history of Annam.

The Viet general Tran Binh Trong was captured in the province of Hung Yen. To Toghan, who had tried to tempt him by offering him North Annam, he replied: "I prefer to be a demon in the South than a King in the North."[9] He was consequently beheaded. The situation was desperate. Many prominent dignitaries, such as the king's brother Prince Tran Ich Tac, joined the Mongols. But Tran Hung Dao was unshakable. Finally the tide turned. General Tran Nhat Duat, with the help of a remnant Sung forces, routed the Mongols at Ham Tu. Then two other generals—Tran Quang Khai and Pham Ngu Lao—dislodged Toghan from Chuong Duong and forced him to retreat to Bac Ninh. The capital, Thang Long, was liberated. Then Tran Hung Dao encircled Toghan, isolating him from the rest of his forces. In the ensuing battle of Tay Ket, Sogetu was killed and Omar fled back to China in a small boat.

In Bac Giang, the Mongol troops were experiencing the rigors of a tropical summer and the ravages of cholera. Toghan decided to retreat and, on his way back to China, fell into an ambush set by Tran Hung Dao at Van Kiep. He escaped and, with a small retinue, went back to Peking, where he found his father, Kublai Khan, busy preparing for the invasion of Japan. The humiliating defeat in Annam called for immediate reprisal. The emperor at once suspended his preparations against Japan to organize a second invasion of the south.

This time, he mobilized 300,000 men and an armada of five-hundred junks. He named Tran Ich Tac king of Annam, to replace Tran Nhan Tong. Again the Viets had to abandon Thang Long, which they had recaptured not so long before. But the will of heaven now sided with Vietnam. At Van Don, General Tran Khanh Du seized by surprise a Mongol logistics convoy with its huge stock. Many high ranking officers were also captured. Deprived of his supplies, Omar had to move to Van Kiep. Then Toghan ordered a general retreat to the Bach-Dang-Giang River, on the bottom of which Tran Hung Dao had planted bronze stakes, thus reenacting Ngo Quyen's feat of three hundred years before. When the Mongol junks were impaled at low tide, a bloody battle ensued, which changed to red the color of the Bach-Dang-Giang River. During his retreat to China, Toghan lost two more generals, and he himself had to hide in a bronze duct. It was a total victory for the Viets.

Tran Nhan Tong realized that war was not the solution for peaceful coexistence with China. The following year, he sent a delegation to Kublai Khan. As a gesture of goodwill, he also returned all prisoners of war, except Omar, who was accused of innumerable war crimes. But in the end, political considerations prevailed, and Tran Nhan Tong decided to let Omar go. He had not counted on the shrewdness of Tran Hung Dao, who had Omar's junk sabotaged on the high seas.

The Mongols were not used to suffering defeat. They were preparing for a rematch when Kublai Khan died in 1294. But his successor renounced his policy as being in vain.

Back at Thang Long, Tran Hung Dao and many others were proclaimed national heroes, and their portraits were worshipped in temples. As for the collaborators, as a gesture of appeasement the Highest King decided to burn their political records. Only those involved in high treason were subjected to death, deportation, or loss of their family name. Because of his royal lineage, Tran Ich Tac was spared from death, but for the rest of his life he was to be addressed as "A Tran," a pejorative term meaning female. Although it might not have been very fair to the memories of Ladies Trung and Trieu, it did keep Prince Tran Ich Tac alive.

By their tenacity and their political wisdom, the two Tran kings were finally successful in securing the independence of Annam. Their dynastic legitimacy may be controversial but, when it comes to success and failure in political enterprises, they should be credited for their resistance to the Mongolian dream of universal domination. In that period, Tran Hung Dao emerged as a legendary figure, comparable to the immortal Kuan Wu of the Three Kingdoms era. Both had given the highest example of loyalty to their king. Tran Hung Dao had resisted the temptation to avenge his father's honor even though he had the opportunity to do so by seizing the throne. More than his military achievements, his fidelity saved the independence of Vietnam.

Tran Anh Tong (1298–1314)

In 1290, the Highest King Tran Thanh Tong died. In 1293, Tran Nhan Tong went into semiretirement leaving the throne to his son Tran Thuyen, who became King Tran Anh Tong. Tran Anh Tong's rule was almost free of troubles, for besides Marshall Tran Hung Dao, who was now a living deity, he also had at his service General Tran Quang Khai, the victor of the Chuong Duong battle. After the passing of both, he started to experience problems with Laos, a kingdom to the northwest (Map 12) whose people had killed Ly Bon when he relied on their hospitality. The Laos frequently organized raids against Thanh Hoa and Nghe An. They fled when Viet troops appeared and came back when the troops left. Tran Anh Tong finally succeeded in keeping them at bay.

Huyen Tran Princess

In contrast, relations with Champa had improved to such an extent that Tran Nhan Tong, the Highest King, was able to do some sightseeing there. He was so pleased with the Cham king, Che Man, that he promised to give him in marriage his daughter, the exquisite Princess Huyen Tran. When he returned to Annam, he forgot. Che Man sent an emissary to arrange the wedding, but after ethnocentric considerations the court refused. For the Viets, the Chams were a barbarian people. Consequently, they wanted to protect their princess, whom they compared poetically to a "cinnamon tree, in the middle of the forest, on which any Man or Muong could climb."[10]

To iron out these problems, Che Man had to offer as additional gifts the two districts of O and Ly, an offer Tran Anh Tong could not resist. He promptly gave away his glamorous sister. But she was out of luck, for a year later Che Man died and she had to follow him on the pyre in order to comply with the Cham-Indian tradition. At this news, Tran Anh Tong expedited a commando under Tran Khac Chung to take his sister back to Annam. It so happened that Tran Khac Chung was her former lover. Princess Huyen Tran boarded his junk, and it took a full year for the journey back home, a trip that usually took not more than three months.[11]

Left alone, the Chams were not very happy. The reaction of Che Chi, Che Man's successor, was quite understandable. He retook the two districts of O and Ly. So Anh Tong invaded Champa, took Che Chi prisoner, and recovered O

Map 12
Annam with the Tran, c. 1306

CHINA
(Yuan)

LAOS

CAMBODIA

Quang Tri

and Ly (Map 13), which became Thuan Chau and Hoa Chau (Thuan Hoa). The recovery of this land, which extended from south of Quang Tri to north of Quang Nam, marked the second stage of the march to the south. When it was assigned to Nguyen Hoang, Thuan Hoa became the cradle of the Nguyen dynasty. Tran Anh Tong gave the Cham throne to Che Chi's brother and took Che Chi to Annam where, despite good treatment from Tran Anh Tong, he died of a broken heart. Although Tran Anh Tong ordered a royal funeral for him, it was not enough to assuage the hatred the Chams harbored toward the Viets.

After the passing of the Highest King Tran Nhan Tong in 1304, Tran Anh Tong relinquished the throne to his heir, Prince Manh, and took the title of Highest King. He died in 1320.

Tran Anh Tong was not a flamboyant ruler. He was erudite and trustworthy. He was mostly a man of his word—when it suited him. At the onset of his reign, when the Highest King Tran Nhan Tong paid a visit to his palace, the entire court was present to pay homage, but Tran Anh Tong was in his bedroom sleeping off his wine. The Highest King was so offended that he summoned the

Map 13
The O and Ly Districts, c. 1312

CHINA

LAO

CAMBODIA

Quang Tri

← O and LY

Quang Nam

CHAMPA

court to his own residence. Awakened, Tran Anh Tong hurried out and on his way ran into a minor scholar named Doan Nhu Hai whom he forced to write a long request for pardon. Then he went to his father's residence and kowtowed. The old king read the petition, gave a long sermon, and then pardoned his son. Back at his palace, Tran Anh Tong promoted Doan Nhu Hai to a mandarin rank and kept him at his side as his personal advisor. But the beauty was that from then on, Tran Anh Tong ceased to drink and obeyed his father's orders, except on one occasion, when he was instructed to tattoo his thighs with a dragon symbol in accordance with royal tradition. Obviously his aversion for tattoos was stronger than his love for paintings. He was also a man with an unalterable sense of humor. When he was terminally ill, his wife sent for a fortune-teller. He brushed her away, paraphrasing Confucius: Since this fortune-teller is not dead, what does he know about death?[12] Tran Anh Tong's reign was a period of peace and prosperity for Annam.

Tran Minh Tong (1314–1329)

Prince Manh took the title of Tran Minh Tong. He was a man of good intent, but had no vision. At the beginning of his reign, there were still prominent leaders, such as Pham Ngu Lao, Doan Nhu Hai, Mac Dinh Chi, and Chu Van An. But they were unable to cope with the perennial palace intrigues. Tran Minh Tong had his father-in-law, the famous general Tran Quoc Chan, command his expeditions against Champa. Since the queen had not yet borne a son, the court split into two camps. One demanded that Prince Vuong, a concubine's son, be named heir; the other wished to wait for the queen to bear a son. Prince Vuong's party launched a defamation campaign against General Tran Quoc Chan, the father of the queen, accusing him of plotting a coup. As a consequence, General Tran Quoc Chan, the victor of many campaigns, was thrown in jail and denied food and water. He was so thirsty that his daughter the queen took a shower with her garments on and later extracted water from the cloth for her father to drink. Afterwards, he died. Later Tran Minh Tong was told of his mistake, but there was nothing he could do. In 1329, he turned the throne over to Prince Vuong and took the title of Highest King.

Tran Hien Tong (1329–1341)

Prince Vuong was given the name of Tran Hien Tong. He was only ten years old, so power remained in the hands of his grandfather, Tran Minh Tong, the new Highest King and a cohort of bad advisors. Besides a few skirmishes with some minority tribes in which his troops were beaten more often than not and with Laos in which he lost one of his generals, Tran Minh Tong could secure only temporary periods of peace. Nevertheless, he had a huge commemorative plaque engraved on a rock mountain facing toward Laos stating that

while he, the highest king of the Tran sixth generation, was on his pacification tour, all leaders of the Qui, Cam, Xa, and Lac tribes, all royal heirs of Champa, Cambodia, and Thailand had come and competed to pay homage, all except the short-sighted Bong, King of Laos, who feared punishment and had not appeared yet. In the winter the Highest King had ordered his generals and other barbarian warriors to invade enemy territory, and Bong fled away with the wind.[13]

Tran Minh Tong was credited with the abolition of body tattoos, which had in the past gained the Viets the reputation of being barbarians.

Tran Du Tong (1341–1369)

Tran Hien Tong died in 1341 leaving no heir. The Highest King Tran Minh Tong therefore enthroned his own young brother Hao as Tran Du Tong. As long as the Highest King Tran Minh Tong was alive, Tran Du Tong retained only a nominal power. After Tran Minh Tong passed away, many competent ministers died. The last one, Chu Van An, resigned because Tran Du Tong refused to behead all seven of his opponents. On his own Tran Du Tong did not make good use of his royal power. He began to build palaces, lakes, and hills for enjoyment. His palace became a casino where rich bourgeois came to challenge the king at raucous gambling parties, an infamous saloon where wealthy drunkards staged drinking tournaments, and a chaotic theater for the turbulent fans of base Peking opera produced and played by shameless members of the royal family. Peking opera, called "Hat Bo" by the Viet, had been introduced by the Chinese singer Ly Nguyen Cat who came to Vietnam with the Mongols. Ly Nguyen Cat stayed after the Mongols left. He founded many schools, and soon "Hat Bo" became a national recreation.

Besides theatrical performances, the princes and princesses indulged in such trivial tasks as the cultivation of vegetables on the banks of the Lich River, in direct competition with the peasants. They even had their servants involved in the sale of folding paper fans on the market. As for the mandarin members of the government, they got their promotions through drinking contests under the king's supervision. The king himself gave performances of his own. During official audiences, when he felt happy, he just got off his throne and danced with his ministers.

And since it was so easy to be king, everybody tried. Ngo Be revolted in Hai Duong. At Luong Giang, an adventurer named Nguyen Thanh proclaimed himself King Linh Duc Vuong. In Nong Cong another, Nguyen Ki, called himself King Lo Vuong. The monk Pham Su On and his forces from the district of Quoc Oai occupied the capital in three days and forced the court to flee to Bac Giang. All these events marked the end of the Tran.

Abroad, problems with Champa arose after the death of their king, Che A-nan. Two factions disputed the throne, and while Bo De took power, his opponent, Che Mo, fled to Annam for help. In 1353, Tran Du Tong sent Che Mo back to Champa with a strong military escort. They were beaten off in Quang Ngai. In 1367, a strong expedition under generals Tran The Hung and Do Tu Binh fell into a Cham ambush. Tran The Hung was captured.

In 1369, Tran Du Tong died without a son. But he had named as his heir Duong Nhat Le. Duong Nhat Le was the son of a couple of Hat Bo actors. During an opera performance, Tran Du Tong had been so attracted by a gorgeous actress that he had made her his concubine, although she was two months pregnant. The court, citing illegitimacy, decided to name Tran Du Tong's brother Cung Dinh Vuong to succeed him. But the queen mother upheld the late king's decision, supporting Duong Nhat Le against her own son. After two years of debauchery, Duong Nhat Le killed both the queen mother and Cung Dinh Vuong, triggering a rebellion from Prince Kinh. As for Prince Cung Tinh Vuong Phu, he ran for his life to the Da Giang region, refusing to join the coup.

Finally, taking the advice of Ngo Lang, Duong Nhat Le consented to step down. Prince Cung Tinh Vuong Phu, who had declined power, was forcefully enthroned. When Duong Nhat Le came to pay him homage, Prince Cung Tinh Vuong Phu embraced him, wept, and said he never thought things would end up like this. The scene was so shocking that Prince Kinh swung his sword, yelling at the new king: "Why at this time do you still behave as a child?" Then Prince Kinh threw Duong Nhat Le in jail. There, Duong Nhat Le claimed he had been duped by Ngo Lang and so he killed him. Only then did Prince Cung Tinh Vuong Phu agree to the execution of Duong Nhat Le and his son Lieu.[14]

Tran Nghe Tong (1370–1372)

Cung Tinh Vuong Phu became Tran Nghe Tong, a king Vietnam had no need for. After Duong Nhat Le's execution, his mother fled to Champa, where she asked for Che Bong Nga's help. King Che Bong Nga was a superb warrior and a bright politician. In 1368, he demanded the return of the three counties, Dia Ly, Bo Chinh, and Ma Linh. Annam's refusal provided him with the pretext for launching incessant raids to which the decadent Viets offered no resistance. Under him, Champa had become a redoutable state.

In Annam, power was in the hands of Ho Qui Ly, a royal relative. Ho Qui Ly was of Chinese origins. His ancestor, Ho Hung Dat, had come to Annam during the period of the Five Dynasties. Later, the family moved to Thanh Hoa. He was adopted by Le Huan and became a Le. Ho Qui Ly's father had two sisters, both of whom were married to King Tran Minh Tong. One was the mother of Tran Nghe Tong; the other was the mother of Prince Kinh. In 1372, Tran Nghe Tong transferred power to his younger brother Prince Kinh and retired as the Highest King.[15]

Tran Due Tong (1372–1377)

Prince Kinh became Tran Due Tong. He was married to Queen Le Thi, Ho Qui Ly's cousin. The Cham were still raiding Annam at their leisure, and although Tran Due Tong was more resolute than Tran Nghe Tong, all the power was still in the hands of the latter. In 1376, the king of Champa, Che Bong Nga, sent as tribute fifteen trays of gold, but Do Tu Binh, who was then military governor of Hoa Chau, kept it for himself and reported that Champa had refused to pay homage. Tran Due Tong decided to retaliate, but the court opposed him for fear of losing to Che Bong Nga. Tran Due Tong then succeeded in forcing the Highest King Tran Nghe Tong to approve his plan. Then he enrolled the population of Thanh Hoa and Nghe An in his army and made Do Tu Binh chief of staff. Before the campaign began, Tran Due Tong had Tran Nghe Tong review his troops at Bach-Hac. Then he moved by sea to reach the mouth of Nhat Le River in Dong Hoi. There, he paused for more training. In 1377, he arrived in Qui Nhon, and after having seized the two fortresses of Thach Kieu and Ky Mang, he attacked Do Ban, the capital of Champa. He perished on the field and lost seventy percent of his troops. Do Tu Binh and his assistant Le Qui Ly fled back to Thang Long, where Do Tu Binh was demoted to the rank of private.

At the news of her husband's death, Queen Le Thi shaved her head and retired as a nun. Contrary to the Trans, who were descended from uneducated fishermen, Le Qui Ly's family was more cultured, as was exemplified by the queen herself.

Tran Phe De (1377–1388)

In 1377, the Highest King Tran Nghe Tong named Tran Due Tong's son Hien to succeed his father under the title of Tran Phe De. As might be expected, Tran Phe De was under the complete domination of his uncle Tran Nghe Tong, who had still not found a way to stop the Chams. From 1377 through 1378, Che Bong Nga twice assailed Thang Long, after having raided many provinces. In 1383, Le Qui Ly, with General Nguyen Da Phuong's assistance, managed to overthrow the Chams at Ngu Giang and Than Dau. But they came back later and captured General Mat On, causing Tran Nghe Tong to fear for his life. He and Tran Phe De boarded a junk and, despite the court trying to retain the skiff by begging them in tears to stand and fight, the two kings shoved off and shamelessly fled away. This scene was to be repeated later when the Cham invaded the capital of Annam. Tran Nghe Tong did nothing to stop foreign aggression and later, when he had troubles with the Ming, was even satisfied with this impertinent advice from a scornful minister: "Your Majesty must serve the Ming as your own father and love the Cham as your own sons, then your kingdom will be free of troubles!"[16] Only sheer cowardice could tolerate such an effrontery.

At no time did Tran Nghe Tong learn from past experience and reorganize his forces against future attacks. The only thing he did was to go and bury his treasure in the nearby mountains to keep it out of the reach of his Viet subjects and his Cham foes. To fight the invaders, he went so low as to ask for the help of a Buddhist monk, Dai Tang Thien Su, and his followers.

THE END OF THE MONGOLS

But dynastic decadence had also reached the omnipotent Yuan in China. Originally, they were a nomadic tribe whose sole preoccupation was waging war. Their first ruler, the ferocious Genghis Khan, succeeded in unifying all the Mongol tribes before annihilating the foreign dynasties in the north—the Liao, the Hsi Hsia, and the Ch'in. They were expert in riding horses and shooting bows, and they spread terror over all of Asia and Europe, destroying everything along their way. Only immediate submission could sometimes save cities from total destruction at their hands. As Genghis Khan used to say, "The greatest joy is to conquer one's enemies, to seize their property, to see their families in tears, to ride their horses and to possess their daughters and wives."[17] The mere appearance of the disheveled Mongol warriors sufficed to sow panic, for by tradition the "Mongols were forbidden to wash or bathe from the cradle to the grave, and also forbidden to wash anything in running water."[18]

The concept of permanent settlements was completely alien to the Mongols. For them, capitals and cities constituted an intolerable infringement on their nomadic culture. When they first seized a Chinese province, they decided to exterminate the entire Chinese population and turn the land into pasture to feed their dwarf horses. But to prevent a holocaust, Genghis Khan's advisor, a Kitan named Yelu Chu T'sai, suggested making a profit by levying a tax on the Chinese. Genghis Khan readily agreed. The capacity to learn and to adapt was the determining factor in the Yuan's political success. After their conquests in central and western Asia were completed, they turned to South China, where they overthrew the Southern Sung. But they were not insensitive to the splendors of China's second Golden Age and easily adapted to Chinese sedentary culture. As a matter of fact, Chinese remained the official language for the affairs of the empire.

Genghis Khan died in 1227, and Ogodei Khan (1229–1241) was selected by the Mongols to succeed him. Contact with the West proved to be fatal to that otherwise good man. Soon he indulged in drinking, but instead of the traditional kumy,[19] he directed his preference toward grape wine, probably from France. As a result, power fell into the hands of his shrewd wife, who actually encouraged him in the dangerous pursuit of personal happiness. Ogodei Khan eventually died, probably of a cirrhosis.

Kublai Khan succeeded him and, in 1257, annexed Yunnan and Burma without major problems. He was enthroned in 1260 as the first emperor of the Yuan dynasty of China. He was a wise ruler and had an extraordinary gift for international diplomacy. After having given free rein to both Confucianism and Taoism, he welcomed Buddhism as the third leg of the religious tripod which he used to secure the stability of his empire. He also opened the doors to foreigners. Among them, Marco Polo was the most trusted—he served in Kublai Khan's civil service from 1271 through 1297.

Because many of his military campaigns did not reach positive conclusions, Kublai Khan did not reach Genghis Khan's stature. His aggression against Japan in 1281 turned out to be a total disaster. His fleet was half destroyed by a storm, and the troops that succeeded in reaching the coast were hacked to the last by hardy samurai. He was no luckier three years later in Java. From 1283 to 1285, Kublai Khan's expeditions against Champa were mere frustration, and as we have seen, in 1287 he finally got kicked out by Annam.

Nevertheless, the Mongols had conquered enough land to experience administrative problems. Decentralization had to be carried out, which ultimately weakened the central authority. Expansion to the west under the T'ang had put China in direct contact with Islam. In 756, more than 4,000 Arab mercenaries joined the Chinese against the Turkish rebel An Lu Shan. After the war, they remained in western China to found Islamic communities. Yunnan not only converted to the new religion, but rejected allegiance to the Yuan because they were Buddhist. That Yunnan secession completed the pattern of decay that led to the end of the Yuan dynasty in China.

Underneath, there was also the silent opposition of the *shih*, the class of scholars who had been kept away from administrative posts and now found themselves in the midst of popular unrest. In spite of a late decision allowing them to take part in national examinations for public service, the will of heaven had changed and the *shih* rallied the malcontents. The last Yuan emperor, Togan Timur, thought nothing would be better than a total holocaust for his Chinese subjects. The Chinese reached the same conclusion about their rulers. Secret societies mushroomed. Most were of Taoist inspiration, such as the White Lotus. Other independent groups also emerged, some made famous by the world renowned author Kim Dung in his 1960s novels.

The peasants, led by Chu Yuan Chung, revolted. In 1368, on the occasion of the mid-Autumn festival, tracts reading "Death to the Mongols" were inserted into the traditional cakes which were cut in every house at the time of the rising moon. When the papers were discovered, each Chinese family slew its Mongol guests. Throughout China, there was immense carnage, to which the last Yuan emperor responded by fleeing back to Karakorum, his ancestral home. The Mongol adventure in China had lasted 108 years.

UNDER THE MING DYNASTY

Chu Yuan Chung proclaimed himself Emperor Hung Wu and began the Ming dynasty as Ming T'ai Tsu. He was the son of poor peasants who had died in a famine in the Huai valley. He grew up as a shepherd, became a Buddhist monk, and finally found himself a powerful brigand. His success came from his common sense. Instead of looting and destroying everything, he held a few strategic bases which he consolidated for further expansion. In 1356, he took Nanking and installed his capital there. He pursued the conquest of eastern China and acceded the throne in 1368, after throwing the Yuan out of Peking. In 1372, the famous Ming general Hsu Ta, with 250,000 men, ravaged Karakorum, the ancestral abode of the Mongols, forcing them to flee far into Siberia. Ming T'ai Tsu then recovered Yunnan and established his authority in Central Asia. Korea and Annam pledged their allegiance to the Ming.

In 1384, the Ming having destroyed the Yuan, began to reorganize the empire. They pressed Annam to deliver 5,000 tons of supplies to the Ming troops in Yunnan and the next year demanded tribute in rice and precious wood. This made Tran Nghe Tong become more and more dependent on Ho Qui Ly (Le Qui Ly), on whom he incessantly bestowed the highest honors. He proclaimed: "Academically and militarily perfect, Le Qui Ly is as virtuous as the King."[20] It is interesting to note that to thank the king, Le Qui Ly wrote a poem in the new Viet script, known as Nom, showing his intent to divorce Chinese culture. But under the Tran, Chinese was still the language of the government.

Tran Thuan Tong (1388-1398)

The young King Tran Phe De, realizing the noxious influence of Le Qui Ly, decided to eliminate him. But before he took action, the plot was discovered and all the plotters were put to death. As for Tran Phe De, he was demoted to the rank of duke. Since he was only a nephew of Tran Nghe Tong, Le Qui Ly had no difficulty in convincing Tran Nghe Tong to name another heir. Tran Nghe Tong appointed his youngest son, Prince Chieu Dinh Vuong, who became Tran Thuan Tong. Later, at Le Qui Ly's insistence, Tran Nghe Tong forced Tran Phe De to strangle himself.

Tran Thuan Tong ascended the throne amid chaos. In 1389, Che Bong Nga again invaded Thanh Hoa. Le Qui Ly, after a brief resistance at Co Vo, fled back to the capital, leaving his lieutenants behind to deal with the puissant Chams. Che Bong Nga's fleet reached the Red River, and a terrified Tran Nghe Tong assigned General Tran Khat Chan to the quasi-impossible task of stopping him. Their morale had reached an abyss; their farewell scene was in itself a tragedy. The weeping general prostrated himself and offered his life to the king, who accepted his sacrifice, crying in terror. But the fortunes of war do not always depend on science or bravery; the will of heaven also makes a difference. Tran Khat Chan, not yearning to fight, moved his troops to Thai Binh Province to prepare their defense. Che Bong Nga sailed up the Red River to meet the enemy forces. A perfidious servant of his, who had joined the Viets some time ago, pointed out his boat to Tran Khat Chan, who rushed to shoot at it. The junk was destroyed, valiant Che Bong Nga perished, and the Cham troops retreated. His head was presented to the Highest King Tran Nghe Tong, who had no shame in claiming credit for the victory and compared himself to Han Kao Tsu receiving Hsiang Yu's head. But Tran Nghe Tong was wise enough to realize the danger presented by Le Qui Ly's increasing power. So he used a display of flattery to deter the potential traitor. One day, repeating Liu Pei's last words to his faithful K'un Min, he said: "You belong to the family, that's why I have given you all powers. Now the kingdom is weak and I am old, if later you can help my son, please do so. Otherwise take over!" In reply, Le Qui Ly kowtowed, threw away his cap, wept, and said in complete hypocrisy: "Once Tran Phe De had tried to kill me; without your protection I would be now swallowing my smile underground. I have no ulterior motives. May the Heaven and the Earth destroy me if I will not serve loyally."[21]

Le Qui Ly (1400–1407)

By the time Tran Nghe Tong died in 1394, Annam had lost the ability to exist as an independent nation. Tran Nghe Tong had from the very beginning of his reign set a pattern of defection. While everybody was fighting for him, he fled away and hid until he was forcefully brought back to be enthroned. Instead of repairing the havoc caused by Champa's unrelenting raids, during which he repeatedly abandoned his subjects despite their supplications to stay and fight with them, he raised taxes to build palaces and amusement lakes and wasted his time finding new caches for his riches. His lack of concern for his people finally led them to destitution, famine, and revolts, paving the way for Le Qui Ly's usurpation.

The war against Champa resulted in growing expenses. Natural catastrophes, the ensuing loss of crops, and more and more taxes led the peasants to abandon their land or sell it to the rich, for whom they went to work afterward. This increased the serf class. In 1389, Pham Su On's forces occupied Thang Long for three days, compelling the Highest King, together with Tran Thuan Tong and the court, to take refuge in Bac Giang.

History has not done justice to Le Qui Ly. His usurpation was the only way to put an end to monarchic apathy and incompetence. He was the last hope for a strong Annam because he had the will and the means to lead the people. His reforms could stop the decay of the state and restore grandeur to the nation. And since nobody could carry out the reforms but him, he had to seize power and eliminate his opponents. Le Qui Ly's behavior was due more to national interest than to personal ambition. He started out in a very low position at the court in 1371, under Tran Nghe Tong's reign. Later he was promoted regional governor and married the king's sister, Princess Huy Ninh, who was the widow of Prince Tran Nhan Vinh. In 1375, he became army chief of staff. In 1380, he won a naval battle against the Cham and took over the army command made available by the demotion of General Do Tu Binh after his defeat by Che Bong Nga at Qui Nhon. In 1387, with royal compliments, he was promoted to supreme commander of all Annam forces. In 1394, he was the highest dignitary at the court. In 1398, since there were no more honors the king could bestow on him, he proclaimed himself "Royal Virtue Renovator" and "National Regent."

He started a series of bold reforms, reminiscent of the Han's Wang Mang's and the Northern Sung Wang An Shih's. In 1396, to cope with economic disasters, Le Qui Ly made use of paper money for the first time in Vietnam's history. Symbolic sketches marked the value of the bills. Seaweed was used on the lowest currency while dragons were portrayed on bills of the highest value. Turtles and phoenixes were on the middle-range bills. But Le Qui Ly alienated the entire nation by forcing the people to exchange their copper coins against government bills. They did not like this because paper was perishable and not easy to stow. The first victims were the nobles and the religious groups.

Besides the reorganization of the armed forces, to which he introduced newly designed combat boats and the consolidation of the infantry with a revised chain of command, he placed his entire administration in uniform.

Provinces and districts were staffed with university graduates, and land was redistributed to limit the rapacity of the landlords. The number of slaves was limited by the rank and position of their owners. Private property was limited, so that the peasants would have their fair share. To protect them from the abuses of princes and dignitaries, he assigned them to work on dams and dikes, to create for themselves more cultivable land. He also sent entire families to colonize the provinces seized from Champa, providing them with the necessary agricultural implements, including plowshares and traction animals. Rice depots were created to help the population in periods of famine. A hospital was established to provide free care for the people.

Le Qui Ly's cultural realizations were also unique. He promoted the Vietnamese Nom to supplant Chinese script. He also denounced the Sung Golden Age, castigated Confucius, and showed his inclination toward the Legalist doctrine. During his thirty years in public life, he directed his efforts toward the restriction of dynastic powers and the ending of aristocratic rule.

Tran Thieu De (1398–1400)

In 1397, after he had built a new western capital at Yen Ton (Thanh Hoa), where he transferred the court so it would be far away from the scrutiny of the Thang Long populace,[22] Le Qui Ly sent an astrologer to convince Tran Thuan Tong to relinquish power and devote his life to the search for immortality. Acknowledging the veiled threat, the king abdicated in favor of his three-year-old son, Prince An, who was named Tran Thieu De. In 1399, Le Qui Ly dispatched his aide Nguyen Can to poison Tran Thuan Tong. He promised to have Nguyen Can executed if he failed in his mission. So with many apologies Nguyen Can gave the poison to Tran Thuan Tong, who bravely swallowed it, probably with the idea of doing a favor for Nguyen Can. But against all expectations he remained alive, causing Nguyen Can to fear for his own existence. Finally the cavalry general Pham Kha Vinh finished the repugnant work by strangling Tran Thuan Tong. In 1400, King Tran Thieu De was summarily deposed. His life was spared because he was the son of Le Qui Ly's daughter. The Tran dynasty, which had lasted for 175 years, was praised for its resistance to the Mongols, but was also blamed by traditional historians for its incestuous practices.

For public consumption, Le Qui Ly declared he "accepted the throne only at Thieu De's request and because the entire Court had insisted three times."[23] He changed his name to Ho Qui Ly and Annam became Dai Ngu for a short period. A few months later, he gave power to his son Ho Han Thuong and became Highest King in pure monarchic tradition.

In Champa, King La Khai, who had just died, was succeeded by his son Ba Dich Lai. Le Qui Ly sent a 150,000 man sea and land expedition under Admiral Do Man and General Tran Tung. Bad coordination between them resulted in the retreat of the Viet troops and the demotion of Tran Tung. Then the Chams set a trap for Le Qui Ly. They offered him two huge ivory plates, then told the Ming that Le Qui Ly had seized the tribute reserved for their emperor. To prevent a clash with the Chinese, Le Qui Ly had to relinquish the precious gifts and transfer them to Peking. Then on the occasion of the ceremony of loyalty at Don Son, the high dignitaries started a plot against Le Qui Ly. But some lost their courage, prompting Le Qui Ly to call in his troops for the rescue. His reaction was ruthless. Three hundred and seventy princes, generals, and high mandarins were executed. The bloody cleansing lasted a year, and all internal opposition was annihilated.

Now Le Qui Ly had to deal with the Ming personally. In 1403, on the occasion of the coronation of Emperor Ming T'ai Tsu, he sent an envoy to pay homage. Claiming that the Tran dynasty was extinct, he begged for the investiture of Ho Han Thuong, who was a Tran grandson and also Le Qui Ly's own son. Ming T'ai Tsu, after conducting an investigation, confirmed Ho Han Thuong as king of Annam.

In 1402, Le Qui Ly had General Do Man invade Champa and compel King Ba Dich Lai to yield Quang Nam and Quang Nghia. In 1403, another expedition, with 200,000 men, failed to take Do Ban (Qui Nhon) after a thirty-day siege.

While Annam was preoccupied with Champa, a slave of Tran Nguyen Huy who called himself Tran Thiem Binh fled to Yen King via Lao and Yunnan. There he claimed to be a son of King Tran Nghe Tong. He denounced the Ho usurpation and asked for Chinese intervention. The Chinese emperor, who was actually rather interested in recovering Annam for his empire, sent a secret agent to investigate. When Le Qui Ly learned about that covert mission, he dispatched his killers to hunt the Chinese spy. But it was too late. The spy had crossed the border a few hours before, with a lethal report against Le Qui Ly in his pocket. To prevent further complications, the Viets had to hand over fifty-nine districts to the Ming. Then, with a typically twisted mind, Le Qui Ly hired native assassins to poison all the Chinese governors. This idea was so ludicrous that Ming T'ai Tsu could not believe his ears and had to dispatch a team of Viet food experts to verify the situation.[24] In 1406, Ming T'ai Tsu ordered 5,000 troops under generals Han Quan and Hoang Trung to escort Tran Thiem Binh back to Annam. At the border, they were promptly surrounded by Viet forces and had to hand over Tran Thiem Binh in exchange for their own safety. Needless to say, Tran Thiem Binh was put to death as a traitor.

Later, the Ming sent two armies under the command of Marshall Chu Nang. On his way to the south, that illustrious warrior died of disease at Long Chau, and his assistant, General Truong Phu, took the command. Three battles would decide Le Qui Ly's fate. He was defeated at Da Bang, Moc Pham Giang, and Ham Tu and had his dispirited general, Nguy Thuc, beheaded for suggesting that "he, the king, should burn himself instead of dying at the hands of the enemy."[25] Later, Le Qui Ly retreated to a mountain, where he was told by the elderly that the name of the place was a bad omen for him. Actually, they misrepresented the spelling to induce him to leave the area. But Le Qui Ly knew better and had them all beheaded. Too intelligent to accept their fabrications, he persisted in staying in the area and was captured with his entire retinue. After a long period in a Chinese jail, he concluded his life as a petty patrol guard somewhere in the province of Kwangsi. This was the will of heaven.

THE LATER TRAN DYNASTY

Gian Dinh De (1407–1409)

In 1407 in the province of Ninh Binh, Gian Dinh Vuong, a young son of King Tran Nghe Tong, proclaimed himself Emperor Gian Dinh De. After a few skirmishes, he was defeated and fled to Nghe An. At that time, Dang Tat, a Viet general who had become the Ming governor of Hoa Chau, probably in a display of remorse killed several Ming officers and joined Gian Dinh De. In Dong Trieu, Tran Nguyet Ho also revolted, but he was soon captured by the Ming. His troops also rallied around Gian Dinh De. A victory by Dang Tat over the pro-Ming Pham The Cang gave Gian Dinh De control of the three important provinces of Thanh Hoa, Nghe An, and Quang Binh. The troops later marched on the eastern capital of Thang Long, and at Bo Co they confronted 40,000 troops from Yunnan under the command of the Chinese generals Moc Thanh and Lu Nghi. The ensuing death of Lu Nghi threw the Chinese into disarray and caused a general retreat. Gian Dinh De decided to follow them in hot pursuit, but Dang Tat disagreed, preferring to wait for reinforcements. Gian Dinh De, who had always doubted Dang Tat's loyalty, began to question his behavior. Later, based on unfounded reports, he had Dang Tat and his chief of staff, Nguyen Canh Chan, summarily executed. It was a fatal mistake, for it destroyed the morale of the troops, which was what Annam needed the most in order to survive.

Tran Quy Khoat (1403–1413)

Dang Dung and Nguyen Canh Di, sons of the two victims, deserted and joined Tran Quy Khoat, a grandson of Tran Nghe Tong, who was fighting his own war in Ha Tinh. Tran Quy Khoat proclaimed himself King Trung Quang. To consolidate the Viet forces, he came up with a bold scheme. While Gian Dinh De was fighting the Ming at Ngu Thien, he had him kidnapped and brought to his quarters where he appointed him as the Highest King, thus establishing Viet unity of command.

To quell the turmoil, Ming T'ai Tsu sent General Truong Phu back to Annam. Soon, Gian Dinh De was captured and Tran Quy Khoat retreated to Nghe An. Truong Phu pursued his advance, sowing terror and destruction on his way. Viet bodies formed mountains; their fresh intestines dangled on trees; their remains were boiled to obtain fat. In 1412, Tran Quy Khoat and Nguyen Canh Di scored a small victory at Hong Chau. But lack of coordination resulted in defeat, forcing both to move back to Nghe An. The next year, under Truong Phu's pressure, they again retreated to Hoa Chau. Tran Quy Khoat had several times sent envoys to Ming T'ai Tsu to apply for recognition, but they were all put to death. Now he had Nguyen Bieu directly approach Truong Phu. But Nguyen Bieu was no diplomat. Instead of using peaceful words he started a violent diatribe against the Ming. As a result, he was decapitated. Some time later, Truong Phu, well informed of the conditions of Tran Quy Khoat's forces, moved to break the Viet defense. But at night his junk fell into the hands of a commando under General Nguyen Suy and Dang Dung. In the ensuing confusion, Truong Phu escaped on a small boat. But realizing the Viets were outnumbered, he counterattacked and forced Dang Dung to retreat. That was the last battle for Tran Quy Khoat and his followers. They took refuge in the mountains and never recovered their strength. Later they were captured by Truong Phu and sent to China. On the way, Tran Quy Khoat and Dang Dung threw themselves into the ocean. A temple in Ha Tinh was erected to commemorate Dang Dung. The later Tran, as they were called, lasted only seven years. But against foreign domination, they followed a pattern of resistance which was to last forever.

For the fourth time, Annam was under Chinese domination. The Ming intervention under the pretense of restoring the legitimate monarch never fooled anybody. But by asking for their intervention, the Tran took the blame for having "opened the Jungle to the Tiger."[26]

After their victory, the Ming were shrewd enough to have some Viet scholars, dignitaries, and nobles issue a manifesto stating that since the Tran dynasty was extinguished, China should reintegrate Annam into the empire as Chiao Chih province. Then they reorganized Annam into seventeen districts under three departments: administration, justice, and construction. Truong Phu was ordered to ferret out Viet scholars and aristocrats and to appoint them to the local administration after training in China. But not all Viets turned into Chinese collaborators. Many rebelled.

In 1414, having reestablished calm in Annam, Truong Phu and Moc Thanh returned to China, not without a large retinue of coerced beauties. Hoang Phuc stayed behind to implement Ming policy. Men were not allowed to cut their hair, and women had to wear long pants with smocks. Provinces and districts were to build temples and shrines for worship of the Chinese spirits and gods. Physicians, diviners, Buddhist and Taoist monks, and Confucian scholars were all enrolled as teachers in the new Chinese schools that were opened around the country. Books on Buddhism and Taoism were imported from China, while Viet works and annals from previous dynasties were shipped to China where they disappeared. Periodically, outstanding scholars were selected to attend the National Administration Institute before being appointed to government posts. Postal services were organized to transport mail by horse between Dong Quan and Gia Lam and by boat from Dong Trieu to Van Ninh, China. Military service was carried out by draft in the north, which was the most heavily populated area. But from Thanh Hoa down to the south, where the population density was low, peasants had to assure their own defense. Identity cards were created reflecting the census records. The entire territory was divided into the same divisions that exist today: hamlets, villages, districts, provinces. As for taxes, a salt tax was added to the land tax, which was increased.

Natural resources were exploited to the fullest extent. Gold mines were opened. Mountains were explored for elephant tusks, rhinoceros horns, and tiger bones, all of which were considered precious Chinese medications. The seas were surveyed for pearls. Forests yielded precious woods (teak and sandalwood) and medicinal plants. It was the worst period in the history of Vietnam. The people suffered, not only from the abuses of foreign exploitation, but also from the zeal of the Viet officers who ruled the country for the Ming. Eager to please their Chinese masters, they devised schemes to plunder their own countrymen and to curb their grievances. Thus, revolts flared up everywhere, producing a climate of unrest.

NOTES

1. James Legge, trans., *The Works of Mencius* (reprint, Hong Kong: Hong Kong University Press, 1970), vol. 2, p. 170.

2. Le Thanh Khoi, *Histoire du Viet Nam* (Paris: Sudestasie, 1992), p. 131.

3. Tran Trong Kim, *Viet Nam Su Luoc* (reprint Los Angeles: Dai Nam), B.I, p. 87.

4. Ibid., p. 99.

5. Some affirm that it also gives women's gaits a wanton look.

6. Tran Trong Kim, *Viet Nam, Su Luoc* B.I, p. 127.

7. He was a forebear of the usurper Mac Dang Dung.

8. Binh Thu Yeu Luoc, *Essentials of Military Arts*, proclamation.

9. Tran Trong Kim, *Viet Nam, Su Luoc* B.I, p. 144.

10. The Man and the Muong are minority tribes.

11. Pham van Son, *Viet Su Tan Bien* (reprint, Los Angeles: Dai Nam, n.d.), B.II, p. 275.

12. Ibid., p. 269.

13. Tran Trong Kim, *Viet Nam Su Luoc*, B.I, pp. 170, 171.

14. Pham Van Son, *Viet Su Tan Bien*, B.II, pp. 290-91.

15. Prince Kinh was the one who had forcefully put Nghe Tong on the throne.

16. Tran Trong Kim, *Viet Nam, Su Luoc*, B.I, p. 181.

17. Arthur Cotterell, *China, a Cultural History* (New York: Penguin, 1988), p. 189.

18. C.P. Fitzgerald, *China: A Short Cultural History* (New York: Praeger, 1950), p. 432.

19. Kumy is fermented mare's milk.

20. Tran Trong Kim, *Viet Nam Su Luoc*, B.I, p. 181.

21. Pham van Son, *Viet Su Tan Bien*, B.II, p. 340.

22. Thang Long (Hanoi) was the eastern capital (Dong Do).

23. Pham van Son, *Viet Su Tan Bien*, B.II, p. 345.

24. They were the same experts previously dispatched to China as part of the Viet tribute.

25. Pham van Son, *Viet Su Tan Bien*, B.II, p. 357.

26. "Tha cop ve rung" in Vietnamese.

4

THE LIBERATORS

After Le Qui Ly's defeat to the Ming in 1406, Vietnam was back under Chinese domination.

LE LOI AND NGUYEN TRAI

In 1418, Le Loi, a rich farmer from the province of Thanh Hoa, started a rebellion. He was supported by the generals Le Kien and Le Thach. Later, at Loi Giang, he met Nguyen Trai, an extraordinary figure who had been a scholar under Le Qui Ly. Nguyen Trai's maternal great grandfather was Tran Quang Khai, the winner of the Chuong Duong battle. When his father, Nguyen Phi Khanh, a highly respected scholar, was deported to China by the Ming, Nguyen Trai followed him. But at the Nam Quan frontier, his father told him that instead of crying he should go back and do his best to avenge his father and his country. So he did. When he met with Le Loi, he had in his pocket a plan to defeat the Chinese. Le Loi made Nguyen Trai his advisor. Ultimately, Nguyen Trai encountered a most unjust fate, losing both his love and his life.

Nguyen Trai had first to secure Le Loi's legitimacy as the Binh Dinh Vuong (King Pacificator) by employing an artifice once used in China.[1] With a stylus moistened with animal fat, he wrote on the leaves of trees in the forest. "Le Loi is the king, Nguyen Trai is his servant." After ants ate away the fat, the leaves displayed the perforated slogan. This prompted people to cry "prophecy," and thousands of peasants joined in.[2] As they were not strong enough to sustain conventional warfare, Le Loi and Nguyen Trai decided to wage guerrilla warfare. Fifteen centuries later, General Vo Nguyen Giap was to use the same strategy against the French, before the final showdown at Dien Bien Phu.

Le Loi chose Chi Linh, in the Ha Tinh mountains, as the operational base from which he launched several attacks and took control of Nghe An. But at Cam Thuy he was driven back, leaving behind his wife and children, who were captured. In 1419, he reappeared at Nga Lac and succeeded in killing the Ming general Nguyen Sao. Ultimately he was surrounded. He owed his life to an officer named Le Lai who substituted for him and was captured and executed. In recognition of his sacrifice, Le Loi announced that Le Lai's memorial would precede his own by one day. Since Le Loi passed away on September 22, Le Lai's ceremony was set for September 21.

While Le Loi was trying to enlist the support of neighboring Laos, revolts erupted in several provinces of Annam, including Phan Lieu in Nghe An, Le Thanh in Ha Hong, Nguyen Dat in Khoai Chau, Ha Cau in Hoang Giam, and Le Nga in Thuy Duong. The Ming forces had to thin out to fight the insurgents. This gave Le Loi some respite and he reinforced his own troops. In 1421, the Ming general Tran Tri encircled Ba Lam, but was repulsed and left 1,000 dead on the battlefield. Lao forces under the Ming, pretending to be Le Loi's allies, surprised the Viets at night. They succeeded in killing their general Le Thach, who had been one of Le Loi's earliest supporters, but failed to secure their position. The following year, a violent battle against the combined Ming and Lao troops forced Le Loi to withdraw to Chi Linh. This was a severe setback. Because of a shortage of supplies, Le Loi's demoralized troops were forced to eat plants and grass and even to kill horses and elephants for food. In 1423, Le Loi called for a cease-fire, which was quickly accepted by the Ming. For a time, both parties exchanged trade until suspicion arose among the Ming, who detained Le Tran, the Viet envoy. Le Loi withdrew to Lu Son Mountain. The following year, he resumed the war and attacked the Ming outpost at Nghe An forcing general Tran Tri to flee to the Chinese headquarters at Dong Quan. He left behind his lieutenant, Ly An, to hold down the fort. Le Loi then seized the post of Da Cang, after dislodging the Ming general Luong Nhu Hot. From there, he set an ambush in the vicinity of Tra Long, where he killed the Ming general Tran Trung and 2,000 of his men. The booty was considerable and included one hundred horses. Cam Banh, the Chinese governor of the Tra Long district, surrendered.

A punitive expedition led by Ming marshall Tran Hiep fell into an ambush at Kha Luu. Two Ming generals were massacred, and their troops were swept back toward Nghe An. The following year, when Le Loi laid siege to Nghe An, the local population rallied under his command. Again Tran Tri fled to Dong Quan. A Ming convoy of 300 supply junks was dispatched from Dong Quan, but was intercepted at Dien Chau by Viet troops under Dinh Le. One Chinese general and 300 troops were killed. Then with the support of Le Sat and Luu Nhan Chu, Dinh Le rode directly to Thanh Hoa, the western capital, with a reinforcement of 2,000 elite troops. The recapture of Thanh Hoa marked the completion of Le Loi's campaign in the south.

Next the Viets moved to the north. Pham Van Xao intercepted 10,000 troops from Yunnan at Xa Loc and forced them to retreat to Tam Giang. At that time, Annam had enough troops to stage both guerrilla and conventional warfare simultaneously. Besides reassembling forces for knocking down Dong Quan, the Viets proceeded with ambushes and harassments elsewhere. To rescue Dong Quan, the Chinese military leader Phuong Chinh left Nghe An by sea, thus giving Le Loi the opportunity to attack the unprotected garrison. From Peking, Emperor Yung Lo dispatched the famous General Wang Tong with 50,000 troops. The Viets, with only 3,000 troops and two elephants, met the Chinese at Tuy Dong. But the Ming suffered a serious defeat. They had lost all their artillery and had to melt the famous Quy Dien bells and the Pho Minh bronze urn to make new guns. Two Chinese generals were killed, and the rest, including Wang Tong, the commander in chief, escaped to Dong Quan. Le Loi let them in and then called for their surrender. However, knowing that they were all high ranking officers who would rather die than surrender, he decided on a stratagem that would allow them to save face. Since their mission had been to reestablish the Tran king, if one were found, they would have accomplished their task. At that time, a man named Ho Ong, who claimed to be a grandson of Tran Nghe Tong, was eager to assume power. Le Loi officially proclaimed Tran Cao King of the South. Wang Tong, well aware of the Viets' designs, pretended ignorance and agreed to the peace talks. Actually he was trying to gain time, having secretly called for help from China, but his messenger was caught. Le Loi accused the Chinese of duplicity and broke off the negotiations. He seized Gia Lam, Thi Cau, Tam Dai, Phu Lang Thuong, and Ky On while increasing pressure on Dong Quan.

In 1427, in a last attempt to save Dong Quan, two Chinese armies converged on the fortified place. The first one, consisting of 100,000 men and 20,000 horses under Marshall Lieu Thang, marched down through Yunnan, and the second, under the old general Moc Thanh, progressed across Kwangsi. At My Dong, the Viets were surrounded and General Dinh Le lost his life. In another encounter, the Viet leader Ly Trien was killed. To reinforce discipline among the troops and the populace, Le Loi issued martial law. At Chi Lang, 10,000 men and five elephants moved to meet Lieu Thang. Not used to fighting in muddy land, the Chinese, despite their numerical superiority, were promptly defeated. Lieu Thang and his lieutenant Luong Minh were killed. Another general committed suicide, and two more were captured. As for Moc Thanh, he preferred to withdraw. In the process, he lost 10,000 men, but succeeded in saving his own life. Although the general consensus was for a military solution, Nguyen Trai advised that only negotiation could put an end to the conflict. When Wang Tong renewed his peace offer, repeating that he was satisfied with the restoration of the Tran, Le Loi dispatched an envoy to the Ming emperor for formal recognition. Emperor Yung Lo had his Minister of Rites, Ly Ty, go to Annam and appoint Tran Cao king. At the same time, the Ming withdrew their governor, ending thirteen years of Chinese domination. The celebrated *Report on the Pacification of China* (*Binh Ngo Dai Cao*) written by Nguyen Trai describes one of the most heroic periods in the history of Vietnam. After seven years of bloody battles, Vietnam emerged a victorious nation, setting an example for neighboring states.

As for Tran Cao, he tired of being a puppet and also feared for his life. He escaped to the Ngoc Ma district, where he was caught by Le Loi's men and forced to take poison.

THE LE DYNASTY

Le Thai To (1428–1433)

In 1428, Le Loi acceded the throne as Le Thai To, the founder of the Le Dynasty. An envoy was dispatched to Peking to ask for Emperor Yung Lo's recognition, but to no avail. The Chinese insisted on having a Tran king. After several attempts, Le Thai To resorted to a ruse by asking leading dignitaries and eminent elders to certify in writing that the Tran dynasty was extinct. Yung Lo had to give his approval, but because he was still grieving the loss of his two senior generals Lieu Thang and Luong Minh, he demanded that every three years the Annam tribute include two gold images of his dead heroes.

Le Thai To rewarded his loyal companions. Nguyen Trai was appointed first minister, and Le Van first general. In total 227 were proclaimed national heroes. As for the troops, 60 percent were demobilized, and the balance were divided into five rotating groups, four being sent home at a time for rice cultivation. The economy was in shambles, causing Le Thai To to enforce austerity measures. Public celebrations were limited, and family entertainments had to be justified. Gamblers were not welcome—those without an occupation would have three fingers cut off, while those having a job lost only one. As for drunkards, 100 strikes of the rod were supposed to make them less thirsty. Land reform was also carried out. Excess land, due to the death of its owner or to lack of cultivation during the war, was redistributed to war veterans and poor peasants. Villages were reorganized in three classes: great villages with more than 100 inhabitants, intermediary villages with over 50 inhabitants, and small villages with over 10 inhabitants. Annam was divided into four administrative zones, north, south, east, and west.

After ten years of war, moral standards had fallen, and so strict enforcement of penalties was required. Sentences were classified into five categories. Retribution for misdemeanors consisted of 10 to 50 strokes of the rod at primary stage, and 60 to 100 strokes at the secondary stage. At the next level, punishments consisted of lowering civil status down to either that of a palace slave, elephants guardian, or remote settlement guard. Higher crimes were punished by deportation to Nghe An, hard labor in Bo Chinh, or banishment to Tan Binh. As for capital punishment, it went from strangulation to decapitation, then to decapitation with public exposure, and finally, the worst of all, live disembowelment.

In the field of education, Le Thai To created an Institute of National Examination for the sons of dignitaries and for outstanding commoners. Confucian schools were opened at the provincial and district levels. All mandarins had to attend academic review. Buddhists and Taoist monks had to be licensed, and those who failed religious examinations were to return to secular life and pursue productive occupations.

Le Thai To died in 1434. His rule was marked by Vietnam's return to independence. Although his public achievements were outstanding, his personal behavior was not above criticism. He was involved in court intrigues and was criticized for killing two of his old followers and for having sequestered Nguyen Trai. In politics, gratitude is not necessarily a virtue, and when the Sung emperor Chao Kuan Yin accused his fellow generals of coveting his throne, he did not have to produce any proof, for he was referring to a political reality.

Le Thai Tong (1434–1442)

Le Thai To's son, who was only eleven years old, succeeded him as Le Thai Tong, under the regency of Le Sat. Although he was among the first to join Le Loi, Le Sat was by no means an educated man. He was unable to grasp the obligations of his high position and soon became corrupted by power. Those who disagreed with him were dismissed or executed. Le Thai Tong, realizing that Le Sat was a liability, had him murdered. But when freed of constraints, Le Thai Tong was even worse. He directed his youthful energy to lustful pursuits. His achievements as a ruler were limited. He made a few changes in the educational and monetary fields. Those who passed their doctoral examinations had their names engraved on a stone in the Temple of Education. The tradition lasted until recent times. The rate of currency was modified to 60 piasters per coin, but did not necessarily profit the populace. To regulate trade, silk and woven material were given standard sizes. Manufactured paper was counted at 100 sheets per set. But Le Thai Tong should have focused on the droughts and floods that were causing much misery among the peasants. As a result, a few minor uprisings took place. The peasants were restrained only by the loving memory of his father, Le Thai To (Le Loi).

In 1442, a tragic scandal—the "Le Chi Farm Case"—rocked the prestige of the monarchy. Following review of his troops at Chi Linh, Le Thai Tong paid a visit to old Nguyen Trai, who was living in retirement nearby with his attractive concubine Nguyen Thi Lo. That night, although "droit de cuissage"[3] was not in the Viet tradition, Nguyen Thi Lo had to serve the young king. He was so pleased with her that the next day he took her with him back to the palace. They arrived at Bac Ninh at night and stayed at the Le Chi farm. At dawn, Nguyen Thi Lo sprang out of bed, hysterically crying for help. A physician ran in to find the king growing "colder and colder."[4] Efforts to revive him were in vain. Le Thai Tong died of exhaustion at the age of twenty. The court condemned Nguyen Thi Lo to death and had Nguyen Trai and his entire family down to the third generation executed. The punishment was unprecedented, given the unique position of Nguyen Trai. He had contributed to the founding of the Le dynasty and to the independence of Annam. In Confucian terms, he was the father of the nation and as such his person was untouchable. The court's actions could only have been due to deeper, darker motives. Indeed, according to some reports, the royal succession had been on the palace agenda for some time. Queen Tuyen Tu and Le Thai Tong's other consorts were fighting for their own offspring. Prince Nhi Dan had been banned from the succession because his mother had made certain mistakes. Another concubine, Hue Phi, was chastised for having resorted to black magic to mesmerize the inconstant Tran Thai Tong. Another, Ngo Tiep Du,[5] was pregnant for ten months without any sign of prompt delivery. Suspicious of evil spirits, Le Thai Tong had her tied to a pole in his park and ordered archers to shoot at her womb. Thanks to the intervention of Le Thang, the king's cousin, she was spared from death and was sent to live in the royal stables. Later, following Nguyen Trai's intervention, she was released to Nguyen Thi Lo's custody. When Ngo Tiep Du finally delivered her son, Prince Tu Thanh, who later became the illustrious Le Thanh Tong, Nguyen Thi Lo helped them to escape. The sensual Nguyen Thi Lo was, at that time, in charge of teaching etiquette to the ladies of the court. According to some sources she was already a favorite of Thai Tong. So whether or not Nguyen Thi Lo met the king for the first time in Nguyen Trai's house seems irrelevant. Anyway, she had already been singled out for her participation in various palace intrigues, so her association with the king's death came as no surprise. As for Nguyen Trai, he was considered an obstacle to Queen Tuyen Tu's ambition to become regent after Le Thai Tong's death.

Le Nhan Tong (1443–1459)

The two-year-old Prince Bang Co succeeded Le Thai Tong with the name of Le Nhan Tong, under the regency of the queen mother Tuyen Tu. His rule was relatively calm and was marked by a few reforms in the fields of education and justice. War against Champa continued with the sack of the capital Do Ban and the capture of King Bi Cai, who was taken to Annam with his entire harem. He was replaced on the throne by a relative.

In 1453, Le Nhan Tong took the reins of power. In 1459, he and the queen mother were assassinated by his half-brother Nghi Dan, who declared himself king. The self-appointed monarch killed many court dignitaries, thus arousing general discontent. In 1460, he was assassinated by a handful of high officers who offered the throne to Prince Cung Vuong. Prince Cung Vuong declined. As a last resort, they went to Prince Tu Thanh,[6] who without Cung Vuong's abstention could never have acceded the throne.

Le Thanh Tong (the Vietnamese Hammurabi)
(1460–1497) and the Hong Duc Code

Tu Thanh was one of the greatest rulers Vietnam has ever had. He took the name of Le Thanh Tong, the only historic king with a legend. His mother, Lady Tiep Du, dreamed that the Emperor of Heaven would appoint a celestial dignitary to be her son and that he would rule Annam. But he found the country too small, so the Emperor of Heaven also gave him Champa. But he was not satisfied; he wanted more and more, including all of China. The Emperor of Heaven became so infuriated that he lost control, struck him on the head, and kicked him down to earth. This explains why Le Thanh Tong was born with a scar on his forehead.

Le Thanh Tong's achievements made Vietnam a mature nation. His legal innovations were reminiscent of Hammurabi's code. They were not only ahead of their time, but also dealt with almost the same concerns: marriage and family; property and theft; judges and accusers; and slavery. But while the Babylonian laws tended to uphold the theocratic foundations of government, the Viet laws worked against the established social order. In promulgating his code, Hammurabi remained obedient to his gods, but Le Thanh Tong denounced the Confucian catechism.

Moreover, the Viet rules did not call for punitive justice on the basis of an eye for an eye and a tooth for a tooth, but rather sought rehabilitation through more humane treatment. Application of penalties depended not on the nature of the crime but rather on the offender's capacity for sustaining punishment, so that the expected reformation could be obtained. For example, different penalties were used for the same infractions, for example, flagellation might be used for women and cudgeling for men. Corporal punishment was reduced for seniors and minors, the handicapped and the sick.

While Hammurabi focused on the protection of trade, Le Thanh Tong was concerned with the social condition of the oppressed classes, of women, peasants, and slaves. Le Thanh Tong first defined the rights of peasants, whom he justly considered to be the building blocks of the nation. Although the choice of village notables had once been left to the village elders, communal polls were introduced to obtain basic popular participation. The tenure of a village chief was reduced to only one term so that no one could monopolize power. Land ownership was limited for government officers, and those found with extra property were severely disciplined. Pressure to dispossess peasants was considered an act of robbery. If cooks who worked in the kitchens of dignitaries forced peddlers to sell at loss, or market supervisors tolerated such abuses, they were marked with tattoos. However, peasants also had responsibilities. Failure to cultivate the land or the unjustified killing of working cattle was cause for severe penalties. Social order was enforced by a series of legal constraints. In order to stem prostitution, no female under fifteen could sell herself without proper transaction documents. And for the first time in Vietnam's history, the notion of statutory rape was introduced by fixing the age of a woman at twelve. Men who seduced others' wives or concubines were subjected to 100 strikes of the cane. The sentence was increased if the accused belonged to the influential class because they were supposed to set a good example. Abortion was forbidden. Death resulting from abortion was subject to criminal justice. Despite all his efforts, Le Thanh Tong could go no further. Actors and singers still shared social prejudice with prostitutes. Although they had the basic rights of citizens, their sons were not allowed to participate in academic examination, and their daughters were not allowed to marry into the nobility. As for slaves, while slaves taken in war served at the absolute discretion of their masters, those serving in the government were not considered the property of their superiors. Therefore, the killing of such slaves was severely punished. Condemning people on the basis of anonymous denunciations was proscribed. Judges who postponed trials in order to extort money from the parties involved were themselves disciplined.

But above all, Le Thanh Tong's civil code was incredibly liberal in its treatment of women's rights. No marriage could be arranged by parents against the will of their daughter. If during the period before the wedding the man was sentenced for a crime or became incapacitated, either physically or financially, the girl had the right to apply for annulment. In such a case, all wedding gifts were returned to the man. But if the woman fell into an identical situation, the man was not allowed to rescind the marriage. Intimate relations between the parties were forbidden before the marriage was officially approved. Married women maintained the right to their own family inheritance but were no longer bound by the law of collective liability with their own family.[7] Concubines received a fair share of their husband's inheritance. Husbands absent for more than five months without reason risked losing their wives.

Beside the new laws, Le Thanh Tong issued a 24-article code of conduct, calling, for example, for parents to educate their children, husbands and wives to live in faithfulness to each other, citizens to help each other, employees to be loyal to their employers, peasants to work hard, and traders to be honest. Although this code of conduct did not call for penalization, it served as a basic warning. As for infractions of the penal code, misdemeanors involved flagellation for women, but for the same offense men were beaten with wooden rods covered with bronze. Punishment for higher infractions involved community service and face marking. Capital punishment, which could be by strangulation, decapitation with public exposure of the head, or live dissection, was used for those accused of the ten capital crimes, among which was high treason, destruction of ancestral shrines, desertion to the enemy, murder of parents or senior family members, insulting parents or refusing to mourn them, and unauthorized use of royal privileges. Children were authorized to bear punishment for their parents. The sick, handicapped, and elderly were not tortured or submitted to other physical punishment. No one was to be tortured more than three times. Except for capital punishment, caning was limited to a maximum of 100 strikes. Petty thieves were sent to guard remote camps, but powerful brigands were beheaded. Nobles and dignitaries who forced peasants to work for them were severely penalized. Le Thanh Tong's laws called the Hong Duc Code, lasted for centuries, until they were replaced by the retrograde Gia Long Code, a copy of the laws of China's Ch'ing dynasty.

Le Thanh Tong's military achievements were no less grand. He was responsible for the submission of neighboring countries such as Laos and completed the conquest of Champa. At that time, Cham Tra Duyet, who had seized power after having killed King Bi Do, sent his brother Tra Toan to the Ming emperor to ask for the throne of Annam. Meanwhile he continued to make incursions. In 1470, Le Thanh Tong issued a proclamation condemning Champa's hostile behavior and mobilized 260,000 men. Leading 1,700 junks and 100,000 troops through the mouths of the Sa Ky River in Quang Ngai and the Cuu Toa River in Quang Nam, Le Thanh Tong met the Cham at Mo No Mountain. The encounter cost Champa the life of one general and 300 men. At Do Ban, their capital, they lost 40,000 troops and 30,000 prisoners were taken, including King Tra Toan and his family. It was Champa's final defeat (Map 14). Le Thanh Tong gave the throne to the general Bo Tri Tri while Tra Toai, a brother of Tra Toan, fled to China to beg for Ming intervention. When the Viet forces reached Nghe An on their way back to Annam, Tra Toan died. Le Thanh Tong had his head hung on the bow of his junk under a white flag bearing the inscription "Head of Tra Toan, King of Champa." The following month, Le Thanh Tong divided Champa into three administrative districts: two under the rule of Viet governors and an insignificant third under Bo Tri Tri. The Ming showed some concern, but fell short of carrying out positive action against Annam. Some authors deny that Le Thanh Tong had any imperialistic designs. But given the magnitude of the forces he took to Champa, it is obvious that he had a plan in mind. Furthermore, the fact that he left many troops behind upon his withdrawal is an indication of more than simple retaliation.

In 1479, Le Thanh Tong again issued a proclamation against the Bon Man, a major tribe on the border of Laos. This time an expeditionary corps of 200,000 was dispatched to the mountainous Lao border. After a difficult battle, out of 90,000 Bon Man, only a few thousand were left. The region was then divided into nine districts under Cam Dong, a native chosen to be governor by Le Thanh Tong. In the past, the Lao tribes had been alternately perfidious allies and treacherous foes. Their elimination removed a factor of uncertainty in the west.

Le Thanh Tong died in 1497. His contributions were immense. At the top of the administration, the king shared power with a full cabinet, which included a prime minister who oversaw the ministers of the interior, finance, public works, defense and justice. Besides protecting the peasantry, Le Thanh Tong also focused on agriculture by increasing irrigation, building dams and dikes, and staffing them with inspectors. He and his mandarins were fervent Confucianists. They built schools, increased the number of examinations, and recruited masses of scholars. The Confucian Temple of Literature was enlarged to form the Na-

Map 14
Nam Tien: The March to the South (with Dates of Occupation)

tional College. A National Academy was created with twenty-eight high ranking scholars under the king himself. Among the total of thirty *trang* (those with the highest academic degree) who emerged in a span of 800 years from the Ly through the Nguyen, nine were from the Le Thanh Tong period. Le Thanh Tong also championed historic studies and commissioned Ngo Si Lien to write a 15-volume history of Vietnam. Cartography was developed, and more maps of Vietnam were drawn. Le Thanh Tong did not favor Buddhism, which he considered vexatious superstition. Therefore, under the pretext of austerity, he prohibited the building of pagodas, temples, and Buddhist libraries, the printing of Buddhist books, and the making of bronze bells. However, he carried out the ritual worship of his ancestors in accordance with Confucian teachings.

Despite his political wisdom, Le Thanh Tong did not keep out of court intrigues. The famous general Le Lang was executed because he originally supported Prince Cung Vuong for the throne. Cung Vuong himself was condemned to die in prison, although without his abstention Le Thanh Tong would never be enthroned. But Le Thanh Tong did not forget the devotion of Nguyen Trai and Nguyen Thi Lo. Their descendants were rehabilitated and promoted to high posts.

Le Thanh Tong, who was by no means a modest monarch, boasted about his fourteen sons and twenty daughters to such an extent that one of his closest advisors said bluntly that they were nothing but trouble. This was not an opinion, it was a prediction. His succession resulted in a pandemonium unprecedented in the history of Vietnam. For having killed an innocent who was his own brother and the architect of his ascension, his own descendents would meet just retribution from heaven.

Le Hien Tong (1497–1504)

Le Thanh Tong's eldest son, Prince Tang, acceded the throne as Le Hien Tong. He was quite a conservative king and was devoted to keeping his father's work unchanged. Nevertheless, he showed an interest in agriculture and waterworks and built roads to improve transportation. In the educational field, he carried out regular examinations. He died in 1504 after only seven years of rule. After him came the deluge.

Le Tuc Tong (1504)

His brother Prince Thuan, the third son of Le Thanh Tong, succeeded as Le Tuc Tong, but died six months later.

Le Uy Muc (1505–1509)

The court named Le Tuc Tong's elder brother, Prince Tuan, to succeed him as King Le Uy Muc. Once on the throne, Le Uy Muc managed to murder his grandmother, Le Thai Tong's wife, and two ministers, Dam Van Le and Nguyen Quang Bat, because they had originally opposed his accession to the throne.

Le Uy Muc was another insane monarch who was to mark the end of his dynasty. Every night he entertained himself with court ladies whom he strangled at dawn. During the daytime, he enjoyed having his palace guards club each other to death. Soon discontent spread around. Realizing his life was in jeopardy, Le Uy Muc recruited the best martial arts experts as body guards. One of them was a poor fisherman named Mac Dang Dung. He was a descendant of the famous scholar Mac Dinh Chi. Soon he was promoted to a high position, which caused many mandarins to resign in protest. Le Uy Muc dismissed the rest, leaving the court in a vacuum that Mac Dang Dung and his supporters rushed to fill. Dissatisfaction also reached the royal family.

Le Tuong Duc (1510–1516)

In 1509, Le Uy Muc precipitated his end by locking up his own cousin Gian Tu Cong. Liberated after having bribed the prison warden, Gian Tu Cong organized a coup and put Le Uy Muc to death. Then he set himself upon the throne as King Le Tuong Duc. He was no better. Although he was not a blood-thirsty character, he had expensive tastes that led him to build huge palaces and mobilize thousands of people. He also built war junks for his palace maids to row on his artificial lakes. Defying dynastic rules, Confucian precepts, the court's opposition, and the clamor of the populace, he took his father's concubines into his own harem. To replenish a depleted treasury, he increased taxes.

Revolts flared up throughout the country. At Dong Trieu, a monk named Tran Cao, who claimed to be a descendant of the Tran, with his son Thang and a Cham general, seized the entire province of Hai Duong. To make things worse, Tran Cao also proclaimed himself to be the Living Buddha. To obtain invincibility his troops donned black uniforms. As a result, thousands of superstitious peasants joined his ranks.

Then as if he did not already have enough troubles, Le Tuong Duc made a fatal mistake. For no reason, he had his senior general Trinh Duy San flogged in public. This was the ultimate loss of face that prompted Trinh Duy San, with the help of his two lieutenants, Le Quang Do and Trinh Chi Sam, to kill Le Tuong Duc.

The mandarins were divided over the king's succession. The debate was hot enough for Trinh Duy San to chop his opponent's head off in the presence of a terrified court. He put his candidate, Prince Quang Tri, on the throne, but a few days later his brother, Tran Duy Dai, for reasons unknown took Prince Quang Tri to Thanh Hoa where he put him to death.

The news of King Le Tuong Duc's murder reached his general Nguyen Hoang Du, who was fighting against Tran Cao at Bo De, near Thang Long. To avenge his king, Nguyen Hoang Du left the field and went back to sack the eastern capital, Thang Long.

Le Chieu Tong (1516–1524)

Since Thang Long had been destroyed, Trinh Duy San moved to Thanh Hoa, where he enthroned Prince Y as King Le Chieu Tong. Meanwhile, the former monk Tran Cao entered Thang Long, which had been left without defense. Then Trinh Duy San, with Trinh Tuy and Nguyen Hoang Du, forced Tran Cao to retreat to Lang Son. After moving back to Thang Long, Le Chieu Tong sent Trinh Duy San against Tran Cao. Unfortunately Trinh Duy San was killed in the ensuing battle, and Tran Cao again threatened Thang Long. At that point, Count Tran Chan was called to the rescue and badly mauled the rebel forces, compelling Tran Cao to retire to Lang Nguyen. There, dispirited, he resolved to transfer powers to his son and to resume his career as a monk, hoping to avert possible retribution in case of final defeat.

The death of Tran Duy San left the warlords without leadership, and soon Nguyen Hoang Du began to fight against Trinh Tuy. Tran Chan sided with Trinh Tuy, compelling Nguyen Hoang Du to withdraw to Thanh Hoa. At the court, Le Chieu Tong executed Trinh Duy Dai, Trinh Duy San's brother, who was plotting against him.[8] Then, suspecting Tran Chan of conspiracy, Le Chieu Tong had him murdered also. In retaliation, Tran Chan's supporters attacked the capital, and Le Chieu Tong fled to Gia Lam. Isolated and without resources, as a last resort, he called on Mac Dang Dung for help. As expected, Mac Dang Dung demanded full power and obtained it. Then, after subduing all the opposition, he challenged the king's authority. Realizing the threat, King Le Chieu Tong fled to join Mac Dang Dung's opponents in Son Tay.

Le Cung Hoang (1524–1527)

Mac Dang Dung named Le Chieu Tong's brother, Prince Xuan, to succeed him as Le Cung Hoang. Although at that time Le Chieu Tong's forces were strong enough to invoke a victory over Mac Dang Dung, Le Chieu Tong was doomed. Frightened and confused, he made many mistakes. For no reason, he put to death General Nguyen Ba Ky, an associate of the mighty warlord Trinh Tuy, who had come to his support. In reprisal, Trinh Tuy arrested the king and took him to Thanh Hoa. In 1524, Mac Dang Dung defeated Trinh Tuy. He then had King Le Chieu Tong assassinated at Dong Ha. In 1527, under considerable pressure, the Le dignitaries issued a proclamation to put Mac Dang Dung on the throne. Since King Le Cung Hoang and his mother were the last obstacles in his way, he had them both slain. Those who opposed his usurpation were executed; others committed suicide.

The Le dynasty, after 100 years of rule that was often prestigious, ended in pity and sorrow. Another Le dynasty, founded in exile with the help of Nguyen Kim survived in the south as the Later Le. From then on, Annam was clearly divided into two parts. The North, from Son Nam up, belonged to the Mac or Northern dynasty, and the South, from Thanh Hoa down, was nominally under the Later Le or Southern dynasty.

THE NORTHERN DYNASTY

Thai To Mac Dang Dung (1527–1529)

Unlike Le Qui Ly or China's Wang Mang, Mac Dang Dung, who came to power as Thai To Mac Dang Dung, had no political vision, no reforms for his people, not even an idea for the survival of his dynasty. During the three years he was king, he just kept up the Le customs, and then simulating the Tran, he relinquished power to his son Mac Dang Doanh and became the Highest King.

He was to bear the responsibility for destroying the unity of Vietnam and for its division in North and South. He took the throne in 1527 facing opposition mostly from Thanh Hoa, where Le Cong Nguyen, Nguyen Nga, and Nguyen Tho Tuong rebelled but were later subdued. At Ma Giang, Le Y scored a few successes before being captured.

In 1537, based on complaints from the Le family, the Ming Emperor Cheng Tung dispatched an army under General Chiu Luan (Cuu Loan) to Nam Quan, where an imperial edict for the capture of Mac Dang Dung was issued. Mac Dang Dung immediately declared allegiance to the emperor and offered him numerous presents. But the Ming kept up their pressure and in 1540 sent out word that they were ready to invade Annam. Mac Dang Dung and a retinue of forty dignitaries, bare chested and in chains as sign of their submission,[9] went to kowtow to the Ming at Nam Quan and ceded to them five Viet districts. With additional bribes, Mac Dang Dung finally succeeded in obtaining Chinese recognition as a second class governor.[10]

In 1529, Thai To Mac Dang Dung died and was replaced by Thai Tong Mac Dang Doanh (1530-1540). In 1541, Mac Dang Doanh was followed by his son Hien Tong Mac Phuc Hai (1541-1546). In 1546, Tuyen Tong Mac Phuc Nguyen (1546-1561) succeeded Mac Phuc Hai.

THE LATER LE OR SOUTHERN DYNASTY

Le Trang Tong (1533–1548)

Nguyen Hoang Du, after being forced back to Thanh Hoa following his defeat at the hands of Trinh Tuy and Mac Dang Dung, died leaving a son, Nguyen Kim, who escaped to Laos after Mac Dang Dung's coup. In 1532 at Sam Chau, in Laos, Nguyen Kim enthroned Le Chieu Tong's youngest son, Prince Duy Ninh, as King Le Trang Tong. Furthermore, to strengthen his support, he married his daughter, Ngoc Bao, to the famous warrior Trinh Kiem, a native of the district of Quang Hoa. Trinh Kiem was known for his filial devotion. As his mother used to have chicken to eat, he stole them, being too poor to be honest. He was caught and was pardoned by the local magistrate because of his filial devotion. But his vengeful neighbors set a trap and buried his mother alive. Disconsolate, he left the village and went to work as a servant in Nguyen Kim's house, until he was singled out for his martial ability. With Nguyen Kim, he built up an army at Sam Chau from which they launched a series of raids against Annam.

In 1540, Nguyen Kim attacked Nghe An. In 1542, Le Trang Tong gave assault to Nghe An and Thanh Hoa. In 1543, both celebrated their first success by taking the western capital, Thanh Hoa, after the false submission of the Mac governor, Duong Chap Nhat. In 1545, Nguyen Kim marched on Son Nam, but at Yen Mo he was poisoned by Duong Chap Nhat under Mac Dang Dung's secret instructions. Then, power passed on to Trinh Kiem, who withdrew to

Thanh Hoa where he installed his headquarters. He built a palace and consolidated his forces by enlisting the southern population.

Le Trung Tong (1548–1556)

In 1548, the southern king Le Trang Tong died at Thanh Hoa, and his son, Prince Duy Huyen, was enthroned as Le Trung Tong. Mac Phuc Hai made an unsuccessful attempt to seize Thanh Hoa. At the passing of Le Trung Tong, there was no successor, and all power was in the hands of Trinh Kiem.

Le Anh Tong (1556–1573)

The temptation to seize the power was strong, but under the advice of the Viet Nostradamus, Nguyen Binh Khiem alias Trang Trinh, Trinh Kiem put Duy Bang, the nephew of Le Thai Tong, on the throne as Le Anh Tong. Until 1558, the two sides opposed each other in incessant combat with no clear conclusion. In 1561, Mac Phuc Nguyen passed away, and his son Mac Mau Hop succeeded him.

In 1570, in the South, Trinh Kiem died and was replaced by his eldest son, Trinh Coi, who appeared to be a detestable leader. His young brothers, Trinh Tung and Trinh Bach, began fighting against him. Taking advantage of the turmoil, Mac Kinh Dien invaded Thanh Hoa with 100,000 troops and forced the submission of Trinh Coi. Mac Kinh Dien then pushed further on, to An Truong. From there he hoped to capture Le Anh Tong, who had moved to Dong Son where he reorganized his forces and named Trinh Tung his prime minister and commander in chief. Mac Kinh Dien's efforts were to no avail, and he had to withdraw. Trinh Tung soon became corrupted by power. His arrogance caused Le Anh Tong to fear for his crown, and the king began plotting against his own prime minister. The plot was discovered in time for Trinh Tung to kill Le Anh Tong's accomplices and for the king to flee to Nghe An with four of his sons. Trinh Tung wasted no time in enthroning the seven-year-old Prince Duy Dam as King Le The Tong. By then, his men had caught Le Anh Tong hiding in a sugarcane field. Le Anh Tong was taken to Loi Duong where he was put to death. To the public, it was reported that he had committed suicide.

Trinh Tung then went back to his defensive strategy, inflicting losses to the Mac Kinh Dien's forces whenever they ventured to the South. In 1583, with his troops well fed and trained, Trinh Tung began to raid the North successfully. In 1591, he took Thang Long, after a victorious encounter with King Mac Mau Hop. But for unknown reasons, he went back to Thanh Hoa, leaving Thang Long at the mercy of Mac Mau Hop. Strangely enough, Mac Mau Hop did not even try to reoccupy the abandoned capital. Actually, he was too preoccupied with a scheme to murder his general, Bui Van Khue, in order to possess his wife Nguyen Thi, to whom he was fatally attracted. Bui Van Khue escaped to Ninh Binh with his gorgeous spouse, but Mac Mau Hop sent his men after them, leaving Bui Van Khue no other choice than to surrender to Trinh Tung. With Bui Van Khue's help, Trinh Tung succeeded in defeating the Mac Mau Hop in Nam Dinh, capturing seventy war junks and General Tran Bach Nien, who promptly surrendered. After a series of reverses, Mac Mau Hop relinquished the throne to his son Mac Toan and took direct command of his army. Seventeen of his senior officers, dedicated to preserving their own conjugal happiness, followed Bui Van Khue's example and joined the Le.

After his last debacle at Vu Giang, Mac Mau Hop fled and sought refuge in a pagoda at Phuong Nhon. He was captured, brought back to Thang Long, and decapitated after three days of torture. His head was exposed at Thanh Hoa. The son of Mac Kinh Dien, who was named Mac Kinh Chi, proclaimed himself king and managed to rebuild a 70,000 man force. Mac Toan, Mac Mau Hop's heir, also submitted to the new ruler.

After his general failed to defeat Mac Kinh Chi, who was a distinguished warrior, Trinh Tung decided to confront him personally in Cam Giang and Thanh Lam where Mac Kinh Chi and sixty members of his court were captured. In 1592, a last attempt was made by General Mac Ngoc Lien to restore the Mac dynasty with Mac Kinh Cung, another son of Mac Kinh Dien. But again, they had to flee to Cao Bang. The remnants of the Mac dynasty continued to resist for thirty-five more years. They had ruled the North for sixty-five years, but history shows they made no significant accomplishments. For 100 years, their presence on the political scene contributed only to slowing down the growth of Vietnam.

Le The Tong (1573–1599)

In 1573, Le Anh Tong, who had been enthroned by Trinh Kiem, did not enjoy the support of Trinh Kiem's successor Trinh Tung. Therefore he fled to Nghe An, but he was captured by Trinh Tung and put to death. He was replaced on the throne by his fifth son, Duy Dam, who was named King Le The Tong. During Le The Tong's reign, Trinh Tung succeeded in eliminating the Mac.

Le Kinh Tong (1600–1619)

From that time, the Le became a pawn on the political chessboard in which the Trinh opposed the Nguyen. Le The Tong died in his bed, but his successor Le Kinh Tong, formerly Prince Duy Tan, did not have the same fortune. In 1619, tired of being Trinh Tung's puppet, he conspired with Trinh Tung's youngest son, Trinh Xuan, to eliminate his father. Trinh Tung reacted by throwing his son into prison and forcing Le Kinh Tong to hang himself.

Le Than Tong (1619–1643)

Le Kinh Tong's son Duy Ky ascended to the throne as Le Than Tong. He had no major problems with the Trinh during his nominal rule and abdicated as the Highest King to his son Duy Huu. In fact, his relations with the Trinh were so good that he would be allowed a second reign later on.

Le Chan Tong (1634–1649)

Duy Huu succeeded Le Than Tong and was invested as Le Chan Tong, King of Annam, by Kwei Wang from Kwangsi Province.[11] The war between the Trinh and the Nguyen had begun. When Le Chan Tong died without an heir, Trinh Trang called Le Than Tong back to the throne until he himself passed away in 1662.

From 1662 through 1788, nine Le kings reigned at the pleasure of the Trinh, until the Tay Son put an end to Trinh rule, causing the last Le King, Le Chieu Thong, to seek shelter in China. Despite his efforts to regain the throne, that unfortunate monarch ended up as a miserable refugee, betrayed and despised by his perfidious Chinese allies.

NOTES

1. During the Ch'in period, Chen Ching hid in a fish's belly a piece of silk on which he had written "Chen Ching is the king."
2. Pham Van Son, *Viet Su Tan Bien*, B.II, p. 428.
3. The right of the suzerain over his *subjects'* brides.
4. Pham Van Son, *Viet Su Tan Bien*, B.II, p. 502.
5. She was to be the mother of the most celebrated King Le Thanh Tong.
6. The Future Le Thanh Tong.
7. Once married, a woman shared common liability only with her husband's family.
8. Trinh Duy Dai had killed King Quang Tri not so long before.
9. Pham Van Son disagrees with Tran Trong Kim on this point (B.III, p. 41).
10. Mac Dang Dung's behavior is severely criticized by Tran Trong Kim.
11. By order of the Ming emperor.

5

THE VIETNAMESE
SHOGUNS

Despite the collapse of the Mac, the Later Le, installed in exile by Nguyen Kim, could hardly regain control of the country.

TRINH AND NGUYEN

When Nguyen Kim died during a campaign against the Mac, military power passed to his son-in-law and assistant Trinh Kiem. To prevent Nguyen Uong's and Nguyen Hoang's claims to the succession of their father Nguyen Kim, Trinh Kiem had Nguyen Uong murdered. The surviving Nguyen Hoang, fearing the same fate, feigned insanity to divert Trinh Kiem's attention. But he secretly dispatched an emissary to seek advice from Nguyen Binh Khiem, who had counselled Trinh Kiem before. He was told to put himself in safety behind the Hoanh Son Mountains. So Nguyen Hoang begged his sister Ngoc Bao, Trinh Kiem's wife, for assignment anywhere in the South. Seizing the opportunity to get rid of a cumbersome relative, Trinh Kiem readily agreed. In 1558, Nguyen Hoang was transferred to an insignificant area peopled only "with coughing monkeys and crowing storks."[1] All his relatives and troops in Thanh Hoa and Nghe An joined him and settled in that wild part of Quang Tri Province. Soon, his behavior and his political wisdom brought Nguyen Hoang unprecedented popular support. In 1569, he craftily initiated a visit to the capital, where he paid homage to both king and Trinh Kiem, giving Trinh Kiem a little more respect. Hence, for his public display of loyalty, Trinh Kiem imprudently rewarded Nguyen Hoang with the two important provinces of Thuan Hoa and Quang Nam.

In 1572, Trinh Kiem passed away leaving power to his son Trinh Coi, who was immediately challenged by his brother Trinh Tung. The Mac, taking advantage of the Trinh family strife, attacked both the Trinh and the Nguyen. While his defeat forced Trinh Coi to surrender to the Mac, the Nguyen managed to kill the Mac general Lap Bao. Then Trinh Tung, who had succeeded Trinh Coi, evicted the Mac. Afterwards, he proclaimed himself Lord[2] with absolute power over political and military matters. King Le The Tong was relegated to a public relations figure, who opened court meetings and welcomed foreign ambassadors. He was allocated a fixed income from the taxes levied on only 1,000 villages. For his protection, he was assigned 5,000 guards. Seven elephants and twenty junks completed his royal entourage. Under such conditions, it would have been quite easy for Trinh Tung to seize the throne. But he was held back by the presence of the Ming to the north and the Nguyen to the south, although the Trinh and the Nguyen were related through the union of Nguyen Kim's daughter, Ngoc Bao, with Trinh Kiem. The king had become hostage of Trinh Tung.

In 1593, General Mac Ngoc Lien, a Mac remnant, came back from Cao Bang, and Nguyen Hoang brought his troops to Thang Long to help Trinh Tung. Nguyen Hoang's successful campaigns aroused Trinh Tung's jealousy and suspicion. After eight years in the North, Nguyen Hoang realized it was for him the time to go back to the South. Yet he had to find a good excuse, since Trinh Tung preferred to keep him under his direct control.

In 1599, King Le The Tong died leaving the throne to his son Duy Tan, who became known as Le Kinh Tong. Bui Van Khue and his associates Pham Ngan and Ngo Dinh Ham began a revolt against Trinh Tung in Nam Dinh, threatening nearby Thang Long. Afraid of losing his royal hostage, Trinh Tung moved king Le Kinh Tong to Thanh Hoa, the western capital, leaving Thang Long without defense. Mac Kinh Cung, son of Mac Kinh Dien, came back from the Mac refuge in Cao Bang and installed Bui Thi, Mac Mau Hop's mother, as queen mother in Thang Long. During the confusion, under the pretense of going to fight the Bui insurgents, Nguyen Hoang sailed back to Thuan Hoa with his forces.

Soon, discord surged among the three rebels. Bui Van Khue and Pham Ngan killed each other while Ngo Dinh Ham joined the Mac. After putting the king in safety at Thanh Hoa, Trinh Tung recaptured Thang Long. Bui Thi was put to death, and Mac Kinh Cung escaped to Cao Bang. Again the king had to move back to Thang Long.

Down in the South, Nguyen Hoang, still fearing Trinh Tung's reprisal for his defection, managed to marry his daughter Ngoc Tu to Trinh Trang, Trinh Tung's eldest son. This was against cultural taboos since he was her own nephew, but it was a good choice anyway, since the other son, Trinh Xuan, was in disgrace, having once tried to overthrow his father.

In 1623, Trinh Tung was terminally ill and decided that the lordship should be shared by his two sons, Trinh Trang and Trinh Xuan. The youngest, Trinh Xuan, was to be vice lord. Rejecting his Father's decision, Trinh Xuan revolted. Trinh Tung retaliated by luring him to the village of Hoang Mai, where he had him executed. A few days later, Trinh Tung expired in the Thanh Xuan Pagoda in the province of Hadong. His death induced another Mac remnant, Mac Kinh

Khoan, a nephew of Mac Kinh Cung, to proclaim himself King Khanh Vuong in Thai Nguyen. In the ensuing encounter, Mac Kinh Cung was killed and Mac Kinh Khoan fled to China. In 1625, the latter made his submission to the Le and with Ming protection was maintained at Cao Bang, which became a tributary province to Vietnam. Later, under the Ch'ing, the Mac lost their Chinese support, and in 1660 Lord Trinh Tac recovered Cao Bang. The Mac lasted 100 years before total extinction.

The disappearance of the Mac should have put an end to the political division of the country and united all parties under the legitimate Le dynasty. But, as in China during the time of the decaying Chou dynasty, the Trinh and the Nguyen reenacted the tragedy of the contending states. On the surface, the two Lords maintained a cordial entente, but finally a time of confrontation came. During the next fifty years, while the Trinh were trying to enlist the support of the Dutch, the Nguyen were helped by the Portuguese. Thuan Hoa and Quang Nam became powerful strongholds with huge caches of food and supplies. Assisted by Joao da Cruz, the Nguyen created a modern artillery. Although their infantry was numerically inferior, only 50,000 compared to Trinh's 100,000, it was better trained and equipped. Their officers were highly qualified. As for their navy, each of the 500 galleys was staffed with twenty-five rowers and outfitted with one fore and two aft cannons. There were a total of 15,000 Nam Ha sailors.

To stop the Northern invasion, the Nguyen built a wall twenty feet high and six miles long at Dong Hoi. Dao Duy Tu also built the famous Luy Thay, an eleven mile long fortress at Tran Ninh. Both proved to be vital to the defense of Nam Ha.

THE END OF CHINA'S MING DYNASTY

In China, ominous changes were taking place. The Ming dynasty, which was going through many ordeals, was coming to an end. When the first Ming emperor, Chu Yuan Chung, also known as Hung Wu, died in 1398, his heir passed away before his coronation. Power went therefore to his sixteen-year-old son Hui Ti. He was immediately challenged by his uncle, Prince Yen, and had to escape disguised as a Buddhist monk. Prince Yen acceded the throne and became Emperor Yung Lo, while Hui Ti was hiding around the country disguised as a monk mendicant. When the former king was discovered in 1441, only the silence of an influential eunuch allowed him to carry on with his miserable life.

Indeed, it was a time of the good eunuchs, and among them was Admiral Cheng Ho. He was a fabulous figure. Sixty-five years before Vasco da Gama, his 70,000 seamen crisscrossed the China Sea and the Indian Ocean, establishing nominal Ming suzerainty over Indonesia, Malaysia, and Ceylon. He took the Chinese flag as far as the Persian Gulf and East Africa. He almost discovered Australia, having reached Timor. But it was clearly an aberration for the Chinese to use their fleet for diplomatic purposes rather than for international trade, which was carried out by land along the Silk Road and, in the south, the Burma

Road from India to Yunnan through Assam and Upper Burma. Perhaps Admiral Cheng Ho had in mind the commercial value of his explorations, but his death had far-reaching consequences for China. It not only put an end to Chinese maritime predominance, but also gave way for the Western expansion at the expense of China.

After Cheng Ho, the reemergence of bad eunuchs led to disaster. In 1443, the eunuch Wan Ch'in, Emperor Cheng T'ing's pet, managed to mount an expedition against the Mongols, not really to fight the barbarians, but to have the emperor stop at his hometown, Huai Lai, and bestow on him the supreme honor of being his guest. As ludicrous as it was, the emperor not only accepted his plan, but also named him commander in chief of the expedition. No wonder the Chinese were badly mauled at their first encounter with the terrible Mongols. However, Wan Ch'in would not give up his idée fixe. Despite the beating, he persisted in having at his house that fatal party, during which the Chinese were surrounded by the barbarians. Wan Ch'in and his officers were massacred. As for Emperor Cheng T'ing, even the war-hardened Mongol chief was quite stunned to find him sitting quietly on the bloody floor amid his people who had been butchered like pigs. History is left to wonder whether his passivity was the display of rare courage or of an intoxicated condition. Anyway, he was taken hostage by the Mongols for further transactions with the Chinese. But the Chinese had the upper hand—they simply put his young brother Ching Ti on the throne. Having lost his bargaining value, Cheng T'ing succeeded in winning the friendship of his captors who later released him without condition. He was even reinstated on the throne when Ching Ti died. Among those who rejoiced at that event were his Mongol friends. And long after he died, his successors Ch'eng Hua and Hung Ch'i enjoyed a pleasant truce with the barbarians.

In 1510, under Emperor Ch'eng Te (1505–1520), a scandal broke out with the arrest of eunuch Liu Chin, who was accused of corruption. He "was found possessed of gold and silver, coined and unminted to the value of 251,583,600 taels. He also had 24 lbs of unmounted precious stones, 2 suits of armour in solid gold, 500 gold plates, 3,000 gold rings and brooches, and 4,062 belts adorned with gems.''[3] That was probably what was left after the police search. The cache was sent to the imperial treasury and later helped Yang Ting Ho and Chang Ku Cheng build their reputations as outstanding ministers, having secured the prosperity of China under two emperors, Chia Ching (1520-1566) and Wan Li (1577-1620). But they had their share of troubles with many pirates financed by the Japanese nobility, which considered it perfectly honorable to ransack China. Finally, in 1592, the shogun Hideyoshi invaded Korea, driving China into a six-year war to defend its Korean vassal. When Hideyoshi died, the Japanese withdrew. The Chinese were relieved, but exhausted.

CHINA'S CH'ING DYNASTY

Then came the Manchus. After the end of the Yuan dynasty, they revolted and were granted autonomy by the Ming. In 1618, Nurhachi succeeded in unifying the four Manchu provinces under his kingdom of Kirin. He then proclaimed the Ch'ing dynasty. Soon, taking advantage of the Ming troubles, he invaded Liao Tung. In 1629, he completed the conquest of Liao Tung but was stopped at Shan Hai Kuan pass by the Chinese general Wu San Kuei. In 1644, the Manchu emperor T'ai Tsung died leaving the throne to his seven-year-old son. Given the ensuing succession problems, the Manchus would have rather kept quiet for a while before attempting anything against China. But heaven decided otherwise.

At that time, the Chinese brigand Li Tzu Cheng from Shensi Province had conquered the entire west of China and Peking, causing Emperor Ch'ing Cheng to hang himself from a tree in his palace garden on Coal Hill. Then, Li Tzu Cheng proclaimed himself emperor and called for the union of all Chinese against foreign invaders. But he made a double mistake, first by taking Wu San Kuei's concubine into his own harem and second by refusing to give her back. Wu San Kuei, who was more of a passionate lover than a fervent patriot, wasted no time to attack Li Tzu Cheng, but, on his way, he learned that Li Tzu Cheng had captured Peking. Wu San Kuei went back to the border where he borrowed some troops from the Manchus in exchange for letting them through the pass of Shan Hai Kuan. With the help of the Manchu mercenaries he dislodged Li Tzu Cheng and chased him around until he could kill him. Meanwhile Peking was left open to Manchu occupation, and the Manchus soon declared it their capital, and their king Shun Chih the emperor of China. For the beautiful eyes of a cabaret singer, General Wu San Kuei had lost North China to the Manchus without a single shot.

To get rid of their awkward associate, the Ch'ing dispatched Wu San Kuei to pacify the south at his own expense. After eighteen years of fighting his own war, Wu finally proclaimed himself king of the southwest, of Kwangsi, while two other Chinese warlords shared the east coast.

In the north, the Ch'ing emperor Shun Chih (1644-1661) appeared to be completely detached from earthly preoccupations. He drifted further and further into Buddhist meditations. In 1661, he secretly relinquished the power to a minor, K'ang Hsi, and settled in a pagoda near Peking as a buddhist monk. K'ang Hsi (1662-1722) was a born ruler. In 1673, at the age of sixteen, he discharged his regents and took the reins of power. At that time Wu San Kuei, in a late burst of patriotism, broke his alliance with the Manchus, but he was old and sick and was unable to carry out his war. He died in 1678. His sons started fighting among themselves, prompting K'ang Hsi to seize their capital and to exterminate all the Wus. The Ch'ing were to rule China for 268 years, until Sun Yat-sen's revolution of 1911, which marked the second turning point in the history of China.

Vietnam was enjoying relative peace. Although the Chinese would have liked to have resumed their domination, at that time Vietnam had reached a prominence that forced the respect of her neighbors. Its triumph over the Mongols, its conquest of Champa, its pacification of Laos, the glorious reign of Le Thai To, and the prestige of Le Thanh Tong were subjects of continual debate among

Chinese politicians. Eunuch Uong Truc had once suggested sending an expedition against Le Thanh Tong, but minister Du Tu Tuan declared, "A war against Annam will cause the destruction of the southeast."[4] Besides, in a report to the Ming Emperor, Vietnam had been described as "a land in the southeast, not of low culture, having distinct customs, and if we called them barbarian no other barbarian could rival them. On contrary, Annam is a civilized country that must be treated with circumspection."[5] At the onset of Mac rule, an attempt had been made to subdue Annam, but those in charge of the campaign promptly seized the first opportunity to abort the effort, partly due to Mac bribery, partly out of fear of a protracted and unproductive war.

THE CIVIL WAR IN VIETNAM

The Chinese abstention gave a free hand to both the Trinh and the Nguyen to wage their fratricidal war under the helpless Le. Actually, the Trinh had never trusted the Nguyen because the latter were related to the Mac. Mac Canh Huong, one of Mac Kinh Dien's brothers, married Nguyen Hoang's sister-in-law, and Nguyen Hoang's heir, Lord Sai, married Mac Kinh Dien's daughter. Furthermore, during the eight years he spent in the North, Nguyen Hoang was involved in military and political espionage. He was also suspected of having had a part in Bui Van Khue's uprising.

Trinh Tung opened the hostilities by sending a letter blaming Nguyen Hoang for his desertion. He was wise enough to treat it as a family affair, calling Nguyen Hoang his uncle. Nguyen Hoang replied with extreme courtesy, reserving the most amicable welcome for his emissary. He begged pardon and renewed his allegiance. Finally, he craftily wrapped up the dispute by giving the hand of his daughter to Trinh Tung's heir, Trinh Trang. So much for Trinh Tung's ego. Actually Nguyen Hoang was ready for a bigger confrontation. During the sixty years the Trinh were busy fighting the Mac, the Nguyen were organizing the South, incorporating Champa, pacifying the west, building up an efficient administration, producing heavy guns with the help of the Portuguese Joao da Cruz, and gathering local tribes, the Chams, Laos, and Viets, into their brotherhood. While the Trinh displayed only arrogance and contempt, the Nguyen showed kindness and appreciation. When it came to enlisting popular support, their behavior made quite a difference, and despite numerous attempts, the Trinh could never impose their authority on the South.

Nguyen Hoang died in 1613. If Trinh Trang ever had any filial respect for his father-in-law that might have kept him from opening hostilities, Nguyen Hoang's passing put an end to such a situation. Nguyen Hoang was succeeded by his sixth son, Nguyen Phuc Nguyen (1613-1635), known as Lord Sai. In the political arena, he was the perfect match for Trinh Trang, for both were canny and ambitious.

In 1620, Trinh Trang conspired with Lord Sai's brothers, Nguyen Phuc Hap and Nguyen Phuc Trach, to overthrow him. Trinh Trang moved 5,000 troops to nearby Dong Hoi. To isolate Lord Sai, Nguyen Phuc Hap and Nguyen Phuc Trach told him to send his famous General Tuyen against Bac Ha in the North. Suspecting some scheme, General Tuyen advised Lord Sai to assign his own brother Ve instead. Consequently, the two conspirators were compelled to throw off their masks and carry out their coup in the open. They were captured by General Tuyen and sent to jail, where they died of shame, according to Lord Sai's official version. As for Trinh Trang, he fled surreptitiously back to Bac Ha.

In 1624, Trinh Trang used another stratagem to get Lord Sai out of his Thuan Hoa stronghold. Since for a long time Nam Ha had not sent any tribute to Thang Long, Trinh Trang had King Le Than Tong (1619-1643) issue a severe admonishment to Lord Sai asking him to deliver tribute and to dispatch his son to the court for homage. In response, Lord Sai gave a warm welcome to the royal envoy and complained about the floods and droughts which had deprived him of the joy of serving his king. Thus, Trinh Trang's ambassador went home happy, but with empty hands. Then another emissary was sent to ask for thirty elephants and thirty junks as the Nam Ha share of the tribute to the Ming. Again Lord Sai dodged the request.

In 1626, Trinh Trang moved 5,000 troops to Ha Tinh and, at the same time, had a royal decree issued promoting Lord Sai to the ducal rank commanding him to join the Trinh in fighting revolts in the North. Lord Sai's counselor, Dao Duy Tu, advised him to accept the promotion in order to gain time while Dao Duy Tu completed a defensive wall, called the Luy Thay, from Truong Duc Mountain to the Bac Ha coast.

When the wall was ready, Dao Duy Tu managed a trick of his own. He had a double-bottom tray specially made to conceal the royal decree together with Lord Sai's reply rejecting that decree. Then, an envoy went to Thang Long and presented the tray with precious gifts displayed on the top. Lord Trinh Trang graciously accepted it. According to protocol, the envoy was supposed to come back later to recover the tray with the king's reply. Instead, he left furtively, thus arousing Lord Trinh Trang's suspicion. By the time Trinh Trang discovered the subterfuge, The Nam Ha envoy was back in safety in Thuan Hoa.[6] Trinh Trang flew into a rage. Not only had Lord Sai rejected his authority, but the highly sophisticated style of his message was an insult to his intelligence. To translate it into common language, he had to appeal to the most erudite scholars.

In 1627, Trinh Trang led a force of 200,000 infantry troops, 500 elephants and 500 war junks. This time he was determined to crush the Nguyen once and for all. Instead, his forces were partly swept by the Nguyen artillery and partly trampled upon by their own elephants, who were terrified by the explosions. Meanwhile, Trinh Trang got the news that in Thang Long his brothers Trinh Gia and Trinh Nhac had started a coup against him. Before realizing it was a hoax staged by the Nguyen, he had gone to the North. It was not such a bad decision after all. He arrived in time to take care of another uprising by some Mac remnants.

In the winter of 1631, on Dao Duy Tu's advice, the Nguyen raided the district of Nam Bo Chinh, put the Trinh governor to death, and replaced him with their general Truong Phuc Phan. Dao Duy Tu was a remarkable politician. A native of Thanh Hoa Province, he was the son of an opera actor and, as such, was denied the right to take the national examinations in spite of his extraordinary intelligence. This induced him to change his name. One day he appeared uninvited at a meeting of scholars and won the debate. This scholastic fame led to his employment with the Nguyen in 1627.

In 1634, a son of Lord Sai, Nguyen Anh,[7] who was assigned to the command of Quang Binh, conspired with Trinh Trang. Both agreed that Trinh Trang would send a gun signal for Nguyen Anh to rise up in Quang Binh. But while Trinh Trang was moving his forces to Dong Hoi, Nguyen Anh was replaced by another commander. Subsequently, when Trinh Trang gave his signal, there was no answer. Trinh Trang decided to pause a few weeks and wait for news of Nguyen Anh. This long period of inactivity caused his troops to become lax, and when they had to confront the Nguyen forces, they were severely mauled and had to withdraw to the North. The following year, 1635, Lord Sai died and was succeeded by his eldest son, Nguyen Phuc Lan (1635-1648), who was called Lord Thuong. Nguyen Anh revolted again, with the support of some Japanese traders from Fai Fo. This time he was captured and put to death.

In 1643, taking advantage of the Nguyen succession problems, Trinh Trang again invaded the South. This third campaign was cut short by the hot weather that killed hundreds of northern troops.

In 1648, Trinh Trang set out on his fourth campaign. His troops were stopped at Dao Duy Tu's wall, Luy Thay. But in Quang Binh, a night attack with 100 elephants led by Nguyen Phuc Tan, a son of Lord Thuong, provoked a disaster for the Trinh. They lost several generals and 3,000 soldiers.

Meanwhile, Lord Thuong died, ending a successful career of victories over the Trinh and the ensuing annexation of the district of Nam Bo Chinh. The important province of Nha Trang had also been taken away from Champa. Nguyen Phuc Tan succeeded him as Lord Hien. In the North, King Le Chan Tong passed away without an heir, and Trinh Trang had to reinstall the Highest King Le Than Tong on the throne.

In 1655, Lord Hien carried out the only offensive ever initiated by the South. He ordered General Nguyen Huu Tien to cross the Linh Giang River and take Bac Bo Chinh, where the Trinh general Pham Tat Toan surrendered. The Nguyen troops pushed further up to secure the citadel of Ha Trung while the Trinh swept back to Nghe An. The Trinh general Le Van Hieu died of an infected wound. Pursuing their advance, the Nguyen generals Nguyen Huu Tien and Nguyen Huu Dat took seven more districts in the North. Trinh Trang had to assign his son Trinh Toan to the Nghe An front. Trinh Toan was a skilled soldier and was highly respected by his troops. He succeeded in slowing down the Nguyen forces.

In 1657, Trinh Trang died and was succeeded by Trinh Tac (1657-1681), an arrogant lord who never kowtowed to the king and never signed his petitions to the king.[8] He even had the insolence to have his seat installed next to the throne. Jealous of Trinh Toan's popularity, Trinh Tac set out to destroy him. First, when Trinh Toan was engaged on the battlefield, he sentenced him for not having attended their father's funeral. Trinh Toan was replaced in his command by Trinh Tac's son Trinh Can. Then he was sent to jail, where he died. Later, Trinh Can led an attack from Nghe An and was defeated. The following year, the Trinh recorded some gains, none of which were decisive.

The two forces continued skirmishes during which an incident occurred that had disastrous consequences for the Nguyen. One night the Southern general Nguyen Huu Dat secretly left his position to go and report personally to Lord Hien. Informed of the fact, his colleague Nguyen Huu Tien declared that Nguyen Huu Dat lacked esprit de corps and decided to teach him a lesson. Under the pretense of attacking the Trinh, he had Nguyen Huu Dat's units put in reinforcement position. Then without Nguyen Huu Dat's knowledge, he ordered a general retreat back to the South, leaving Nguyen Huu Dat alone to deal with the enemy. When Trinh Can's troops arrived, Nguyen Huu Dat was in serious jeopardy. With Trinh Can at his pursuit, he managed to escape and joined Nguyen Huu Tien's forces who were already in the South. Although afterwards both fought fiercely against Trinh Can, they lost all of the seven districts they had seized previously. Because of Nguyen Huu Tien that successful campaign turned into a bitter deadlock.

In 1661, Trinh Tac engaged in his sixth campaign, again bringing King Le Than Tong to the South. The Trinh believed the presence of the king gave an aura of legitimacy to their military actions, and they never missed the opportunity to take him along. Besides, they probably preferred to keep him under close surveillance. For the Nguyen, as royal authority had been usurped, their duty was to fight for the legitimate authority, either that of the Le king or that of the Nguyen lord.

The northern troops under Trinh Can collided with the Nguyen at Nam Bo Chinh, where Nguyen Huu Dat offered stubborn resistance. A year later, in 1662, short of supplies and victories, the Trinh withdrew with Nguyen Huu Dat in pursuit. Back at Thang Long, King Le Than Tong died and was succeeded by Prince Duy Vu, who became King Le Huyen Tong. After eight years of rule, Le Huyen Tong passed away, leaving the throne to his brother Duy Hoi, who took the title of Le Gia Tong.

In 1672, the Trinh resumed their southern conquest for the seventh time. Again Trinh Can met with the irrepressible Nguyen Huu Dat, reinforced by Lord Hien and his fourth brother Hiep. In spite of their frenetic efforts, the Trinh failed to take the Tran Ninh Wall, which had been erected by Dao Duy Tu before breaking off relations with the Trinh. Meanwhile, Trinh Can fell sick at Linh Giang, and the northern troops had to retreat. From that time, the Trinh renounced further hostilities, until the Tay Son appeared. The North-South war had lasted for forty-five years, from 1627 through 1672. The Trinh failed to establish supremacy in Vietnam in spite of seven campaigns, some stretching over several years. From then on, for a century, the Linh Giang River was to mark the peaceful separation of the two Vietnams.

ONE HUNDRED YEARS OF PEACE (1672–1772)

The North

Peace, as far as the Trinh were concerned, was not caused by a sudden urge for reconciliation with the South. Actually, there were problems with China. After the Ch'ing overthrew the Ming, Trinh Tac had to renegotiate recognition with the new emperor and fighting a war was not the proper way to go about it. However, the Ch'ing themselves had succession problems, which compelled the Trinh to wait until 1667 for K'ang Hsi's approval. In the meantime, the last Mac had lost Ch'ing support by reckless alliance with the rebelling Wu San Kuei. Seizing the opportunity, Trinh Tac sent General Dinh Van Ta to throw Mac Kinh Vu out of Cao Bang. Mac Kinh Vu fled to China, were he was captured. He was the last remnant of the extinct Mac dynasty.

Le Hi Tong (1676–1705)

At the death of Le Than Tong, his wife, a member of the Trinh family, was four months pregnant. Trinh Tac took her back to his palace where her son, Duy Hop, was raised. Later he succeeded Le Gia Tong, who left no heir. Duy Hop took the name of Le Hi Tong and ruled for twenty-nine years before retiring as the Highest King. As for Trinh Tac, he died in 1682 and was succeeded by Trinh Can.

In spite of their failure to conquer the South, the Trinh maintained an effective and often remarkable administration of the North. Their army, which in 1585 had only 56,000 troops under Trinh Tung, had expanded to more than 200,000 men in 1627 under Trinh Trang. But with the truce, these forces turned to other tasks, and before the end of the period of peace, there were only 115,000 draftees and 4,000 26-oar galleys, each equipped with 14-pound guns and staffed with 50 sailors. The troops were divided into elite units, which were traditionally recruited in Thanh Hoa and Nghe An provinces and assigned to the capital for the protection of the lord and the king, and first class troops, who came from the regions of Son Nam, Bac Ninh, Hai Duong, and Son Tay and were deployed in the provinces for combat in times of war and for cultivation in times of peace. Trinh Cuong opened a military academy for sons of dignitaries. Every three years, people were allowed to attend martial arts tests focusing on the use of bows, swords, and lances and combined horseback riding and bow shooting. Academic tests were given after these basic requirements were met. Trinh Cuong also promoted a land survey for subsequent taxation.

In the field of justice, the right to replace retribution with payment in cash was suppressed. With few exceptions, penalties were to be carried out strictly in accordance with the law.

As for Trinh Tac, he seemed to have concentrated on education. Under him, in 1664, the mandarin Pham Cong Tru introduced the decimal system. Printing blocks were made locally, and as a result, import of books from China was prohibited. Unfortunately Trinh Tac's efforts to liberalize the national examination by making it open to all those able to pay the registration fee ended in disaster. Thousands of people bottled up the entrance gates, trampling on each other and causing confusion and death. The system then degenerated into an "examination market" because, with the connivance of the responsible officials, any candidate could pay an indigent scholar to sit for him on the examination bench.

Under Trinh Giang, the financial system was reformed and modern accounting principles and budget forecasts were introduced. The exploitation of minerals, including gold, silver, copper, and tin, which had been in the hands of numerous groups of Chinese, was now restricted. To eradicate feudalism, the government ceased to grant rewards on the basis of land ownership. Salaries and pensions were used to pay for services or bonuses. Government officers were not allowed to possess land within their jurisdiction. Coinage privileges, which had been reserved for provincial authorities, were transferred to the central government, and two factories for minting coins were installed in the capital.

In 1740, temples were erected for national heroes such as Hung Dao Vuong[9] and Chinese heroes such as Kuan Vu.[10] Vietnam's history was formally recorded by royal historians, among whom were four scholars of great repute, Nguyen Hoan, Le Qui Don, Ngo Thoi Si, and Nguyen Du, author of the national masterpiece *Kim Van Kieu*.

Le Duy Phuong (1729–1732)

In 1729, Trinh Cuong coerced King Du Tong into abdicating in favor of Prince Le Duy Phuong. After Trinh Cuong's death, his successor, Trinh Giang, accused Le Duy Phuong of adultery with the late king's widow. Subsequently Le Duy Phuong was dethroned and murdered in 1732. That marked the beginning of the end for the Trinh.

Le Thuan Tong (1732–1735)

Although the succession was provided with the accession of Le Thuan Tong, one of Du Tong's sons, the news of King Le Duy Phuong's assassination shocked popular conscience and revolts erupted everywhere.

REVOLTS IN THE NORTH: PRINCES AND OUTLAWS

Critical tasks such as the maintenance of dams and dikes were neglected. Administrative decadence had started with Trinh Cuong. In 1702, the Ma and

Chu rivers in Thanh Hoa flooded causing the loss of all crops. The following year, famine spread to the Red River delta, threatening the capital, Thang Long. Then drought came, and when it ended, the Red River overflowed, submerging Son Nam and Son Tay. Afterward, the Chu and the Ma surged again, destroying thousands of houses, cattle, and crops. This time, the people ate tree bark, herbs, and leaves and died by the thousands. Although Trinh Cuong declared tax exemption and called for the cooperation of the rich to provide relief, swarms of peasants left their land. Famine persisted in Thanh Hoa and Nghe An provinces from 1726 through 1728. During the following years, 1729 and 1730, floods ravaged Bac Ninh and Hung Yen.

Trinh Giang, who was in power, showed little concern for his people. Instead, he indulged in sadistic amusements, building underground palaces because he had a psychotic fear of thunderbolts. Like the Chinese emperors, he left power in the hands of his eunuchs, whose only concern was to line their own pockets.

Thus, under the slogan ''For Le, against Trinh,'' peasants and bandits went on the rampage while princes and aristocrats joined together in open rebellion. In 1686, the Nung minorities in Tuyen Quang revolted. At the beginning of the eighteenth century, revolts flared up in Son Tay and Kinh Bac, Lai Chau and Cao Bang. In 1734, the Muong tribe arose in Thanh Hoa.

Later, in 1738, more important movements occurred, under Bonze Nguyen Duong Hung in Son Tay and Thai Nguyen. The following year, three princes entered the arena. Two, Le Duy Mat and Le Duy Qui, were sons of the late King Le Du Tong and therefore brothers of the current king, Le Thuan Tong. The other was Le Duy Chuc, a son of the late King Le Hi Tong. All were princes by blood. Together they charted the murder of Trinh Giang. But Le Duy Chuc and Le Duy Qui died suddenly, and Le Duy Mat had to flee away.

Finally, in 1740, Trinh Giang's own ministers Nguyen Quy Canh and Nguyen Cong Thai had to depose him in favor of his brother Trinh Doanh. But the rebellion took more than ten years to put down. Meanwhile, the rebels killed Governor Hoang Kim Qua. Lord Trinh Doanh dispatched Pham Ngu Phuc and Pham Dinh Trong against them. A minor rebel leader named Vu Dinh Dung was captured and executed. But a former civil servant, Nguyen Huu Cau, had built up enormous popularity by sharing his loot with the poor peasants. Brave and resourceful, he might lose a battle one day and come back the next with ten thousands of new recruits. In 1743, Nguyen Huu Cau killed Admiral Trinh Bang and seized the entire Gulf of Tonking littoral. He named himself commander of the western popular army. In 1749, after winning two battles in Bac Giang Province, he negotiated his submission in exchange for a ducal title. Trinh Doanh agreed and dispatched orders to General Pham Dinh Trong to cease hostilities. But the general rejected the lord's order, stating that on the battlefield, the commander's authority prevails. Actually, he had a personal score to settle with Nguyen Huu Cau because once, for some reason, Nguyen Huu Cau had dug up General Pham Dinh Trong's mother's remains and thrown them into the river. Nguyen Huu Cau was finally captured at Hoang Mai, on the coast of Nghe

An, in 1751. He was one of the two leaders of greatest repute. The other was Nguyen Danh Phuong.

In 1744, after several successes, Nguyen Danh Phuong, a remnant of the Son Tay band, established himself as The Heavenly Lord at the head of 10,000 followers in the mountainous region of Ngoc Boi, west of Thang Long. There he built palaces, levied taxes, and appointed ministers. In 1750, Trinh Doanh himself had to take command of the operations against Nguyen Danh Phuong. First he was repelled by stubborn resistance. To force a victory, he had to proclaim martial law for his troops. Nguyen Danh Phuong was finally captured.

Nguyen Huu Cau and Nguyen Danh Phuong ended in ignominy. At the celebration of the Trinh Doanh's victory, Nguyen Danh Phuong had to serve drinks to the troops and Nguyen Huu Cau had to blow the trumpet to amuse them. That was their last performance, for both were executed the following day.

Another leader, Hoang Cong Chat, who was entrenched in the Hung Hoa mountainous region, and was supported by the minorities, was defeated in 1769.

Among the three prince rebels, Le Duy Mat was the only survivor. The deaths of Le Duy Qui and Le Duy Chuc had never been clarified. According to some reports, they had been killed by the Trinh; others claimed they had died of disease. Anyway, after many trials and tribulations, Le Duy Mat succeeded in establishing a base in Nghe An with the support of poor peasants and minorities. His princely status lent legitimacy to his action. Also, he was delivering good deeds. He forgave tax arrears, distributed the lands of the rich to the poor, and even dug canals. In 1764, he asked in vain for help from the newly enthroned King Nguyen Phuc Khoat, who had also turned a deaf ear to the Trinh when they applied for the right to pursue Le Duy Mat.

In 1767, upon the death of Trinh Doanh, Le Duy Mat attacked the Trinh forces and lost. He took refuge in Tran Ninh. In 1769, Lord Trinh Sam, after having tried in vain to negotiate with Le Duy Mat, assailed his stronghold in Tran Ninh. If it had not been for the treason of his own people, Le Duy Mat could have expected successful resistance, but his son-in-law opened the citadel to the Trinh troops. Refusing to surrender, Le Duy Mat set a mine and blew himself up, together with his entire family.

The elimination of rebels did not resolve the country's problems, and despite the end of the war, the peasants continued to eat bark and rats.

THE MARCH TO THE SOUTH (NAM TIEN)

While the Trinh were dealing with revolts, the Nguyen were gradually developing a new form of administration which took into account the situation that had resulted from the piecemeal annexation of Champa.

When Nguyen Hoang, fearing for his life, asked for that wild land snatched from Champa, he was reenacting the story of China's Liu Pang who volunteered to go to the remote land of Ba Thuc in order to put distance between him and his archenemy Hsiang Yu.[11] Later, Nguyen Hoang staged a very successful journey to Thang Long where mighty Lord Tung, elated by his calculated adulation, imprudently rewarded him with the two additional regions of Thuan Hoa and Quang Nam. These were rich lands left behind by Governor Nguyen Ba Huynh, who had been promoted to the administration of Nghe An. Thuan-Quang, as it was called, became a haven for all kinds of humanity, ex-convicts, young adventurers, political opponents, scholars unhappy with examination scores, traffickers in various goods, soldiers, peasants, artisans, and traders. All were in search of a land where they could unleash their talents, their ambitions, or their schemes. The gradual conquest of Champa and Cambodia would fulfill their dreams. In 1611, Nguyen Hoang took Phu Yen from a Champa once reduced by Le Thanh Tong's partition. In 1617, the Viet occupied Tran Bien Dinh. In 1653, following the revolt of the Cham king Ba Tham, Khanh Hoa was annexed in reprisal. In 1693, it was the turn for the Thuan Phu district. In 1697, what was left of Champa became the provinces of Phan Ri and Phan Rang. From then on, Nam Ha became a colonial power and began looking further away to the remote kingdom of Cambodia as the second phase in its southward expansion. At that time, the abdication of King Soryopor in favor of his son Chey Chetta II came to Vietnam as a blessing from heaven.

Chey Chetta II (Chat Tri) was not comfortable with Thailand's domination, although he had been invested by the Thai. Preferring Viet protection, he married the beautiful princess Ngoc Van and formally opened Baria to Viet immigration. Actually, many Viets had already established small colonies in Cambodia, and on several occasions, Viet troops had been sent there to assure their safety. But under Chey Chetta II, a systematic pattern developed with the exodus of the entire population of Quang Binh.

In 1679, Chinese general Duong Ngan Dich and his assistant Hoang Tien, from Kwangsi province, rejected Ch'ing rule and surrendered to the Nguyen with 3,000 soldiers and 50 galleys. They were assigned to the Cambodian provinces of Gia Dinh, Bienhoa, and Mytho. These Chinese colonies soon became the economic backbone of Nam Ha. Their ports were crowded with affluent merchants from all over the world, from Spain, Portugal, Holland, France, Great Britain, Japan, Java, China, and Siam.

Meanwhile, Ha Tien, in the Gulf of Siam, was a haven for international adventurers and, as such, attracted a Chinese illicit trader named Mac Cuu. He obtained from the Cambodian administration authorization to open gambling houses, which became extremely profitable. With the proceeds, he built up prosperous villages at Kampot, Phu Quoc, Rach Gia, and Ca Mau, but eventually he bid allegiance to the Viets and was appointed governor of Ha Tien.

In 1688, Hoang Tien killed Duong Ngan Dich and together with Ang Non (Nac Ong Non) revolted against Ang Sor[12] and the Nguyen. After the Nguyen victory over Ang Non, Hoang Tien was arrested and executed by Nguyen Phuc Tran (Lord Nghia). In 1698, Nguyen Huu Kinh, son of the famous Nguyen Huu Dat, was assigned to the reorganization of Cambodia. In addition to the 200,000 original settlers there, he moved in a large population from Quang Binh. The

Map 15
The Nguyen Annexation of South Cambodia and Ha Tien

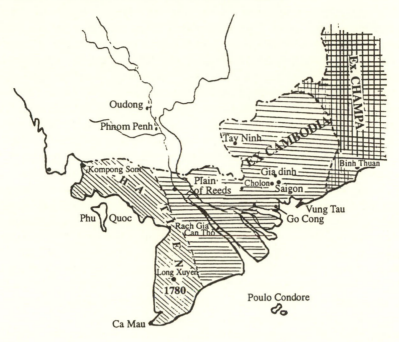

expansion continued as the Viet experienced their first taste of imperialism (Map 14).

In 1715, the Cambodian rulers again had succession problems, and again each side sought the help of its ally, Siam or Nam Ha. The Siamese decided to attack both the Vietnamese and their Cambodian protégés. With 3,000 troops, they stormed Ha Tien, forcing Mac Cuu to retreat to Kampot. When the conflict ended with the Nguyen victory, Mac Cuu was reinstated by Lord Nguyen Phuc Chu. He died in 1735, leaving Ha Tien in a state of full expansion. Under Mac Thien Tu, his wise successor, Ha Tien became a minikingdom with its own complete cultural, economic, and administrative structure.

Soon, the Cambodians resumed their family dispute. Their allies, the Thai, invaded Ha Tien and were beaten off by Mac Thien Tu after heroic battles. As for the Cambodians, each time they fought among themselves, they had to pay for foreign help. So, they yielded Kampot and Kompong Som to Mac Thien Tu, after having offered North Bassac to the Nguyen. Without a single shot, Nguyen Vu Vuong (1738-1765) received the six famous provinces now called Luc Tinh.

In 1780, Mac Thien Tu died without an heir and Ha Tien was annexed to the Nguyen kingdom (Map 15).

REVOLTS IN THE SOUTH: THE TAY SON

The 100 years of truce had not brought the expected results in terms of economic development or political stability. This was due to the fact that the Viet rulers, bound to Confucian culture, had not given the merchant class the necessary support. Even the traditionally respected scholars had lost their social status and were reduced to sordid poverty. The country had no economic policy and no trade agreements with the numerous foreign merchants who were flocking to the prosperous Viet ports. Instead, the Portuguese, Spaniards, Dutch, and Chinese, and later the French, English, and Japanese were subjected to constant abuse from government agents.

Peace was the pretext for spending on the construction of more palaces and temples. The fact that certain Buddhist monks were granted princely privileges indicates that the people had also lost the traditional protection of the clergy. Now, to increase their revenues, even the Buddhist monks collected taxes. Depravity and corruption were rampant. The fiscal measures decreed by the governments of both the North and South had no other objective than to tax thoroughly the land, the people, and the professions.

In the North, maintenance of dams and dikes, which had been the traditional duty of the ruler, was neglected, resulting in rupture of the Ma and Chu rivers in Thanh Hoa and the subsequent destruction of crops. Famine spread to the entire Red River delta. People ate bark, leaves, and grass and died. From 1715 through 1769, revolts surged in Son Tay, Lai Chau, Son Nam, Mo Trach, Cao Bang, and Thanh Hoa. All were quickly quelled.

In the South, the picture was even worse. The aristocracy's wealth contrasted sharply with the peasants' poverty. In 1744, following the Trinh example, the Nguyen named themselves Princes (Vuong), after having built a magnificent capital in Phu Xuan (Hue). Soon, the court and the aristocracy indulged in a lavish style of living. They resided in brick and stone houses filled with decorations, silk curtains, and precious wood furniture. They dressed in brocades and rare silk while the poor dwelled in empty straw huts and wore raw cotton loincloths. While the rich heated themselves with aromatic stoves, the peasants covered themselves with palm leaves. For the rich "gold and silver were like sand, and rice was nothing but mud."[13]

With Vu Vuong Nguyen Phuc Khoat (1738-1765), taxes were increased to pay for court expenses. Tribes were forced to produce more forest products, such as precious woods, honey, beeswax, rhinoceros horns, and elephant tusks. The population of Quang Nam paid high taxes to work in the gold mines which belonged to the mandarins. In 1765, Vu Vuong Nguyen Phuc Khoat died. His ninth son, Nguyen Phuc Hieu, was to succeed him, but the powerful Truong Phuc Loan, who was Vu Vuong Nguyen Phuc Khoat's father-in-law, drew up another will giving the powers to his own grandson Nguyen Phuc Thuan. Nguyen Phuc Thuan took the throne as Dinh Vuong. Since he was only twelve years old, Truong Phuc Loan was his self-appointed regent. Those who opposed him were either imprisoned or executed. After placing his family in key posts, he began to appropriate government sources of revenue, including the important port taxes. His wealth was immeasurable. "After a flood, the gold he put to dry irradiated his entire yard."[14]

All these abuses led to the insolvency of the peasants, who were compelled to abandon their land to the rich. Since taxes had often gone unpaid for ten years, more and more collectors were hired to recover the arrears. Some rulers tried to limit the rights of the upper class, but changed their minds for fear of reaction from the court.

In the South also, revolts erupted among the Viets and tribes alike. From 1695 through 1771, merchants and ethnic minorities attempted four times to change their conditions. In 1695, the merchant Linh revolted in Quang Ngai and Qui Nhon. In 1708, the Baria tribes rose up. In 1747, the merchant Ly Van Quang with 300 men seized the port of Bien Hoa. In 1770, the Sre tribe revolted in Quang Ngai.

But coinage was to be the catalyst for the biggest revolt in Vietnam's history. Since there was no copper in the South, it had to be imported from China and Japan. When trade was booming, the government had to import more and more copper at increasing prices. Soon, tin coins were produced to alleviate the importation of copper. To make a profit for himself, Truong Phuc Loan sold all the coinage privileges to mandarins and rich merchants. More than 100 private foundries were erected, but there was no control over them. When tin was fraudulently added to copper, the copper currency depreciated. Truong Phuc Loan took no measures to rescue the situation. When tin and copper coins reached parity, rice speculators rushed to stockpile and the price of rice skyrocketed.

In 1768, famine broke out. Discontent grew and opened the door for the Tay Son. This time, the movement was supported by the merchant class, which provided the rebels with subsidies, to complement the more or less legitimate proceeds of their widespread banditry. But no war can bring prosperity to people.

Toward the end of the eighteenth century, the conditions of the peasants became desperate. To survive, they had to eat grass, tree bark, and leaves. Half of the Nam Ha population died. In a letter written in July 1775, Father Labartette, a French priest, described the period when the Tay Son invaded Thuan Hoa and drove the Nguyen king, Dinh Vuong Nguyen Phuc Thuan, to Bien Hoa. He stated that it was as if God had poured down his anger on this unfortunate country which was once populous and prosperous. People were dying of hunger by the thousands, everyone in rags and tatters, covered with scabies, undermined by diseases. Mothers ate their suckling babies. Entire families committed suicide. Chinese mercenaries practiced cannibalism, telling around that human flesh tasted better. Markets were selling human parts. Streets were crowded with decomposing bodies which endangered public health.

The Rise of the Tay Son

They were three brothers. Nguyen Nhac, the eldest, was followed by Nguyen Lu and Nguyen Hue. All were natives of Tay Son, a district of the impassable plateau of An Khe. Their ancestor Ho Hung Dat, from Chiet Giang in China, counted among his descents another well-known figure, Ho Qui Ly. During the period of the Five Dynasties, the family came to Vietnam and first settled in the village of Bao Dat in the Quynh Luu district. Later, the colonization of Champa allowed them to resettle in Tay Son. As history has shown, many Chinese immigrants were adventurers in search of unexplored land where absence of social organization would enable them to build a world of their own. Insatiable ambition coupled with rare intelligence were their common denominators.

For some period, the family, except for Nguyen Lu who was a Buddhist monk, was involved in the modest commerce of betel leaves and areca nuts, to which people were addicted as they later were with tobacco. Nguyen Nhac became a tax collector at a time when people's insolvency required drastic enforcement of the law. As a side job, he chose gambling. One may expect he was, at the beginning, using his own money. But gradually he made random dips into the tax cash. When luck deserted him, to avoid government prosecution he went up to the mountains and practiced banditry. He was a Vietnamese Robin Hood, taking from the rich and sharing with the poor. Since the poor constituted the majority, he won an immense constituency. Among his first followers were a Cham princess, two rich notables, and two Chinese merchants, Ly Tai and Tap Dinh, whom he never trusted despite their close association. Finally he felt strong enough to challenge the government. Although the family name was originally Ho, since the name of Ho was associated with Ho Qui Ly, the usurper, and could cost him dearly, he decided to take his mother's name, Nguyen.

The plateau of An Khe was a strategic point par excellence. Access was extremely dangerous, due to the steep trails and dense vegetation. From the plateau, without being exposed, one could keep a close watch on the Qui Nhon-Thanh Hoa axis. Moreover, wood, horses, elephants, iron, and sulphur abounded in this mountainous region. There was just enough to build up an army, under the protection of the natural obstacles. In 1773, Nguyen Nhac decided to take Qui Nhon without bloodshed. Pretending to be a prisoner, he put himself in a cage and had his men deliver him to the governor. Once inside the citadel, he opened the gate to his forces. Afterwards, from Qui Nhon the Tay Son launched a series of attacks against the Nguyen and by year end secured control of all the area between Quang Nghia and Binh Thuan.

At that time, abuses by Truong Phuc Loan caused Nguyen Phuc Van, a member of the Nguyen family, to ask the Trinh to intervene. Obviously this put an end to the 100-year period of truce.

Trinh Sam wasted no time in responding. In 1774, he charged his general Hoang Ngu Phuc with invading Nam Ha with 30,000 troops. He declared that his only purpose was to punish Truong Phuc Loan. Thanks to the treason of a

Nguyen officer, the Trinh, for the first time, succeeded in taking the famous Tran Ninh Wall and threatened the capital, Phu Xuan. To appease the Trinh, a terrorized court captured Truong Phuc Loan and delivered him to Hoang Ngu Phuc. But the Trinh proclaimed they wanted also to submit the Tay Son. Without further ado, they pursued their march on the Nguyen capital, where no Tay Son resided. The Nguyen general Ton That Thiep and his assistant Nguyen Van Chinh tried to stop the Trinh at Quang Dien, but they were promptly crushed. The Trinh stormed Phu Xuan. The Nguyen remnants fled to Quang Nam. After naming Hoang Ngu Phuc governor of Thuan Hoa, Trinh Sam went back to the North.

As for Dinh Vuong Nguyen Phuc Thuan, after the fall of Phu Xuan, he escaped to Quang Nam. There, he named his nephew Nguyen Phuc Duong his heir and gave him the mission of staying and fighting while he fled to Gia Dinh with another nephew Nguyen Phuc Anh.[15] In Gia Dinh, Dinh Vuong Nguyen Phuc Thuan was defeated by Nguyen Lu, the second Tay Son brother, who seized Saigon. It was for Nguyen Lu a short victory for a Nguyen general, Do Thanh Nhan, threw him out. Nguyen Lu retreated to Qui Nhon, not without taking along the totality of the Saigon rice reserve.

The famine of which Father Labartette has given us a gruesome description was rampant in Thuan Hoa, and both the Trinh and the Nguyen were justly held responsible for that situation. The people were convinced that the Tay Son would put an end to their misery. They welcomed Nguyen Nhac's troops and enlisted en masse.

Hoang Ngu Phuc, an old professional soldier, quickly realized the Tay Son threat. However he could take no immediate action because his 30,000 men were exhausted by the long journey to the South, in addition to an untimely outbreak of flu and cholera.

At that moment, the English and French also tried to intervene. According to a report Major Chevalier sent to Pondichery Governor De Bellecombe, he dispatched to Tourane the vessel *Diligente* under Captain Cuny to assess the situation. There Cuny was approached by the captain of an English vessel and asked to take common action in favor of the Nguyen. As Cuny had no combat mission, he pursued his trip to Macao, leaving the English alone with their threats to bomb the Tay Son. Later, the French warship *Lauriston* arrived, armed with twenty-six heavy guns manned by a small crew of Europeans and natives of Madagascar. The crew's surgeon, named Philibert, was dispatched to meet the Nguyen, who begged for a French landing. Philibert stated that he did not have enough troops for an intervention and furthermore he had to sail to China before the monsoon changed. Major Chevalier concluded his report by expressing his concern over the English intervention in Nam Ha, which might deprive France of further benefits. He suggested that France dispose of the warship *Le Brillant* with 150 European troops and 30 blacks.

As for Hoang Ngu Phuc, his troops, after a rest, crossed the Hai Van Pass and reached Hoa Vinh, where they met with the Tay Son advanced guard commanded by the Cantonese mercenary Tap Dinh. The Cantonese troops, Warriors of high repute, started pummelling the Trinh until enormous reinforcements from the North turned the Tay Son advantage into a setback. That gave Nguyen Nhac, who disliked the ambitious Tap Dinh, a pretext to eliminate him. Well aware of his fate, Tap Dinh fled back to China, where he was captured by the Ch'ing and subsequently beheaded. This battle brought Quang Nam under the Trinh. The Tay Son retreated to Qui Nhon. This would be their only defeat. Later, under Nguyen Hue, the Tay Son would never lose a single battle.

In spite of his victory, Hoang Ngu Phuc had no illusions. He told his entourage that the Tay Son were like a hurricane and he was too old to fight. He was afraid there would be a lot of difficulties with the Tay Son. However, he had no idea how Machiavellian Nguyen Nhac could be. As a matter of fact, the Tay Son were in serious trouble. On their rear, the Nguyen general Tong Phuc Hop, who had recaptured Binh Thuan, Diem Khanh, and Binh Khanh, was intensifying his pressure. Caught between the Trinh and the Nguyen forces, Nguyen Nhac had to make a quick decision. He opted to surrender to the strongest party, the Trinh. He sent an emissary to Hoang Ngu Phuc, offering his allegiance in exchange for control of Quang Ngai, Qui Nhon, and Phu Yen. He even proposed to lead an expedition against the Nguyen in Gia Dinh. Hoang Ngu Phuc readily agreed and granted him the title of ''Tay Son General Leader.'' He dispatched his assistant Nguyen Huu Chinh to perform the investiture ceremony, which included the traditional presentation of a sword, flag, cap, gown, and even a horse. This meeting with the Tay Son was to decide Nguyen Huu Chinh's fate.

To test Nguyen Nhac, Hoang Ngu Phuc instructed him to fight the Nguyen at once. Nguyen Nhac developed a stratagem of his own. First, he married his daughter, Tho Huong, to Nguyen Phuc Duong, the Nguyen heir. Then he forced Nguyen Phuc Duong to proclaim himself lord. As Phuc Duong refused because his uncle the king was still in power at Gia Dinh, Nguyen Nhac pretended to beg for Tong Phuc Hop's help in order to convince Phuc Duong. Phuc Hop, the powerful Nguyen governor of Phu Yen, had no reason to doubt Nguyen Nhac's loyalty. But during the time he took to think it over, Nguyen Hue stormed his Phu Yen headquarters. For this feat, Nguyen Hue was promoted to general. Then Hoang Ngu Phuc fell sick and died in Thuan Hoa, leaving Quang Nam in the hands of the Tay Son.

From then on, the Tay Son had no difficulty in swallowing the last Nguyen positions at Thang Binh and Dien Bang. All of Quang Nam was under their banner. When Nguyen Nhac moved back to Qui Nhon, Nguyen Hue stayed to rule Quang Nam. In the South, Nguyen Lu had succeeded in looting Saigon and in transferring the booty back to Qui Nhon.

In 1776, Trinh Sam officially granted Nguyen Nhac the province of Quang Nam, unaware that in doing so he brought grist to the Tay Son mill. Nguyen Nhac at once proclaimed himself king of Tay Son. He then held the heir Nguyen Phuc Duong in custody at the Thap Thap Pagoda. Later, Nguyen Phuc Duong escaped and joined King Nguyen Phuc Thuan in Gia Dinh. Tap Dinh's former partner Ly Tai, who had also deserted Nguyen Nhac, took Nguyen Phuc Duong to Saigon where he made him King Tan Chinh Vuong, while Nguyen Phuc Thuan became the Highest King Thai Thuong Vuong.

In 1777, Nguyen Lu and Nguyen Hue attacked Gia Dinh with land and sea forces. Ly Tai fled away. Nguyen Phuc Duong escaped to Ba Vat (Vinh Long) and the Highest King, Nguyen Phuc Thuan, took refuge in Long Xuyen. Soon both were captured and put to death. After leaving Governor Chu behind to rule Gia Dinh, the two Nguyen brothers went back to Qui Nhon.

Only one member of the Nguyen family escaped the massacre, the seventeen-year-old Nguyen Phuc Anh, another one of Nguyen Phuc Thuan's nephews. Although he did not have Nguyen Hue's military skill, Nguyen Anh (Nguyen Phuc Anh) was intelligent and tenacious. When Nguyen Hue turned his back, Nguyen Anh reappeared with the support of Do Thanh Nhon, Tong Phuoc Luong, and Le Van Cau, he recaptured Saigon, then attacked Binh Thuan, Diem Khanh, and the remainder of Gia Dinh. After pacification of the area, Nguyen Anh sent an embassy to Siam. At the same time, he invaded Cambodia, where he established a protectorate with Ho Van Lam as his representative.

In 1778, Nguyen Nhac took the title of Emperor Thai Duc and made Qui Nhon the imperial capital. Nguyen Lu and Nguyen Hue were also promoted to higher ranks. At that time, Nguyen Hue had emerged as a military genius known for his blitzkrieg attacks.

In 1780, Nguyen Anh proclaimed himself king of Nam Ha. Then he caused problems for himself by putting to death the famous General Do Thanh Nhan, thus causing many of his supporters to defect.

In 1781, the king of Cambodia, Ton Nac (Outey II), refused to recognize Taksin (Trinh Quoc Anh) as the king of Siam because he was a commoner. Taksin therefore dispatched generals Chakkri and So Si to deal a blow to the Cambodians. Nguyen Anh assigned Nguyen Huu Thoai and Ha Van Lan, with 3,000 troops, to rescue his protectorate. While the two armies were preparing to clash, Chakkri learned that Taksin had imprisoned his wife and family. He promptly entered a friendly pact with Nguyen Huu Thoai, who agreed to let him go. Back to Bangkok, Chakkri put Taksin to death and became the first king of the Rama dynasty, which has lasted until now. But he did not forget what the Viets did for him in a crucial moment. He would help Nguyen Anh against the Tay Son.

In 1782, Nguyen Nhac and Nguyen Hue came down with 100 war junks and, near Can Gio, completely destroyed Nguyen Anh's fleet. Then they went back to Qui Nhon, leaving Do Nhan Trap as governor of Saigon. This time, in the absence of Nguyen Hue, a former officer of Nguyen Phuc Thuan's Chau Van Tiep, formed an army of his own and succeeded in taking back Saigon. He then sent for Nguyen Anh in Phu Quoc.

In 1783, Nguyen Hue and Nguyen Lu were back again, bringing on their junks entire regiments of elephants. Nguyen Hue also took advantage of the direction of the wind, blowing from sea to land, and bombed the Nguyen with incendiary rockets. This time, Nguyen Anh and his family escaped to Phu Quoc. In June, Nguyen Hue arrived at Phu Quoc and Nguyen Anh fled to Poulo Condor (Con Lon) with Nguyen Hue following after him. The pursuit would have been fatal to Nguyen Anh if a typhoon had not appeared providentially and saved his life. After a long detour, Nguyen Anh went back to stay in Phu Quoc. It was a disaster. To survive, Nguyen Anh and his troops had to eat plant roots and banana pulps. At that time, he decided to apply to Pigneau de Behaine for French help.

Chau Van Tiep went to Siam to ask for Chakkri's support. Aware of Nguyen Anh's whereabouts, the king of Siam invited him to Bangkok, where he put at his disposal 20,000 troops and 300 junks.

In 1785, Nguyen Anh went back to Vietnam with those reinforcements. They jostled the Tay Son garrison and took over Rach Gia, Ba That, Tra On, Man Thit, and Sadec. At Man Thit, Chau Van Tiep died of his wounds. Again, Nguyen Hue came down to Gia Dinh. He lured the Nguyen and their Siamese allies into Rach Gam and Rach Xoai Mut, where he destroyed the entire Siamese fleet. Out of 20,000 men, only 2,000 to 3,000 managed to escape to Siam through Cambodia. With Nguyen Hue on his tail, Nguyen Anh managed once again to escape. To foil Tay Son surveillance, he wandered from island to island, from Tran Giang to Tho Chau to Co Cot, before arriving back in Thailand.

The Siamese intervention had been a mistake because not only were they unable to help, but also their barbarian behavior alienated the Viet populace and hence discredited Nguyen Anh's cause. Although he did not complain to Chakkri, Nguyen Anh later declined another Siamese offer. Meanwhile, he urged Pigneau de Behaine to sail to France with his son Prince Canh and some ministers. To make sure he had all he needed, he also sent two Spaniards to Manila to beg for Spanish aid. But they were intercepted by Nguyen Hue.

In April 1785, Le Van Cau joined Nguyen Anh with a retinue of 600 men. At that time, Chakkri had provided Nguyen Anh with Long Ky, an area in the suburbs of Bangkok, where he began to organize the Viet community for rice cultivation, military training, and junk construction. From there, he dispatched specialists in psychological warfare to Cochin China to win hearts and minds and to recruit local forces. He also helped Chakkri repel a Burmese invasion and Malaysian pirates who were infesting Siam's littoral.

In 1786, he received an offer for fifty-six boats from the Portuguese in Goa, but chose to decline it. Since he had just rejected a Siamese proposal for another expedition, he did not wish to hurt Chakkri's feelings.

The familial showdown between Nguyen Nhac and Nguyen Hue provided Nguyen Anh with new incentives for resuming hostilities. Fearing Siamese opposition to his parting, he secretly left for Longxyen with his entire entourage. There he built an army with Nguyen partisans, Tay Son defectors, Chinese pirates, and Cambodian mercenaries. On September 7, 1788, Nguyen Anh defeated Nguyen Lu, who fled back to Qui Nhon where he later died. The discord among the Tay Son prevented any coordinated action against him and hence gave Nguyen Anh more time to reinforce his army. Recruitment centers were established in many places, and arms manufacturing started at once. As a result, in 1790, he had 30,000 men with heavy guns, war junks, and two western type gunboats which he named Huynh Long and Xich Nhan. From Macao, where he had dispatched a purchasing team, he received 20,000 pistols and 2,000 guns. Against payment in rice and sugar, he obtained from the foreign merchants raw iron, cast iron, copper, sulphur, and lead.

From that time, Nguyen Anh carried out seasonal warfare (*giac mua*) taking advantage of climatic conditions. Every year from May through October, his fleet sailed up North to make contact with his infantry forces which had moved on land. After building some fortresses where they left a garrison, they had the northeast winds carry them back home during the winter season.

The Fall of the Tay Son

Only after Nguyen Hue's death in September 1792 did Nguyen Anh venture into sustained operations. In 1793, he succeeded in capturing Qui Nhon, after having secured Dien Khanh, Binh Khang, Phu Yen, and Binh Thuan. Nguyen Nhac had to call on Phu Xuan for help. King Canh Thinh, Nguyen Hue's son, dispatched 17,000 men under General Pham Cong Hung, assisted by Le Trung, Nguyen Van Huan, and Ngo Van So, to the rescue of Qui Nhon. When they entered the capital, Pham Cong Hung kept the command and seized all the royal treasures. Nguyen Nhac was so outraged that he "vomited blood and died."[16] Instead of maintaining the Nguyen Nhac's dynasty, King Canh Thinh had Nguyen Nhac's son Nguyen Bao demoted to the rank of "Duke of the Small Kingdom." It was a political mistake. Soon partisan intrigues within the Phu Xuan court caused the end of the Tay Son.

In 1795, while the Tay Son general Tran Quang Dieu was on the point of recapturing Dien Khanh, a struggle arose among various opposing factions in the capital, Phu Xuan. Tran Quang Dieu had to withdraw and go back to impose peace on the protagonists. Later, when order had been reestablished because of his personal efforts, Tran Quang Dieu found himself stripped of his command. Deprived of their best leader, the Tay Son forces started to disintegrate.

In 1798, Duke Nguyen Bao, unhappy about his dynastic position, conspired to surrender to Nguyen Anh. The plot was unveiled, and he was executed together with Le Trung and Nguyen Van Huan. That incident triggered the defection of many Tay Son officers loyal to Nguyen Bao's father Nguyen Nhac.

In 1799, judging conditions ripe for a final takeover, Nguyen Anh attacked Qui Nhon. For some reason, the Tay Son rescue column was delayed and the Tay Son garrison commander Le Van Thanh had to surrender to Nguyen Anh. The name of Qui Nhon was changed to Binh Dinh (Pacified).

In 1800, the Tay Son general Tran Quang Dieu was assigned to recapture Qui Nhon. His fleet reached the mouth of the Thi Nai and established a defensive base there while his infantry laid siege to Qui Nhon. With the help of French volunteers, Nguyen Anh destroyed the Tay Son fleet. Then, judging the Tay

Son forces at Qui Nhon too strong for direct confrontation, Nguyen Anh made an excellent strategic decision. To defuse Qui Nhon, he chose to attack the capital, Phu Xuan, which was not protected. The capital fell easily into Nguyen Anh's hands in 1801. It was a decisive victory. In response, Tran Quang Dieu intensified his attacks against Qui Nhon, forcing Vo Tanh to surrender in 1802. After asking Tran Quang Dieu for mercy for his garrison, Vo Tanh burned himself to death. His assistant Ngo Tong Chu chose to take poison. Tran Quang Dieu gallantly took Vo Tanh's troops under his protection and gave both Nguyen officers a hero's funeral. Then from Qui Nhon he dispatched a rescue column to Phu Xuan, but it ran short of supplies and could not reach the capital.

At that time, King Canh Thinh who had escaped to the North upon the loss of Phu Xuan, came back with 30,000 troops and crossed the Gianh River. He was escorted by Tran Quang Dieu's wife, Bui Thi Xuan, and 5,000 of her troops. They were stopped at the Tran Ninh Wall. King Canh Thinh ordered a retreat, but Bui Thi Xuan refused and took direct command. She fought until dark and had to withdraw after her lieutenant Nguyen Van Kien had defected to the Nguyen. Both King Canh Thinh and Bui Thi Xuan moved back to Nghe An. Tran Quang Dieu left Qui Nhon to join them.

For Nguyen Anh, the fall of Phu Xuan and Qui Nhon was the conclusion of his war, since along with Gia Dinh, they were the three capitals of the Tay Son. Now, the entire country from the Linh Giang River to Gia Dinh belonged to the Nguyen. At the insistence of his followers, Nguyen Anh took the title of Gia Long, founder of the Nguyen dynasty. He dispatched Trinh Hoai Duc and Ngo Nhan Tinh to China for recognition by the Ch'ing. At the same time, he pursued his march to Bac Ha, where he took Thanh Hoa and other provinces. In many provinces, the Tay Son avoided fighting. King Canh Thinh and his two brothers, Nguyen Quang Thuy and Nguyen Quang Thieu, were captured along with Admiral Tu in the region of Phuong Nhan. Nguyen Quang Thuy and Admiral Tu and his wife committed suicide, and the rest were sent back to Thang Long.

To the defeated Tay Son, Nguyen Anh showed no mercy. Instead, he ordered the most sadistic punishments. Ngo Thoi Nham, the original architect of the Ch'ing defeat, was beaten with steel hooks until his entrails spilled out on the bloody ground. His executioner, Dang Tran Thuong, was settling an old score. Once, as a minor official, he had been flogged for not standing at attention in the presence of Ngo Thoi Nham. Asked how an intelligent man like him could serve the Tay Son, Ngo Thoi Nham who was a fine scholar, replied with a verse of his own:

> In this uncertain world, dukes, dignitaries, who is who?
> Games of the Warring States, games of the Spring-Autumn,
> when you play the games, you can only follow the rules.[17]

Nguyen Anh offered a high position to the outstanding Tran Quang Dieu, who had repeatedly defeated the Nguyen. Tran Quang Dieu, refusing to serve two masters, declined, but asked that his eighty-year-old mother be spared.

Nguyen Anh promptly complied, remembering Tran Quang Dieu's generosity towards the Nguyen troops when he took Qui Nhon not so long before.

As for King Canh Thinh, he was to endure the most abject treatment. He had to witness the desecration of his ancestors' tombs and the sight of Nguyen soldiers urinating on Nguyen Hue's and Nguyen Nhac's bones. Then, yanked by four elephants linked to his limbs, he was torn into four pieces. All that time, without a single word, he kept staring at his father's remains. His own remains were hung at the four gates of the Thang Long market under soldiers' guard.

The worst had yet to come for Bui Thi Xuan and her daughter. As Tran Quang Dieu's wife, Bui Thi Xuan was known not only for her military courage but also for her sensational beauty. According to a French witness, both mother and daughter were delivered totally naked to the monstrous elephants. Many people in the crowd captivated by their splendid features, shouted for their release. But it was in vain. The soldiers struck their gongs and the beasts started to move toward their victims. As her daughter went white with horror, Bui Thi Xuan calmly told her to die with courage for she had no way to help her. The elephant picked the teenager up with its trunk and threw her into the air, up and down as if it were playing with a ball. Then, it laid her down on the ground and trampled her into a pulp.

When her turn came, Bui Thi Xuan's face was as radiant as it had always been when she was fighting on the back of her elephant. When the beast came close, she shouted an order to make it turn around against the troops. The terrified soldiers shot at the monster, forcing it, despite the protestations of the crowd, to go back to the victim. Bui Thi Xuan, coiled in the elephant's trunk, was crushed to death with the horrible sound of broken bones. Blood poured down on the ground like water out of twisted laundry. But as if it wanted to show respect to a valiant commander, the elephant refrained from touching her with his feet. When she was dead, the beast became mad and went on a rampage, howling with rage. The troops and the crowd ran for their lives.

The Tay Son had ruled for only fourteen years (1788–1802) during which time Nguyen Hue had written the most fascinating pages of Vietnam's history. If it had not been for his untimely death, the epic of his conquest of China might have surpassed the classic tales of the Three Kingdoms.

The division into three territories without a central authority was the primary cause of the Tay Son's defeat, for it had prevented the creation of a federal structure without which no political or economic survival was possible. Under the Tay Son, the conditions of the people had not significantly improved. The peasants were still needy, the merchants had lost faith in the cause, and the scholars opposed the abandonment of Chinese script for the Vietnamese Nom script. The war in Gia Dinh was nothing but a hunting party. As Le Thanh Khoi explained, the Tay Son were not interested in securing territories, but only in exterminating the enemy. Once the enemy fled away, the party was over and the hunters went back to the comforts of their homes in Qui Nhon. Nguyen Lu, the lord of Gia Dinh, was clearly incompetent. Curiously, the shrewd Nguyen Nhac limited his vision to a few spoils. Only Nguyen Hue had a program, but he could not carry it out to the end, for he died too early.

As for Nguyen Anh, he proved to be a determined and intelligent foe. At first he maintained a traditional administration, avoiding disruptive reforms. He used psychological warfare by supporting the classical scholars, who glorified him in popular pamphlets and war poems. His entertainment teams contributed to maintaining the morale of the troops. For them, probably under French advice, he even had a hospital. He benefitted from the French training in artillery, naval technique, and construction of Vauban-style forts. He succeeded in holding together peoples as diversified as the Muongs of Thanh Hoa and the Thais of Hung Hoa. His efforts to tighten relations with neighboring countries, particularly Siam and Laos, resulted in friendly assistance which, if not decisive, was nevertheless helpful. In newly conquered territories, he collected no taxes. But the primary cause of his success was that he had enough rice to prevent his troops from living off the peasants. He certainly could afford that luxury after Vietnam swallowed all of Champa at the end of the seventeenth century. As for the march to the south, if from the Tran through the Nguyen each dynasty could claim a share in the systematic extermination of Champa, the annexation of southern Cambodia was to be the merit of the Nguyen alone. Those six provinces of the west, (Luc Tinh), fertile and poetic, would later allow Vietnam to be one of the major rice exporters of Southeast Asia.

NOTES

1. *Khi ho Co gay*, a Vietnamese term.

2. *Chua* in Vietnamese, which has the same meaning as *Shogun* in Japanese.

3. C.P. Fitzgerald, *China: A Short Cultural History*, 3d ed. (New York: Praeger) p. 471.

4. Pham Van Son, *Viet Su Tan Bien* (Los Angeles: Dai Nam), B. II, p. 23.

5. Ibid., B. III, p. 24.

6. The former districts of O and Ri, which had been ceded by the Cham.

7. Not to be confused with the Nguyen Anh, who became King Gia Long.

8. Unless authorized by royal decree, all subjects were required to kowtow to the king, and petitioners were required to sign their petitions. Failure to do so resulted in the crime of lese-majesty.

9. Marshall Tran Hung Dao had been made Prince (Vuong).

10. The red-faced Chinese warrior of the Three Kingdoms era, exalted for his unwavering loyalty.

11. Both were heroes of the Han-Shu epic of the post-Ch'in period. Liu Pang became Emperor Han Cao Tsu.

12. Ang Sor was the Cambodian First King and resided in Pnom Penh.

13. Nguyen Khac Vien, *Histoire du Vietnam* (Paris: Editions Sociales, 1974), p. 84.

14. Le Thanh Khoi, *Histoire du Vietnam* (Paris: Sudestasie, 1992), p. 311.

15. Also known as Nguyen Anh, he later became King Gia Long.

16. This is reminiscent of the Three Kingdoms period, when the Eastern Wu minister Chou Yu (Chau Do) vomited blood and died after being outwitted by his archenemy K'un Min (Khong Minh), Liu Pei's minister.

17. Pham Van Son, *Viet Su Tan Bien* (Los Angeles: Dai Nam), B. IV, p. 244.

6

THE NGUYEN HUE EPIC

Nguyen Hue was endowed with both political wisdom and military genius. With a single slogan "For Le, against Trinh," he conquered all of Bac Ha. In only seven days, he defeated a force of 200,000 Chinese, twice the size of his own army. But what made him unique among the Vietnamese rulers was his daring vision for the conquest of China.

THE INVASION OF BAC HA

In 1776, Nguyen Nhac, having constructed fortresses and palaces in his capital, Qui Nhon, proclaimed himself king of Tay Son.

At that time, Thuan Hoa was under Pham Ngo Cau, an impotent Trinh governor. All of Bac Ha was still affected by the commotion generated by the clash between Trinh Can and Trinh Khai ensuing the death of their father, Lord Trinh Sam. In his last years, Lord Trinh Sam fell under the irresistible spell of the fascinating lady Dang Thi Hue, and consequently designated their son, Trinh Can, as his successor. While Trinh Sam's coffin was still exposed in the palace, the Kieu Binh staged a coup in favor of his eldest son, Trinh Khai. The Kieu Binh were the elite troops traditionally recruited from the three districts of Ha Trung, Thieu Hoa, and Tinh Gia in Thanh Hoa and Nghe An provinces. Because they came from the ancestral abode of the Le dynasty, their loyalty was unquestionable. As the first architects of the Trinh's success, they were granted exceptional privileges. But they gradually got out of control. They became openly involved in brigandage and murder, causing deep misery among the Bac Ha population. Even high dignitaries were not spared. In 1663, under Trinh Tac and King Le Gia Tong, they killed the high mandarin Nguyen Quoc Hoe and ransacked the house of the national hero Pham Cong Tru. In 1740, under Trinh Doanh and King Le Hien Tong, they murdered the high mandarin Nguyen Quy

Canh. Now, for the succession of Lord Trinh Sam, they pitted Trinh Khai against his brother Trinh Can.

The population, which had been suffering from war and natural disasters, also had to carry the unjust burden of government excises. Indeed, the poor and landless had been exempted under former dynasties, but under Trinh Sam they had to pay taxes. In 1786, famine raged in Bac Ha. The Kieu Binh's unchecked abuses added another dimension to the general misery. That anarchy prompted Nguyen Huu Chinh to urge the Tay Son to intervene. When Nguyen Hue objected, stating he had no order from Nguyen Nhac, Nguyen Huu Chinh said that what counted was the result. In this case, there was more to gain than to lose. Furthermore, on the battlefield, the Commander had more authority than the King. His scruples quashed and his ego stirred up, Nguyen Hue ordered Nguyen Huu Chinh to march on Thang Long. Nguyen Huu Chinh crossed over Hai Van Pass and attacked An Nong, where the defeated Trinh general, Hoang Nghia Ho, committed suicide. At Thuan Hoa, Governor Pham Ngo Cau was still worshipping his war spirits when Nguyen Huu Chinh arrived. All the garrison officers were killed or committed suicide. Pham Ngo Cau surrendered and was later executed in Qui Nhon. This battle cost the lives of thousands of starving refugees who had fled to Thuan Hoa looking for food.

The news of Thuan Hoa's fall reached Thang Long, triggering numerous uprisings. The Kieu Binh party vigorously opposed any government attempts to quash the insurgents. No agreement could be reached either to stop the Tay Son invasion. Nguyen Huu Chinh's troops surged along the mouth of the Viet An River and entered Nghe An, which had been abandoned by Bui The Tuy, the son of Bui The Dat.[1] In Thanh Hoa, the Trinh general Ta Danh Thuy escaped leaving behind six million liters of rice,[2] hidden there while tens of thousands were dying of starvation. Nguyen Huu Chinh's army reached first Vi Hoang, the point of rally where the entire Tay Son expedition gathered for the final assault on Thang Long. The Trinh forces intercepted them at Son Nam (Hung Yen). The clash was extremely violent with heavy artillery fire on shore and on the junks. The Tay Son used decoys to lure their opponents. When they realized they had exhausted their munitions aiming at the wrong targets, the Trinh disbanded. The loss of Son Nam was the prelude to the defeat of Bac Ha.

TRINH KHAI, THE LAST TRINH

In a last attempt to protect Thang Long, Trinh Khai deployed his forces in the suburbs. But he was no match for Nguyen Hue. In spite of a few displays of heroism, the Trinh were crushed. Trinh Khai rode his elephant back home to find Tay Son flags displayed all over his palace. He fled in the direction of Son Tay. Arriving at the village of Ha Loi, he stopped to look for the faithful Ly Tran Quan, who had been among his first followers. Although Trinh Khai tried to conceal his identity, Ly Tran Quan's deferential behavior aroused suspicion among his own attendants. Later one of them, Nguyen Trang, arrested Trinh

Khai. Ly Tran Quan desperately begged for Trinh Khai's release. As a last resort, blaming himself for Trinh Khai's condition, Ly Tran Quan apologized and committed hara-kiri in front of Trinh Khai.[3] Another man, Ba Chuc, who was an ex-servant of the Trinh, vainly tried to wrest the prisoner from Nguyen Trang. Finally both agreed to share whatever reward they could yield from the Tay Son. That night, the two men led Trinh Khai to a boat and sailed to the Tay Son camp. On the way, taking advantage of the darkness, Trinh Khai cut his throat, but the wound was too small, so he had to enlarge it with his bare fingers. He died later, at the village of Nhat Chieu. Nguyen Hue ordered his corpse be publicly exposed in front of the palace for three days, but gave him a princely funeral. Nguyen Trang received a promotion from Nguyen Hue, and Ba Chuc met a different fate in the hands of Nguyen Huu Chinh. During the identification of the dead body, Nguyen Huu Chinh asked Ba Chuc how he knew the body was that of Trinh Khai. Chuc replied that he was his servant. Chinh calmly declared that a servant who betrays his master deserves death, not reward, and he had Ba Chuc beheaded at once.[4]

With the death of Trinh Khai, the house of Trinh was in jeopardy. While his two sons, Trinh Bong and Trinh Le, went into hiding, his supporters, the Kieu Binh, started a stampede. But they were tracked down by the population and slaughtered without mercy. As for Bac Ha's regular troops, they went on a rampage. On July 21, 1786, Nguyen Hue entered Thang Long. Discipline was restored among the troops and the population. Justice was expeditious. Robbers, burglars, and rapists were decapitated publicly with no further ado. Possession of rice from illicit trade was condemned. Life and property were respected. Nguyen Hue had even secretly dispatched a group to protect King Le Hien Tong.

On July 26, after having advised the king of his impending visit, Nguyen Hue went with Nguyen Huu Chinh and other high officers to explain courteously that the only aim of the Tay Son was to destroy the Trinh and to reestablish the Le dynasty in accordance with the will of heaven. A few days later, Nguyen Hue returned to the palace at the head of an official delegation, respectfully kowtowed, and presented the national census as a sign of allegiance. The next day King Le Hien Tong bestowed on him the title of duke. Although he accepted it, he was infuriated by the modesty of the title since he had expected to be named Vuong. He sent an emissary to thank the king, but also to mark his displeasure. Nguyen Huu Chinh had to use all his eloquence to calm him down. He even advised King Le Hien Tong to offer Nguyen Hue the hand of his twenty-first daughter, Princess Ngoc Han, who was renowned for her incomparable beauty and her refined education.[5] Nguyen Hue was finally subdued, but the old king Le Hien Tong could not survive so much stress in such a short time. As a Trinh puppet, he never had to worry about his life for he was submissive and unassuming. But he had a visceral fear of the Tay Son, in spite of their friendly manners. He died a few days later at the age of seventy, after forty-seven years of irresponsible reign.

Upon Ngoc Han's pleading, Nguyen Hue agreed to the accession of her brother Prince Duy Ky to the throne as King Le Chieu Thong. That man did not stop making blunders all his life. He started to act against protocol by sitting on the throne in front of his father's coffin. Then he forgot to include his brother-in-law Nguyen Hue among the mourners. His omission hurt Nguyen Hue personally and politically. On the one hand, it implied that Nguyen Hue did not belong to the royal family; on the other, his absence at the funeral destroyed the credit he was trying to build as the protector of the Le. He was so incensed that princess Ngoc Han had to bear the brunt of his rage. Subsequently she had the young king come and beg for his subject's pardon.

After the coronation of Le Chieu Thong, the court performed the posthumous consecration of his late father, King Le Hien Tong. This time, as his son-in-law, Nguyen Hue appeared dressed in a white mourning gown. During the ceremony, he caught a smile on the face of a young attendant and had him beheaded at once for contempt for the king. A shudder went through the entire court, but everybody agreed that Nguyen Hue had observed dynastic rites to the perfection.

Now Nguyen Hue had to deal with his brother the emperor Nguyen Nhac, who was approaching Thang Long with an escort of 2,500 elite troops and 100 elephants, creating an enormous commotion in the capital. His contention was that Nguyen Hue had invaded Bac Ha without his authorization. Actually, he feared Nguyen Hue would keep the North for himself. Anyway, he should have realized that his action would deal a serious blow to Nguyen Hue's ego. He soon had to pay for that psychological error.

King Le Chieu Thong was devastated by the news but, after consulting with his court, decided to surrender to Nguyen Hue's boss. As he entered the capital, Nguyen Nhac found the new king and his entire court kneeling on the sidewalk in total submission. He did not stop, but had Le Chieu Thong ordered to go home. Overnight, the two brothers hammered out their differences, and at dawn, King Le Chieu Thong reappeared humbly offering to share his kingdom with Nguyen Nhac. But Nguyen Nhac emphatically refused saying: "We came here to help you against the Trinh. If Bac Ha had belonged to them, we would take every inch of land. But as it is yours, we shall not touch a single inch. All we hope is for you to secure your kingdom so that our two nations can have a lasting friendship." This was a threefold statement. First, it deemed to appease Bac Ha. Second, it implied that the Le were no longer masters of the South. Third, it was a clear order for Nguyen Hue to pack up and go home.

As they prepared to leave, Vu Van Nham, who hated Nguyen Huu Chinh, suggested that Nguyen Hue leave Nguyen Huu Chinh behind to deal with Bac Ha. He said that the Northern people don't like him. After they kill him, Hue could still go back and take the whole North. Nguyen Hue promptly agreed. On the day of his departure, Nguyen Hue kept Nguyen Huu Chinh at his side, making sure he knew nothing about his plan. That night, the Tay Son left surreptitiously after having secretly bid King Le Chieu Thong farewell and not without taking along all the royal treasures.

At dawn, Nguyen Huu Chinh learned of the news and, with a small retinue, ran down to the pier, where he was stoned by a menacing crowd. He seized a boat after killing its occupants and sailed to the South. He met the Tay Son in Nghe An, where an uneasy Nguyen Hue explained that Bac Ha was not to be trusted and that was why he had left Nguyen Huu Chinh behind to watch. He also said that Nguyen Huu Chinh should stay in Nghe An to prevent any attempt from the North. Chinh was no dupe. He admitted the fact that his boss did not want him, but at that time he saw no way out.

THE SEEDS OF THE TAY SON DIVISION

When he returned to Nam Ha, Nguyen Hue stayed at Phu Xuan and kept for himself all the Bac Ha booty. Nguyen Nhac went home to Qui Nhon. Later, he sent an emissary to summon Nguyen Hue, who refused to comply saying he was still preoccupied with Bac Ha. Then Nguyen Nhac dispatched a second envoy to bestow on Nguyen Hue the title of Bac Binh Vuong (North Pacification King). He also asked Nguyen Hue to turn over the Bac Ha booty. After what had happened in Thang Long, for Nguyen Hue this was the last straw and he taught his eldest brother a good lesson. Without notice, he had Qui Nhon surrounded by his troops. For the defense of Qui Nhon, Nguyen Nhac hurriedly withdrew his forces from Gia Dinh. Finally, convinced he could not resist, Nguyen Nhac resorted to an appeal to their blood ties. Although he was furious at his brother, Nguyen Hue was deeply moved and consented to withdraw. History does not say whether he shared the contested booty with Nguyen Nhac. But by moving his troops from Gia Dinh, Nguyen Nhac made a strategical error with incalculable consequences. It left Gia Dinh to the mercy of Nguyen Anh, who later used it as a springboard for his reconquest of the North.

Then Nguyen Nhac blundered again. He called for a meeting to divide Nam Ha into three parts. As the "Central Emperor," Nguyen Nhac remained in Qui Nhon, in charge of Quang Nghia, Qui Nhon, Phu Yen, and Nha Trang. As Bac Binh Vuong (North Pacification King), Nguyen Hue was stationed in Quang Nam and controlled Phu Xuan and Bac Ha. As Dong Binh Vuong (East Pacification King), Nguyen Lu ruled Gia Dinh, Binh Thuan, Dong Nai, Dalat, and Ha Tien. But the seeds of division were sown; the Central Emperor had lost the control of his empire (Map 16).

NGUYEN HUU CHINH

Nguyen Huu Chinh was born in Nghe An and came from a well-to-do merchant family. He was articulate, courteous and extremely intelligent and later succeeded the Trinh in Bac Ha. A diviner who passed in front of Nguyen Huu Chinh's house at the time of his birth and heard his first cry predicted that Nguyen Huu Chinh would become a "scoundrel of troubled times." So goes the legend. Nguyen Huu Chinh went on to get a master's degree in philosophy.

Map 16
1780: Vietnam with the Tay Son

CHINA
(Ch'ing)

Cao Bang
Lang Son
Thai Nguyen
Thang Long

Luang Prabang

Vientiane

Thanh Hoa

Nghe An

Hoanh Son

Hai Nan

Phu Xuan
Hai Van
Da Nang
Quang Nam
Hoi An

BASSAC

Quang Ngai

Qui Nhon
Phu Yen
Dien Khanh
Nha Thang
Phan Rang
Binh Thuan
Vung Tau

Oudong
Co Cot
Pnom Penk
Sadec
Phu Quoc
Long Xuyen
Go Cong
Camau

⊘ NGUYEN HUE

⊜ NGUYEN NHAC

⊗ NGUYEN LU

However, realizing that in times of war a military career was more profitable, he turned to the study of the science of war, but failed to pass the required examination. He offered his services to the Trinh governor Hoang Ngu Phuc and, following successful campaigns against sea pirates, rapidly became his best general. In 1775, Hoang Ngu Phuc dispatched him to commission Nguyen Nhac, who was then quite impressed by Nguyen Huu Chinh's talents. Back home, Nguyen Huu Chinh reported to Hoang Ngu Phuc that the Tay Son were very ambitious and would not remain in his service for long. After Hoang Ngu Phuc died, Nguyen Huu Chinh continued to serve his adopted son Hoang Dinh Bao, who was involved in the Trinh Sam succession contest. As Hoang Dinh Bao had sided with the losing party, he lost his life. Fearing the same fate, Nguyen Huu Chinh threw his lot in with those trying to revolt against the Trinh. He secretly approached General Vu Ta Giao for help. But Vu Ta Giao refused and Nguyen Huu Chinh had to flee to Qui Nhon with his family and sought Nguyen Nhac's protection. Soon he became the most trusted of Nguyen Nhac's officers. But Nguyen Hue had some misgivings. One day, as Nguyen Huu Chinh tried to convince him to invade Bac Ha, Nguyen Hue raised some objections. Chinh insisted that he not be so concerned because now that Nguyen Huu Chinh had left, no one could find a single good leader in Bac Ha. Nguyen Hue laughed and replied that he was not worried about their leaders, but about Chinh.

In Thang Long, as soon as the Tay Son turned their backs, the Trinh remnants began fighting for Trinh Khai's succession. His two sons, Trinh Bong and Trinh Le, who were hiding from the Tay Son, now reappeared to claim the succession. King Le Chieu Thong appointed Trinh Bong, thus triggering a revolt by Trinh Le, who lost the ensuing battle at Can Muong. Left alone, Trinh Bong gradually unveiled his despotic nature, offending King Le Chieu Thong in many ways and abusing the people more than ever. Bac Ha again sank into chaos. Entire villages rose up, fighting each other, while inundations and tornadoes played their part in destroying houses, animals, and people. Le Chieu Thong tried to enlist a few faithful supporters. Finally he realized that only Nguyen Huu Chinh could deal definitely with the Trinh and sent him an emissary.

In Nghe An, Nguyen Huu Chinh had long understood that he had no future with Nguyen Hue, but had yet to find a way out. When King Le Chieu Thong's envoy arrived, it was for him the light at the end of the tunnel. He left the Nghe An command to his lieutenants Le Duat and Nguyen Huu Due and moved with his troops to the North. On the way, he crushed Trinh Bong's forces and entered Thang Long in triumph. Trinh Bong fled. He sought refuge in religion and was not seen again. Nguyen Huu Chinh took over Trinh Bong's palace and functions after King Le Chieu Thong appointed him commander in chief. Later, the king thought he had made a mistake and plotted the murder of Nguyen Huu Chinh.

Nguyen Huu Chinh was no petty character. Politically and militarily, he was the perfect match for Nguyen Hue, and sheer jealousy was the source of their mutual hatred. His ambition was not limited to the North, he also wanted the South. While consolidating his grip on Bac Ha, he kept a close watch on the

Tay Son. Through Nguyen Huu Due, his man in Nghe An, he learned of the discord among the Tay Son. Nguyen Huu Due was also a complex character. He had once served Nguyen Nhac, and now he was plotting with Nguyen Huu Chinh against Nguyen Hue. The latter, aware of the conspiracy, charged Vu Van Nham with keeping an eye on Nguyen Huu Due.

Vu Van Nham himself was no altar boy. He had been Nguyen Anh's commander at Gia Dinh, and when he lost it to Nguyen Hue, he tried to commit suicide but did not succeed. As he was a good soldier, Nguyen Hue convinced him to join the Tay Son. Later Vu Van Nham managed to marry Nguyen Nhac's daughter and became Nguyen Hue's hatchet man. He was slyly competing with Nguyen Huu Chinh for the Bac Ha command, but lost due to King Le Chieu Thong's preference. From that time on, Vu Van Nham spied on Nguyen Huu Chinh and his men in Nghe An.

Eventually Vu Van Nham's vicious reports led Nguyen Hue to order the arrest of Nguyen Huu Chinh in Thang Long and the transfer of Nguyen Huu Due to Quang Nam. Fearing Nguyen Hue's punishment, Nguyen Huu Due left Nghe An under his assistants and ran for safety to Qui Nhon and Nguyen Nhac's protection. Subsequently, Vu Van Nham took over Nghe An without a single shot. Then he set out for Bac Ha with 10,000 of his best troops. Nguyen Huu Chinh, who had just escaped from a murder attempt by Le Chieu Thong, was coerced into another contest.

At this point, King Le Chieu Thong, unaware of his impending doom, made an absurd move. Counting on the Tay Son family dispute, he sent his minister Tran Cong San to claim back Nghe An Province. When Tran Cong San arrived at Nguyen Hue's headquarters, he learned that Vu Van Nham's troops were on their way to punish Bac Ha. Of course, Nguyen Hue rejected vehemently the king's request, reminding him of the Tay Son's past contributions and accusing him of ingratitude. He sent Tran Cong San into seclusion, but upon Princess Ngoc Han's pleading, he allowed him to go back to Thang Long. With 100 taels donated by the princess, Tran Cong San and his retinue boarded a junk which would later be destroyed by Nguyen Hue's men on the high seas. So all of Bac Ha delegation lost their money and their lives.

On forced marches, Vu Van Nham's troops reached Thanh Hoa, where Le Duat, one of Nguyen Huu Chinh's generals, was killed in the first encounter. The news rocked the capital. Nguyen Huu Chinh dispatched his son, Nguyen Huu Du, to halt the Tay Son but he was defeated at Ha Nam and Ninh Binh. A few miles from Thang Long, in a desperate battle, Nguyen Huu Chinh's troops opposed Vu Van Nham's. The result was the total disintegration of the Bac Ha forces. Then Nguyen Huu Chinh ordered the evacuation of Thang Long. King Le Chieu Thong wished to retreat to ancestral Thanh Hoa, but finally joined Nguyen Huu Chinh and went to Kinh Bac.

In Bac Giang Province, Nguyen Huu Chinh met his fate. His horse was killed under him, and he was captured by the Tay Son Nguyen Van Hoa, along with his son Nguyen Huu Du. Both were taken to Thang Long where a delighted Vu

Van Nham read him a long list of accusations, to which Nguyen Huu Chinh responded that it was because of the circumstances. He died atrociously, torn apart limb from limb by four giant elephants yanking his arms and legs. His son Nguyen Huu Du was beheaded. Nguyen Huu Chinh had had only ten months in which to reorganize the near total collapse of Bac Ha. His efforts to rebuild the North's army and administration were undermined by a hostile court and a suspicious King Le Chieu Thong, who wished him dead. He persisted in being loyal to a chief, Nguyen Hue, who had rejected him. These were the circumstances which history should take into account: what Nguyen Huu Chinh was lacking was not intelligence or talent or even a measure of loyalty, but time, only time.

VU VAN NHAM

Now a word must be said about Vu Van Nham, Nguyen Huu Chinh's rival. In 1786, he surrendered to Nguyen Hue after his demise at Gia Dinh. Then he managed to enter the Tay Son family as King Thai Duc's (Nguyen Nhac) son-in-law and was wise enough to sit on the fence while the two brothers were clashing. But when he and his wife applied for permission to visit Nguyen Nhac in Qui Nhon, he aroused Nguyen Hue's suspicion. In response, Nguyen Hue sent him to Nghe An with the mission of fighting Nguyen Huu Chinh. For canny Nguyen Hue, no matter what the outcome between these two potential traitors, he could always get rid of one—or maybe both, if they managed to kill each other at the same time.

After Vu Van Nham had executed Nguyen Huu Chinh, it was his turn to assume power in Bac Ha. He was not aware that General Ngo Van So, his military counterpart, was Nguyen Hue's spy. One day, following the escape of Le Chieu Thong to China, an argument arose between them over the choice of Prince Le Duy Can as regent. Ngo Van So told Vu Van Nham that they did not need a puppet and to take over Bac Ha. But Vu Van Nham brushed him off saying that he should fight his war and leave the political matter to him. Resenting these harsh words, Ngo Van So willfully reported that Vu Van Nham was eyeing Bac Ha for himself. Since that was all he wished to hear, Nguyen Hue entered Thang Long furtively at night, stormed Vu Van Nham's bedroom, and had him stabbed to death while he was still sleeping. Of course, Ngo Van So was promoted to Vu Van Nham's post.

THE DEFEAT OF THE CH'ING

While Nguyen Huu Chinh was being captured, King Le Chieu Thong managed to escape and arrived in Kinh Bac (Bac Ninh), where he found a rather lukewarm welcome from General Nguyen Canh Thuoc. Frustrated, Le Chieu Thong and his retinue went on to Bao Loc and were greeted by Nguyen Trong Linh. After their defensive dike was overrun, the king fled to the South as he had originally intended. Many trials and tribulations occurred before the king arrived at Nghe An and Thanh Hoa, where traitor Dinh Tich Nhuong, whose family had served the Le for eighteen generations, informed the Tay Son of his whereabouts. Eventually, he had to escape to China where he was granted asylum.

In Peking, the Le Chieu Thong's case was seriously debated within Emperor Ch'ien Lung's circles. The doves, reminiscing about the disaster two hundred years before, wished to stay away from a conflict with the South, but General Sun Shih Yi succeeded in persuading Ch'ien Lung to send 200,000 troops to the Bac Ha border. They were to intervene only if Le Chieu Thong's forces could not deal with the Tay Son. In fact, before leaving Sun Shih Yi unveiled his real intent, telling his Emperor that they should take this opportunity to have Annam back.

The Chinese forces were divided into three armies. The first, from Yunnan, marched on Tuyen Quang; the second, from Kweichow, moved in direction of Cao Bang; and the main corps, under Sun Shih Yi himself, came from Kwangtung and Kwangsi and aimed at Langson.

In Thang Long, Ngo Van So summoned a war meeting. To those who suggested guerrilla tactics, Ngo Thoi Nham, one of Nguyen Hue's advisors, said that they could succeed only with popular support. But since the Ch'ing had come under the Le banner, the Bac Ha people would not fight against their king. The best way was to lure the Chinese deep into the country and let Nguyen Hue exterminate them. Be that as it may, no one was in a position to resist 200,000 Chinese troops.

In 1788, at the first clash on Tam Tan Mountain, the Ch'ing artillery set fire to the Thi Cau citadel, killing hundreds of Tay Son soldiers. As their commander Phan Van Lan forced a retreat through the nearby river, many soldiers died from drowning and the rest were killed by hostile peasants. Finally Phan Van Lan arrived back at the capital with only twenty-eight horsemen. Under these circumstances, Ngo Van So ordered the evacuation of Thang Long.

Sun Shih Yi's troops entered Thang Long, which had been evacuated by Ngo Van So. The Ch'ing transferred the power to Le Chieu Thong, who apparently did not know what to do with it since he went to report to the Chinese headquarters everyday. Toward his own people, Le Chieu Thong was brutal and merciless. Despite war and famine, he compelled the people to supply food and provisions to his court every day. Severe punishments were reserved for those unable to comply.

Then he started a bloody cleansing of his harem. Ladies found pregnant by the Tay Son were disembowelled and their fetuses were thrown to the dogs. Three of his uncles who had married their daughters to the Tay Son had their legs cut off and exposed on the marketplace. Many high dignitaries were put to death or banished. These excesses even outraged the queen mother, who went on to predict the end of the dynasty.

After Le Chieu Thong had been back for a month, his orders reached only the suburbs of Thang Long. Even in Nghe An, the ancestral abode of the Le, nobody was aware of his return. Instead of reorganizing his army, Le Chieu Thong relied solely on the Ch'ing forces. As for Sun Shih Yi, his first success had given him nothing but contempt for the Tay Son. He repeated that defeating Nguyen Hue was as easy as putting things in his pockets. When the Viet prime minister Le Huynh was in Peking, he used to boast that Le Chieu Thong had the support of the entire population. This induced Sun Shih Yi to rely on the Le's cooperation. As Le Huynh was now insisting that he attack the Tay Son, he realized that the Viet had lied to him. He was furious because if Le Huynh had told him the truth, he would not have stopped in Thang Long. He would have pursued the Tay Son to the South. But actually, Sun Shih Yi was enjoying the queen mother's company and so decided to postpone the operations until the spring. When Le Huynh persisted, he sarcastically told him to go ahead and fight himself if he wished.

NGUYEN HUE, EMPEROR QUANG TRUNG

While Le Chieu Thong was busy purging his harem, Nguyen Hue was preparing for war against the Ch'ing. On November 24, 1788, he received from Ngo Van So news of the Chinese invasion. Showing no concern, he told them that the Chinese had come to be massacred.

Since the people of Nghe An wanted a king to lead the war, on December 22, 1788, Nguyen Hue proclaimed himself Emperor Quang Trung. Whether this was a spontaneous idea from his followers or it was at his instigation (history is rather reticent on this point), the obvious result was that now Vietnam had three emperors—two self-appointed, Nguyen Nhac and Nguyen Hue, and the third, Le Chieu Thong, supported by the Chinese. To solve that puzzle, a showdown was inevitable. Nguyen Hue was ready. He had recruited 100,000 men and several hundred elephants.

On December 26, Nguyen Hue issued a proclamation:

The Ch'ing have invaded our country. The men of the North (China) are a different race. In the past, the Trung sisters, Dinh Tien Hoang, Le Dai Hanh, Tran Hung Dao, Le Thai To had thrown them out. Men of conscience and virtue join us in this great undertaking. Do not have two hearts. Traitors will be executed without mercy. They could not blame me for not having warned them.[6]

While Tran Hung Dao's proclamation had referred to Chinese role models, Nguyen Hue only mentioned Viet heroes. After a thousand years, the fight for independence had its own martyrs.

Nguyen Hue's forces unfurled like a tidal wave, covering the distance from Ban Son to Nghe An (around 300 miles) in four days. To preserve the strength of his troops, Nguyen Hue ingeniously set up three-man teams, two in turn carrying a hammock in which the third could rest. When he arrived at the border between Ninh Binh and Thanh Hao, he found Nguyen Van So and his assistant

Nguyen Van Lan ready to accept punishment. But Nguyen Hue comforted them. Actually, he realized that his advisor Ngo Thoi Nham was right. Thang Long was indefensible because the Tay Son were caught between an internal revolt from the Le loyalists and an external offensive by the Ch'ing. Furthermore, it was not such a bad idea to lose the first match in order to give the enemy a false sense of superiority. For Nguyen Hue, too, psychological warfare was an important concept.

Pretending to negotiate, he sent a letter to Sun Shih Yi suggesting he abandon the Le and recognize Quang Trung. As expected, the arrogant Sun Shih Yi tore up the message and put the Viet envoy Tran Danh Binh to death. He even had a price on Nguyen Hue's head, showing he considered him no better than a petty thief. In reply, Nguyen Hue had only this to say: "We shall throw out the Ch'ing in ten days. Today, let's celebrate the Tet[7] in advance. In spring, we will celebrate again in Thang Long."

On December 30, he chased the Le general Hoang Phung Nghia out of Nam Dinh, forcing him to withdraw to Ha Nam. In Ha Dong, the entire Le advance guard was captured.

On January 3, 1789, at the Citadel of Ha Hoi, Nguyen Hue surprised the Ch'ing at night during their sleep. They surrendered without combat.

Before dawn on January 5, Nguyen Hue donned a yellow scarf as a symbol of total sacrifice and led an elephant attack against the heavily fortified post of Ngoc Hoi. Wounded by the enemy's artillery, the Viet elephants became mad and went on a wild rampage, killing thousands of Chinese. The Tay Son infantry followed with thick wooden shields, which they used to pave the way over underground stakes. In total darkness, surrounded by suffocating smoke, waves of Viet soldiers submerged the Chinese positions. The hysterical screams of human beings, the delirious trumpeting of elephants, and bloody eruptions of flesh and bones provided the background for the final hand-to-hand fighting. It was a bitter defeat for the Ch'ing, but the worst was yet to come. When the news of Ngoc Hoi's defeat reached Sun Shih Yi, Nguyen Hue was already in the suburbs of Thang Long. Sun Shih Yi and Le Chieu Thong and his family only had time to escape undressed on unsaddled horses. On his way to the capital, Nguyen Hue conquered the three outposts of Van Dien, Yen Quyet, and Kiem Thuong and killed five Ch'ing generals.

The reinforcements dispatched by Emperor Ch'ien Lung, under Phuc An Khang[8] had to retreat to Bac Ninh because of Tay Son pressure. The two armies from Yunnan and Kweichow, hearing of the disaster, also withdrew without fighting. The Tay Son victory was complete. With only half strength, Nguyen Hue had defeated the 200,000 men of the Ch'ing expeditionary force. This superb campaign had lasted a total of forty-two days—thirty-five were spent in preparation and only seven in actual fighting.

Now, it was the time for negotiations. Phuc An Khang suggested Nguyen Hue write a nice petition to the Ch'ing emperor promising to back him up. Nguyen Hue charged Ngo Si Tham with drafting the message. It was a disaster.

After insinuating that the Ching emperor was responsible for the conflict, it went on to imply that he had been asinine enough to listen to Sun Shih Yi's inventions. The plea ended on a sordid note. It revealed that Sun Shih Yi had become a toy in the hands of Le Chieu Thong's luscious mother, who used him to destroy the Tay Son. Phuc An Khang had not even finished reading it when he hastily destroyed the message. Then he muttered, "You do not really want peace, do you?" Hence Phuc An Khang took the matter into his own hands and persuaded his emperor to recognize Nguyen Hue. In this instance, Ch'ien Lung displayed a rare gift for fair play. He readily agreed on the conditions for Nguyen Hue to come and pay homage in Peking in accordance with tradition. Phuc An Khang suggested that for the emperor to save face, Nguyen Hue should erect a temple for the Chinese warriors he had killed. Naturally, the emperor would have no objection to any other conciliatory gestures. This meant that a great amount of gold and silver had to be offered, of which Phuc An Khang secretly took 100 taels for his mediatory efforts.

THE LAST LE

As for King Le Chieu Thong, he arrived at Nanning together with Sun Shih Yi. But his fate was sealed. Friendly Sun Shih Yi was soon replaced by the Tay Son's accomplice Phuc An Khang, whose ruthless schemes would eventually lead him to destitution and death.

In 1789, Phuc An Khang promised Le Chieu Thong that he would send troops to Annam in the fall. In 1790, he suggested that Le Chieu Thong first go back to his country, but for his own protection he was to wear a Chinese costume and shave his head in Manchu fashion. Le Chieu Thong fell into this vulgar trap. He shaved his head and donned chinese garb. Then Phuc An Khang reported to the emperor that the Viet king had decided to stay in China and had adopted local customs. Happy to see a Viet king renounce his crown to be his simple subject, Ch'ien Lung allocated to Le Chieu Thong a minor title for his subsistence.

Realizing that he had been duped, Le Chieu Thong made a petition in which he asked to be given the two provinces of Thai Nguyen and Tuyen Quang for his dynastic rites, or else to be sent back to Gia Dinh where he could help the Nguyen against the Tay Son. In vain he tried to approach Ch'ien Lung. One day, while the emperor was in his summer garden, he forced the entrance. Apprehended by the guards, Le Chieu Thong and his party were severely beaten and imprisoned for a month. Once out of jail, to prevent further collusion, Phuc An Khang ordered Le Chieu Thong's entourage to be scattered to remote provinces, leaving Le Chieu Thong alone. In 1792, Le Chieu Thong lost his son in a smallpox epidemic. The following year, he succumbed to despair and disease. The Ch'ing Emperor ordered a ducal funeral for him. His tragedy was not a lack of will, but of judgement.

In 1802, the new Nguyen dynasty authorized the transfer of Le Chieu Thong's remains back to Annam. According to the annals, only his heart was found intact. After the funeral, his widow, who had remained in Vietnam during his exile, refused food and died.

When Le Chieu Thong escaped to China, his brother Prince Duy Chi led sporadic resistance in Bao Lac (Tuyen Quang) for more than one year. With his Lao allies from Tran Ninh and Vientiane, he attacked Nghe An. In 1790, General Tran Quang Dieu, with 5,000 troops, pursued the king of Vientiane to the Siam border. Duy Chi was captured and executed. So ended the Later Le dynasty.

NGUYEN HUE'S DREAM

Having reached an accord with the Ch'ing, Nguyen Hue gave himself a ten-year respite to prepare for the conquest of China. If the Mongols and the Man-chus had been able to do it, why not Nguyen Hue?

This early decision to attack China led him to evade any act of personal allegiance to the Chinese. For this reason, he refused to take part in an investiture ceremony. On July 26, 1789, he received notice of the impending ritual, which was to be held in Thang Long in accordance with tradition. Claiming one excuse after another, at Phuc An Khang's secret suggestion he finally dispatched his nephew Pham Cong Tri disguised as Emperor Quang Trung to perform the allegiance ceremony.

From then on, relations between the two countries improved because the Chinese emperor, whose Manchu ancestors had fought against Chinese domination, had developed the greatest admiration for Nguyen Hue, who had defeated him in loyal combat. When Nguyen Hue's mother was in need of thousand-year-old ginseng to cure an illness, the Chinese emperor ordered the use of the imperial relay to dispatch his gift without delay.

When the time came for Nguyen Hue to pay homage in Peking, he dodged again and finally appointed a double. Authors disagreed on the identity of that man. But as Nguyen Hue, he received the warmest welcome from Ch'ien Lung, who did everything to charm him. He was treated as a close member of the imperial circle, sat with the emperor on his personal couch, and enjoyed multiple marks of affection. Rare precious gifts and the highest titles were bestowed on him. Although Prince Quang Thuy had been mistaken for the heir Quang Toan, Ch'ien Lung persisted in taking him for the crown prince of Annam, and when he fell sick, the emperor personally ordered doctors and medications for him.

The Viet delegation numbered 150 persons, including princes, dignitaries, and entertainers. The Phu Xuan royal music and dance troop received a special invitation to teach the Viet arts in the inner court. Finally when the man posing as Nguyen Hue left, Ch'ien Lung gave him the highest mark of affection, an imperial portrait made especially for him and a red leather pouch with gold decoration, usually reserved for the emperor's nearest relatives. Embracing the supposed Nguyen Hue, the emperor said he wished him to consolidate his kingdom so that both could enjoy a long friendship. Not so long before, Nguyen

Nhac had said the same to his king Le Chieu Thong, who was now running for his life.

At home, the real Nguyen Hue was preparing his secret plan for the final elimination of Nguyen Anh. First, Nguyen Nhac and his Chinese mercenaries would attack Gia Dinh from the East. Second, from Phu Xuan, Quang Trung's forces would land at Ha Tien and take Gia Dinh to the rear. Third, another one of Quang Trung's columns, with Khmer troops, would attack from the northwest via the Hauts Plateaux.

Taking advantage of Ch'ien Lung's apparent friendship, Nguyen Hue ventured to ask China for the return of Kwangsi and Kwangtung, which had been part of the original Nan Yueh (Nam Viet). Upon the stern refusal from the Manchu emperor, he intensified his preparations for war. To manufacture more heavy guns, he ordered the confiscation of all copper coins. At the same time, he financed the mighty Heaven and Earth secret society to carry out raids against the Chinese in the important region of Tu Xuyen. Later he openly refused to deliver the two traditional gold statues, part of Vietnam's regular tribute. The Chinese court knew all about these provocations but chose to ignore them.

In 1792, pushing his arrogance further, he wrote Emperor Ch'ien Lung asking for the hand of his daughter with the provinces of Kwangtung and Kwangsi as dowry. To carry his message to Peking, instead of a professional diplomat, this time Nguyen Hue appointed a military expert, Admiral Vu Quoc Cong, whose other mission was to spy on Chinese naval defenses. Contrary to Nguyen Hue's expectations, Emperor Ch'ien Lung showed an unusual willingness to accede his impertinent request. Not only did he give him his daughter, but he also consented to yield Kwangsi. He even pressed the princess to journey to Vietnam at once. Thus, one is left to wonder whether Nguyen Hue had not finally found his nemesis in the person of Ch'ien Lung, whose passive behavior might have concealed some ulterior motives. For the Manchu emperor was shrewd enough later to use his family ties to claim back Vietnam and Kwangsi. The fact that once both had been part of the Chinese province of Chiao Chou could only bring grist to the imperial mill.

But the will of heaven prevailed. Suddenly, on September 16, 1792, Nguyen Hue died, apparently of a stroke. With him ended the most fascinating episode of Vietnam's history. He was the only one among the Viet to have dreamt of the conquest of China. He was also the only one capable of succeeding, for his military genius was unmatched. Even after his death, the Tay Son forces kept drawing the admiration of their enemy. It took Nguyen Anh four campaigns to capture Qui Nhon, where three French officers were in command of the Nguyen troops. One of them, the famous Chaigneau, wrote: "Before, I had nothing but contempt for the Tay Son but now I realize I was deadly wrong. They are an unbeatable force."[9]

Granted, the merchant class had not obtained the benefits they expected when they enrolled in the Tay Son movement. Also the classical scholars, who clung to the Chinese script, would not identify themselves with the efforts to develop a national language such as the Nom. But at least there was peace in the North enabling the development of ceramics, silk production, and the fishing industry. Many Chinese works were translated into Nom, thus enriching the national culture. Under the Tay Son, literature flourished and Vietnam's most celebrated authors, such as Nguyen Du (Kim Van Kieu) and Nguyen Dinh Chieu (Luc Van Tien), and poetesses Ho Xuan Huong, Ba Huyen Thanh Quan, Doan Thi Diem produced numerous works. Princess Ngoc Han, widow of Nguyen Hue, was herself acclaimed for her Ai Tu Van (Lamentations) and Van Te Vua Quang Trung (Eulogy to Emperor Quang Trung). Small Buddhist pagodas were razed to be replaced by larger temples staffed with prominent priests. Those monks who failed to respond to government criteria of virtue and knowledge were returned to productive life. Agriculture and demography were the two pillars of economic policy. Peasants away from their native villages on nonvital assignments, such as extended family visits, had to go back to work their land. Abandoned properties were returned to the community and redistributed for cultivation. In bad years, peasants were exempted from taxes. The Quang Trung coins had replaced Chinese currency, and markets were installed in Nanning, Cao Bang, and Langson to promote international trade. According to some Western observers, the Tay Son had carried out a better policy than their Southern opponents. But no sustained reform could be carried out as long as war existed. First Nguyen Hue had to deal with Nguyen Anh.

NOTES

1. Bui The Dat was the ex-governor of Thuan Hoa. He replaced the late Hoang Ngu Phuc and was in turn replaced by Pham Ngo Cao.

2. Pham Van Son, *Viet Su Tan Bien* (reprint, Los Angeles: Dai Nam, n.d.), B. III, p. 366.

3. According to Pham Van Son, Quan buried himself alive in a coffin. Pham Van Son, *Viet Su Tan Bien*, B. III, p. 371.

4. Ibid., p. 373.

5. By such a marriage, Nguyen Hue would become a prince.

6. Le Thanh Khoi, *Histoire du Vietnam* (Paris: Sudestasie, 1992), p. 325.

7. The Vietnamese New Year.

8. Phuc An Khang was governor of the Kwangsi and Kwangtung provinces. Some Chinese authors suggest he was the illegitimate son of Emperor Ch'ien Lung.

9. Pham Van Son, *Viet Su Tan Bien*, B. IV, p. 222.

7

WESTERN INVOLVEMENT

In the North, the fight against the Mac usurpers led to the emergence of the house of Trinh, which at the onset carried the seeds of familial division since the founder of the Trinh in the North, Trinh Kiem, was the son-in-law of Nguyen Kim, the ancestor of the Nguyen in the South. At Nguyen Kim's passing, Trinh Kiem took the power that should have gone to Nguyen Kim's sons, Nguyen Uong and Nguyen Hoang. Hence despite their passivity the two men were considered potential threats to Trinh hegemony. Nguyen Uong was soon murdered and Nguyen Hoang had to simulate madness to stay alive. Later, he was, at his own request, transferred to Thuan Hoa, a wasteland that had been seized from Champa.

THE ECONOMIC SITUATION IN THE SEVENTEENTH CENTURY

The rivalry between the Trinh and the Nguyen was not confined to politics. It also entailed the economic divergence between the North and the South.

While the Nguyen in the South could expand their territory at the expense of Champa, the Trinh in the North were ruining themselves in a war against the Mac usurpers. They had also to deal with China's Ming dynasty, which supported the Mac. The war was a burden to the people who had to pay more and more taxes without knowing to whom it went, whether to the Le king or to the Trinh lord. Besides the traditional land and personal taxes, the peasants had to pay customs and salt taxes. A tax on mining was also introduced. To levy taxes, the Trinh relied on the census records, but they turned out to be misleading and unfair. So they decided on a fixed individual tax independent of demographic changes. In 1720, a revision took place, but two fundamental problems remained: people and land. Since rich landowners—high dignitaries, princes, and Buddhist Church—and the natives of Thanh Hoa and Nghe An province, which provided the backbone of the Bac Ha army, were exempt from taxation, the peasants had to make up for the loss. To correct this dilemma, the Trinh followed the Nguyen example, seeking territorial expansion to the west.

In the seventeenth century, Laos (Vientiane) was at its apogee under King Souligna-Vongsa, who had married a Le princess. The only territorial agreement was determined by the difference in architectural style—land where houses were built on piles, typical Lao construction, was Lao territory. Later, when King Souligna-Vongsa died, the Trinh helped enthrone his nephew Sai Ong Hue (Trieu Phuc). He became a vassal of Annam. He married into the Trinh family, but soon Laos was divided into three kingdoms: Luang Prabang, under King Sisarath, to the north; Champassak (Bassac), under Sisarath's brother Nokasat to the South; and Vientiane, under Sai Ong Hue, in the middle. The alliance with Vientiane did not bring any definitive benefit to Bac Ha. On the contrary, the expenditures involved in protecting Vientiane against her two neighbors resulted in more financial burdens for the North.

During that period, which corresponded to the 100-year peace, the Nguyen succeeded in securing more productive lands by their march to the south. Although taxes were high for communal and state lands, they were reduced for private property in order to encourage the colonization of Gia Dinh. At that time, the two major colonies of Baria and Bienhoa were already in place in Cambodia under King Chetta II's protection.

Toward the end of the seventeenth century, two Ming renegades, generals Yang Yandi (Duong Ngan Dich) and Chen Sang Chuan (Tran Thuong Xuyen) arrived at Da Nang with 3,000 troops in fifty junks. When they asked for asylum, Lord Hien relocated Yang Yandi at Mytho and Chen Sang Chuan at Bienhoa. Some of the Chinese were involved in trade; the rest cultivated rice. Since they were experienced and hard working, soon their regions became the most prosperous. Bienhoa was renowned for international trade and teemed with crowds of Chinese, Japanese, European, and Malay merchants. At that time, as the Viet counted only 200,000 settlers, to cope with the economic growth the Quang Binh population was moved into the region. Government records indicated a total of 1.5 million inhabitants, with 126,000 in Thuan Hoa. In Gia Dinh, 165,000 were from Quang Binh. There were 55,000 hectares of communal land and 97,000 hectares of private properties under cultivation. Thuan Hoa inhabitants had 0.40 hectare, while in the rest of Nam Ha, the peasants' share was 0.60 hectare.[1]

In the eighteenth century, the march to the south accelerated. Nam Ha extended to the Gulf of Siam with the annexation of Ha Tien, which was left without an heir at the passing of Mac Thien Tu in 1780. Along with the six provinces of the west (Luc Tinh), Ha Tien was a major acquisition. Since the time it had been granted to Mac Cuu, Ha Tien had burgeoned into an autonomous province with a complete administrative structure. It enjoyed political and economic predominance in the Far East.

In the South, the policy of the Nguyen toward protection of private property modified the social structure of Nam Ha. The society was originally one of the peasantry but had added a class of bourgeoisie as a result of private ownership. As the bourgeoisie had specific needs—luxury goods, for example—some peasants moved into industrial production. But agriculture remained the backbone of the economy. And while the North was still plagued with perennial floods, the South enjoyed happy cooperation from the rich and generous Mekong. Not only was land plentiful, but also freedom of settlement completed the conditions for a economic well-being. Peasants were free to choose the land they wanted and to grow whatever they liked without any interference from the government. They were in a certain sense in control of their own destiny since by their farming decisions they also decided on the tax they would have to pay. They extended their activities to the production of such crops as sugarcane, and spices. In exchange for these crops, they were able to get silk fabrics and other goods from the capital or the major ports.

Industrial production converted entire villages into stages of manufacturing chains, each one specializing in one step of the production process. Likewise, in the cities, entire streets were devoted to specialized production. That was a quantum leap, for villages which had been so far living in autarky were now economically interdependent. As salaried labor grew to form another class, it played a role in maintaining social balance with the new bourgeoisie. But as Le Thanh Khoi explains, the mining industry was at the base of capitalism in Vietnam.[2] In Bac Ha, Chinese settlers from Yunnan exploited gold and tin mines for centuries until 1717, when they were limited by an immigration quota policy that caused many to withdraw. Later increased demands required more capital and labor, so the local mandarins and some rich merchants pulled together to furnish funds and hire more Chinese workers. Some enterprises had tens of thousands of employees. The mining industry was less developed in the South, which had limited mineral resources. Some gold mines were operated in Quang Nam by rich mandarins who had to pay a simple royalty to the Nguyen.

Internal Trade

Because of geographical differences, internal trade was carried out in distinctive fashion in the North and in the South. In Bac Ha, local markets were open biweekly on the first and the fifteenth of the lunar month, but in the South, exchanges were made through seagoing junks along the east coast from Gia Dinh to Thuan Quang. Nam Ha delivered cattle, areca, and rice in exchange for precious woods, medicinal plants, silk, salt, fish sauce (*nuoc mam*), and dried fish (*kho ca*). The western Hauts Plateaux got fish sauce, dried fish, salt, copper, and gold and silver jewels from the coastal areas; in return, the littoral received cattle, elephant tusks, natural honey, and other forest products.

To facilitate exchange, the Nguyen created standards for weights and measures. The *thuoc* was equivalent to 13 inches; the *can* was equivalent to 1.34 pounds; and the *ta* was equivalent to 126 pounds.

Coinage became a major problem for both regimes. In the North, the Trinh yielded the privilege of minting coins to the provincial authorities, but when they decided to centralize production in Thang Long, it was too late. The people revolted. In the South, the mandarin Truong Phuc Loan, already unpopular for his usurpation of royal power, gave the privilege of minting coins to private concerns over which he maintained no control. That situation, worsened by tax abuses, hurt the merchant class, which for the first time revolted. The revolt was led by the Tay Son brothers.

External Trade

Particularly in Vietnam, the monsoon season shaped economic and military conditions. With seasonal wars, there was also seasonal trade. Depending on their port of departure, foreign traders had to observe the timetable of the monsoon. Those who came from the North arrived with the northeast winds in October and left in the summer when the winds turned to the opposite direction. Those from the South, took the opposite way (Map 17). As crop gathering did not follow the same seasonal patterns, it ensued that ships had to wait in Vietnam's ports. Thus it became necessary for foreign merchants to install trade offices to purchase crops at harvest time and store them for future shipments. Outside the harvest season, prices could be 40 percent higher. The Portuguese based in nearby Macao used local Chinese and Japanese *compradores* to handle their trade, sometimes under the supervision of Portuguese missionaries. When their ships docked, their crews received hospitality from Portugal's mission or from their company's agents. That arrangement prevented them from being under direct pressure from the lords. Originally there were two ports of trade: in the North, Pho Hien; and in the South, Fai Fo. Later, Ke Cho (Thang Long) was added in Bac Ha, and Cua Han (Tourane) became the second port in Nam Ha. Of the entire peninsula, Fai Fo was the dominant economic outlet. It was a bustling place, originally divided between Chinese and Japanese, who for generations were implanted there with their particular customs and culture.

In 1637, to prevent Western penetration, the Tokugawa shoguns started a period of isolation for Japan, enforcing prohibition of foreign trade along with religious persecution. Entire Christian families followed their Jesuit pastors to Fai Fo. With the disappearance of the Japanese from international trade, the Western powers rushed in to fill the vacuum.

Explorers and Merchants

Actually the West had been around for some time. Archeological finds based on the discovery of Roman coins in the North, date the first European presence to the time of Marcus Aurelius. But the coins could have been brought there by merchants from Central Asia. Later, in 1285, Marco Polo stopped in Champa when he was serving as an official in Kublai Khan's administration. His notes on the island of Poulo Condor later attracted the curiosity of the English and the French.

After the providential error which allowed Columbus to discover the Americas, the Portuguese and the Spanish started to compete for hegemony. To preserve peace among the Catholic powers, Pope Alexander VI issued a bull dividing the world in two by drawing a meridian 100 miles west of the Azores. Thus while Brazil was given to Portugal, the rest of the Americas was placed under Spanish influence. At that time, the Vatican was not interested in the Far East. Therefore the two powers kept fighting each other for the spices route to the east of the Azores. In 1498, Vasco da Gama passed the Cape of Good Hope and reached Calicut, on the west coast of India. Actually, the port which was famous for its cotton fabrics, had been visited by the Portuguese explorer/trader Pero Da Covilha the year before. In 1530, the Spanish and the Portuguese reached an agreement. As a result, the Spanish agreed to stop exploration at the 117-degree meridian east of Molucca.

Under Admiral Albuquerque, the Portuguese settled in Diu and Goa on the west coast of India, after stopping in Ceylon where, according to Joseph Buttinger, they founded Colombo, named after Columbus. Later they sailed to Malacca. From there they controlled the entire Far East from the South China Sea to Java and the Gulf of Siam. With the Portuguese monopoly of the spices route, the capital of international trade moved from Venice to Lisbon. In 1513, the Portuguese established a trading post in Canton. In 1542, they reached Japan. In 1557, Macao became the Goa of China. During that period, the Portuguese wandered up and down the South China Sea along the coast of Vietnam, catching a glimpse of Da Nang in 1535 and building up Fai Fo in 1540. To the west, they reached Ayudhya and Burma.

In 1570, the Spanish seized the Philippines in blatant violation of the 1530 treaty. At that time, the Catholic traders were not to be alone any longer in the Far East. The English and the Dutch were about to enter the arena, determined to have their fair share of the Asian trade. It was also a critical time for Christianity. Islam was firmly entrenched in Java and threatened the entire Indonesian archipelago. Caught between the Protestants and the Mohammedans, the Catholic Portuguese welcomed their Spanish rivals as their natural allies. This did not help much since some time later the English succeeded in destroying the famous armada, crippling irremediably Spanish might.

As for the English, in 1600 they founded their East India Company, but having set their hearts on India, they went to fight the Portuguese there. Only after destroying a Portuguese fleet in the Indian Ocean could the English set foot on India. Then they turned to the more serious affairs in the South China Sea. Their first attempt to land in Vietnam met an ominous fate. In 1613, from their Hirado headquarters in Japan, they dispatched to Nam Ha their first agent, Walter Carwarden. When he landed on the shores of Fai Fo, the English envoy was at once slaughtered by a frantic populace, probably at the instigation of the Portuguese. In 1616, the English succeeded in establishing a post in Bac Ha,

Map 17
Sixteenth-Century Western Trade in Southeast Asia

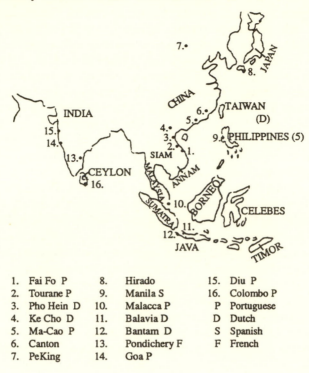

1.	Fai Fo P	8.	Hirado	15.	Diu P	
2.	Tourane P	9.	Manila S	16.	Colombo P	
3.	Pho Hein D	10.	Malacca P	P	Portuguese	
4.	Ke Cho D	11.	Balavia D	D	Dutch	
5.	Ma-Cao P	12.	Bantam D	S	Spanish	
6.	Canton	13.	Pondichery F	F	French	
7.	PeKing	14.	Goa P			

but this time met the crafty Dutch who were determined to drive them to the wall. As a result, the English were expelled in 1625. That also caused the closing of their stations in Japan and Taiwan (Map 17). In 1637, under King Le Than Tong and Lord Trinh Trang, Pho Hien was a crowded place with some 2,000 habitations, second in size only to the capital, Thang Long. In 1654, the Treaty of Westminster forced the Dutch to bury the hatchet with the English, allowing the latter to go back to Southeast Asia. In 1672, under Captain Gyfford, who also resumed operations in Taiwan and Japan, the English opened a factory at Pho Hien side by side with the Dutch. It appeared to be a flash in the pan. In 1674, the Dutch had the Javanese destroy the Bantam post from which the English controlled their Bac Ha operations. In 1683, despite their success in setting up another factory in Thang Long, the English did not fare well because of opposition from the Viet Catholics who were inspired by the Portuguese and the Dutch. To add fuel to the fire, the king, lords, and officers were reluctant to come up with prompt payment for their long-standing debts. Since these circumstances made their enterprise absolutely untenable, finally, in 1697, the English left. In 1778, they attempted a comeback by sending Charles Chapman from Calcutta to reassess general conditions in Nam Ha. Among other things, he recommended supporting Nguyen Anh against the Tay Son. After having proposed Tourane as a base, he also warned against the French. But the American War of Independence prevented England from engaging further in Vietnam.

As for the Dutch, with all the troubles they caused everywhere, it was also curtain time for them. In 1699, only two years after the English, they left Bac Ha, their profits having plummeted down to 10 percent from the original 400 percent. Based on a report from a Dutch resident of Goa, the Dutch started their Asian adventure by prompting Cornelius de Houtnam to undertake the two expeditions to Java in 1595 and 1597. Thrilled by the tremendous profit of 400 percent on their first investments, they rushed to create the United East India Company in 1602, two years after the English. With capital of 6.5 million guilders, this company was more powerful than its English rival. It was, in fact, the merger of more than ten smaller enterprises. It easily obtained from the Dutch government the trade monopoly for a large region, including the Far East, and went on to build factories all over the area. Consequently, Batavia (Djakarta) became the Dutch Goa.

For mercantile and religious reasons, the Dutch were determined to bring the Portuguese to their knees. As the Portuguese had never used civilized manners toward the Asians, the Dutch had no troubles in rallying the natives against their oppressors. Then it turned out that the Dutch were no better, and the natives became more and more reluctant to cooperate. At that point, Jan Pieterzoon Coen appeared with his theory that success in trade could only be obtained by violence. He was ready to demonstrate his theory if the Dutch government paid the right price. He was therefore appointed governor general of the Dutch East Indies. Once in place, Coen put his theories into practice. He killed rival traders and stopped buying spices at high prices. In other words, all of the Far East was to be conquered and the natives were to be forced to grow spice plants solely for the Dutch, at extremely low cost. Those opposed to such a policy were massacred and their crops were either confiscated or destroyed. It was antique colonialism in its simplest expression. But the Dutch had to pay the price. Foreign competition and native hostility compelled them to increase their military defenses to such a point that finally expenses wiped out profits. Hence, the Far East trade became a liability.

Being a part of Southeast Asia, Vietnam was of course part of Coen's area of penetration. The Dutch first came to Nam Ha, where they met their rivals the Portuguese, who had been there for a century. By their military association with the Nguyen, the Portuguese held a predominant position which allowed them to handle trade competition with assassination schemes and diplomatic skirmishes. From Macao, they dispatched an envoy to warn Vu Vuong that "if you accept the Dutch, you would invite the same troubles they had created in India and elsewhere."[3] The Portuguese Jesuit missionaries did not stop offering gratuitous advice with sanctimonious innuendos. As a result, the Dutch had to phase out for a while. Later, Paulus Traudemius, in an effort to revive trade, succeeded in setting up a factory in Quang Nam and from Japan his ships came regularly to Tourane.

In the North, the Dutch were faring better. In 1632, they moved their Pho Hien office to the capital. But the Portuguese kept fueling Lord Trinh's suspicions about the Dutch. He was warned that the Dutch planned to purchase from the Nguyen the Island of Cu Lao Cham, located southeast of Tourane. This led to an inquest during which the Dutchman Hartsingh denied having territorial ambitions on the island. But when asked to provide military support to Bac Ha, he ducked, invoking his higher authorities in Batavia. That incident made the Dutch more cautious, and later they lent a deaf ear when Lord Trinh demanded the participation of three Dutch ships in a Bac Ha expedition against the South. Their refusal prompted the Trinh to retaliate. At that time, five Dutchmen who were involved in supplying arms to the Mac remnants were thrown in jail without further ado. Another incident finally convinced the Dutch that neutrality was not the answer to their problems. In 1641, because of a navigational error, two Dutch ships ran aground at that critical island of Cu Lao Cham. The crews were captured by the Nguyen and the Dutch were expelled, leaving their Fai Fo post to the care of the Japanese. Taking advantage of the Dutch demise in the South, the Trinh increased their pressure and finally the Dutch agreed to receive a diplomatic delegation from Bac Ha. In 1642, Captain Van Liesevelt took the Bac Ha envoys to Batavia on his ship. On the way, for reasons unknown, he stopped at Fai Fo. Made aware of the presence of the Trinh embassy, Lord Thuong put the Bac Ha team and the Dutch crew in confinement in spite of Captain Van Liesevelt's protests.

In 1642, Van Liesevelt came back to Nam Ha with a vengeance. He led with a fleet of five ships, 152 sailors, and seventy infantry troops. He made the mistake of first landing with only ten soldiers. All were killed. In retaliation, his assistant, Captain Van Linga, captured twenty Viets along the coast, had them all put to death. Lord Thuong, in turn, had one Dutchman executed. Captain Van Linga captured another 107 Viets and sailed to the North. Dutch alliance with the Trinh had now materialized.

Finally at the end of 1643, Batavia dispatched to Tourane three warships under the command of Pierre Baeck. There they met with sixty Nam Ha warships. The Dutch command ship was scuttled and the fleet commander committed suicide. Another frigate ran aground and was destroyed. The third one went to seek refuge in the North, but the Trinh lord, frustrated by the incompetence of the Dutch, refused to give them assistance. This incident marked the end of the Dutch. In the North, their days were numbered. Although they had lost the support of the Trinh, they remained in a vain attempt to recoup their losses. In 1663, judging the Bac Ha operations too hazardous, they decided to leave but continued to send their ships periodically for trade. In 1698, under the reign of Le Hi Tong, the Dutch, totally disenchanted, pulled down the curtains on the North.

In the South, all their possessions were seized by the Nguyen, and their staff was sentenced to death. The sentence was later commuted to allow the Dutch repatriation to Batavia on a Chinese merchant ship. In 1650 in Nam Ha, the new Lord Hien opened negotiations with Batavia. The Dutch would return their prisoners, and the Viets agreed to provide assistance to wrecked ships, to reduce taxes for merchandise damaged in shipwrecks, to leave Dutch subjects under their own jurisdiction, and to let the Dutch open a new factory. But in 1698, realizing that a profit margin of 40 percent was not worth all these troubles, the Dutch left Nam Ha. But they remained a colonial power in the Far East having completely annexed Indonesia.

The period of peace had not provided the Viet peasants with any benefits they might have expected, such as tax reductions or agrarian reforms. The foreign trade in arms and munitions had provided foreign merchants with political leverage against the warring lords. But it was cut short in times of peace and was replaced by trade in luxury products, which only profited the lords, their entourages, and also the new class of bourgeoisie who could afford it. Upon arrival in a Vietnamese port, foreign traders had to submit their manifests, together with the mandatory gifts, to the lords and their customs agents. If they were satisfied, then no tax applied. It is quite obvious that the peasants, who were not interested in those products, had to pay for their import one way or another.

In the realm of foreign relations, while all Western powers were geared for international trade, the two Viet governments conspicuously lacked any sustained policy. Finally, since China had become a most promising market, the dispirited Western traders flocked to Canton.

FRANCE AND VIETNAM

France was sitting on the fence for quite a long time, for two main reasons. On the one hand, the French treasury was experiencing cash difficulties because of all the wars the French were fighting in Europe. On the other, the concept of official cooperation between church, state, and business was a long and difficult process that needed time to mature. Obviously, such cooperation was not always productive. If trade was welcomed as a necessity by the two Vietnamese belligerents, the propagation of a foreign faith, conspicuously opposed to Confucianist teachings, would unite them together on the religious front. Aware of this fact, the church first sought the help of the traders, and missionaries went to great lengths to disguise themselves as merchants. In 1533, a certain Ignatio was preaching in Bac Ha. Only half a century later, another priest, Diego Adverte, was allowed to preach in Nam Ha, until some Spanish warships imprudently entered territorial waters without the consent of the Nguyen. Conscious of the natives' reaction to such incidents, he hurried to leave his platform under a frenzied salvo of bamboo arrows. He did not return.

As these private initiatives were too hazardous for the safety of the missionaries, the Portuguese and Japanese merchants in Fai Fo decided to sponsor a group of Jesuits who had recently been expelled from Japan and were waiting for reassignment in Macao. The first Jesuit mission in Nam Ha was thus founded in 1615. Father Busoni was allowed by Lord Sai to preach in the Nam Ha, where Alexandre de Rhodes arrived in 1624. Then the missionaries began to oppose the cult of ancestors, and in 1626, under King Le Than Tong, Father Baldinoti was expelled by Lord Trinh Tung. Later Alexandre de Rhodes went to Thang Long with a clock as a gift for the Trinh. He was allowed to preach in the capital.

The brilliant and hard working Alexandre de Rhodes began to preach in Vietnamese only six months after his arrival. He was credited with having contributed to the creation of *quoc ngu*,[4] in which he published the first catechism. Since his transfer to Thang Long in 1627, he claimed to have baptized in less than two years 6,700 persons, including members of the Trinh family. But his popularity was also the instrument of his demise. He was expelled in 1630 and went to stay in Macao. He kept going back to Vietnam, but finally, in 1645, he received notice of his definitive expulsion. Religious persecutions began to unfold. Papal intransigence against the cult of ancestors jeopardized the missionaries' work. Later, when Prince Canh, son of Gia Long, refused to bow in front of his ancestors' altar, there was an uproar throughout the entire country. Gia Long himself awoke to the dangers of Catholicism. Pigneau de Behaine consequently had to accept ancestor worship as a cultural tradition.

In 1631, both South and North began their push against Western religion. In Nam Ha, Lord Thuong (Nguyen Phuc Lan) prohibited preaching. In 1644, Lord Hien had missionaries executed in Danang. The North followed, and in 1663, Trinh Tac expelled all missionaries and prohibited the practice of the Christian religion. Later, the politics of Monsignor François Pallu in Thailand had ominous repercussions in Vietnam. In 1685, mistaking his desires for reality, Monsignor Pallu reported that the King of Siam and all his subjects were ready to convert to Catholicism if the French would militarily support a political change. The results were deplorable. Not only did the French forces fail, but the fiasco caused a wave of suspicion against the missionaries. In 1696, Trinh Can again expelled all missionaries. In 1712, Lord Trinh Cuong ordered that all Christian believers bear on their foreheads a tattoo saying, "Student of the Dutch religion."[5] In 1754, Trinh Doanh systematically persecuted the Catholics with mass executions.

Back in France, Alexandre de Rhodes relentlessly championed the French presence in Vietnam, going on at length to declare that the country was a sort of El Dorado with fertile land, gold mines, spices, and "so much silk that they used it even for their fishing lines and sailing cords."[6] In Rome, he advocated the training of native priests. In 1658, one year before he died, he received the Papal nod.

The French Foreign Missions Society

In 1664, to carry out Alexandre de Rhodes' project, the famous Societé des Missions Etrangères was founded, with the participation of merchants and missionaries and under the blessing of both the French king and the Pope. A few months before, the French minister of finance, Jean-Baptiste Colbert, had created the French East India Company. If in France the relationship between the two organizations was not conspicuous, in Bac Ha the confusion was such that in 1680 a puzzled English trader reported: "The French have a house in town, but we can not make out whether they are here to seek trade or to conduct religious propaganda."[7]

Toward the end of the seventeenth century, against Portuguese objections, the Pope named the French Monsignor François Pallu as Vicar Apostolic to Ayudhya (Thailand), having also Vietnam under his jurisdiction. Actually Pallu was not a newcomer to the trade. He had been responsible for the Company of China for the propagation of Faith and the Establishment of Commerce, originally founded by the powerful Company of the Holy Sacrament.[8] The project ended in a storm which destroyed Pallu's ship during his first voyage to the Far East.

This time, before leaving France Pallu, in unequivocal terms, thanked the French East India Company for having paid his travel expenses. He assured the Company that his people would endeavor to promote the Company progress in Vietnam.[9]

In Thailand, King Narai was having an irreparable rift with the British and for his protection was seeking alliance with another Western power. Pallu, always on the lookout for intrigues, dispatched Father Tachard to contact the Greek Phaulkon, an influential adviser to King Narai. As usual, the task was undermined by Jesuit interference. In 1682, King Louis XIV dispatched a Jesuit envoy to King Narai and later Phaulkon was converted to Catholicism. In 1684, a mission from Siam under Father Vachet arrived in France to lure the government with the fantastic prospect of having King Narai and his entire kingdom convert to Catholicism, since Phaulkon, the most powerful man in Thailand, had done so himself. The mission came back escorted by two warships under Chevalier de Chamond, a converted Huguenot. In 1685, negotiations conducted separately by the Jesuits and the mission resulted in many trade and military advantages for the French while the matter of religious conversion was skillfully shunned by Phaulkon. As the Jesuits insisted on having a Catholic kingdom similar to the Philippines, Phaulkon suggested that the next king might be more responsive. Father Tachard took the hint and started to devise a coup against King Narai.

To seize Bangkok, France dispatched six warships and some 700 troops out of which 200 were sick upon arrival in Thailand. As the contingent was deemed insufficient, Tachard went back to France to ask for reinforcements. In the meantime, the sudden illness of King Narai led to a separate coup by Siam's General Pra P'etraja. As for Phaulkon, he had his candidate for the throne, over which the Jesuits and the mission disagreed. As a result, both parties refused to intervene and all the French forces retired inside the Bangkok citadel. Left alone, Phaulkon was arrested and executed. A month later, in July 1688, King Narai passed away. The French were allowed to evacuate. That was the end of their adventure in Thailand.

Obviously, Pallu's mission encompassed both matters of church and state for he reported directly to Minister Colbert on politics and trade, while he reserved subjects of religion to the Vatican. There was no doubt that trade served as a cover for religious propagation since as early as 1669, missionaries disguised as merchants had sailed the Red River up and down. That unholy alliance could only arouse the suspicions of Trinh Can who declared that ''the Catholic religion is contrary to natural principles, hurts reason and troubles the people's spirit.''[10] Continual strife between Portuguese missionaries and their French counterparts between Jesuits and Dominicans placed the missions in jeopardy, despite the favor enjoyed by the Jesuits in the South where they succeeded in securing important government posts. The opposition of the Pope to the cult of ancestors and the missionaries' stubbornness in carrying it out forcibly, reinforced the Viet government's will to root out foreign religions.

In 1680, the Company opened a factory in Pho Hien, in North Vietnam. Two years later, in 1682, having lost Bantam to the Dutch, the French also closed their post in Pho Hien.

Actually the problems lay not only on the Viet side. As business was losing steam, the Western merchants resorted to cheating and violence to keep the money rolling in. Furthermore, the anti-Catholic drive was gaining momentum, and the merchants had to share the heat since they were involved in promoting Christianity. In 1686, as the Viet rulers decreed more and more restrictions against them, the Western companies decided to move to Canton, where the huge Chinese market called for all temptations.

Expansion of their trade lines led the traders to seek new bases. The Bantam incident had convinced the French to opt for an independent post. In 1686, the Frenchman Verret first discovered the island of Poulo Condor, which controlled the mouth of Mekong. But, in 1802, the French were outwitted by the English who occupied the island with a garrison of troops from Macassar. In 1805, a Nam Ha governor, Truong Phuc Phan, succeeded in infiltrating a squad of Malays who stirred up the garrison. Since the English had failed to repatriate them as promised, the Macassar soldiers massacred all their English officers, missing two who fled on a boat. Truong Phuc Phan took over Poulo Condor. In 1723, French agents came back for another survey. They found the climate harmful and the land barren. However, their negative report did not fall on deaf ears. When, later in 1907, the French colonial administration was in need of a concentration camp for Vietnamese prisoners, Poulo Condor admirably served the purpose.

In early 1720, a native of Lyon, Pierre Poivre, appeared on the scene in Nam Ha as a missionary, until he ceded to more materialistic temptations and left for

Canton to trade in silk. On his way back to France, he lost his right arm in a battle against the English on the high seas. He preached his own version of the Dutchman Coen's doctrine: "A company wishing to establish itself in Cochin China and to lay solid foundations for advantageous commerce has to start by making itself feared and respected. It will find the means in the general situation of the country and in the Bay of Tourane especially, which is a place that can be easily fortified."[11] His ideas became the dogma of the French colonialists, for a century later, in 1847, they generously gave a show of strength by sinking the Viet fleet in the bay of Tourane.

This idea of using Tourane (Da Nang) as a base in the Far East was also on the mind of Joseph François Dupleix, governor general of the French East India Company. From Pondichery, he directed his efforts toward locating a junction point for all Far East lines and toward establishing trade stations in Vietnam. Informally, he dispatched his Irish relative Baron Jacques O'Friell, then based in Canton, to collect information in both North and South. His envoy official, Monsignor Bennetat, landed in Nam Ha loaded with numerous presents, among them a gilded coach that cost £24,000, a belt of gold, diamonds and rubies, a sophisticated clock, and, of course, a large quantity of pistols and guns. That was enough to secure a trade concession from the Nguyen. The efforts to obtain Tourane came to an end with the hostilities between France and Austria. In India, the French had to fight for their meager possession of Pondichery, and in 1748, Dupleix forced the English to lift the siege. In 1754, he went back to France, where he failed to recover the funds he had advanced to the company. He died in 1763.

The campaign for the Vietnam trade continued with the participation of various circles. An ex-missionary, Thomas de St Phalle, who had been in Vietnam from 1732 to 1741, wrote a wishful report to the French minister of justice in 1753 stating, "They have gold in their mines and rivers and even in the excrement of their ducks."[12]

During that period, Pierre Poivre became an expert on Vietnam. In 1748, the French East India Company dispatched him to open a factory in Tourane. As a representative of both the French government and the East India Company, he arrived on the ship *Machault* loaded with merchandise. Troubles came after he had distributed all his gifts. He realized then that, despite the trade license he had been graciously granted by King Vu Vuong, the only way he could get rid of his merchandise was to give it away too. But, instead of recognizing that the people were too poor to pay for his luxury goods, which they did not need anyway, Poivre set the blame on Vietnam's rulers, whom he justly accused of rapacity and corruption. In 1750, after one year of trials and tribulations, Poivre left Tourane with hundreds of tropical plants in his luggage and a male interpreter named Michel Cuong whom he had abducted for some ambiguous reason. This triggered a ferocious reaction from King Vu Vuong, who proceeded to expel all French missionaries. In turn, the mission expelled Poivre for "serious reasons." According to rumors, Pierre Poivre had sinned. Alerted, the East India

Company governor Dupleix summoned Phu Xuan's (Hue) Resident Bishop Bennetat to Pondichery for an inquiry. Then Bennetat was dispatched to the island of Mauritius to have Michel Cuong released. In his defense, Poivre said that he had acted in retaliation against Michel Cuong for sabotaging his mission in Nam Ha. In 1753, after the so-called hostage was returned in good physical condition, Vu Vuong was pleased enough to authorize the readmission of the mission and the reopening of the French factory in Tourane. In 1757, Bishop Bennetat was expelled and the company was closed down in Nam Ha.

Be that as it may, in the following year, 1758, Admiral Count d'Estaing, with the support of Lally Tollendal, governor of the French Indies, contrived a plan to seize Phu Xuan, the Nam Ha capital, for three days, during which the French would completely loot the royal treasures. The spoils would serve to finance trade in the Philippines and in China. When his expedition reached the vicinity of Sumatra, the aggressive admiral could not resist the temptation of provoking the British. When he later got out of his gung ho battles, the monsoon had changed. There was no more southwest wind to take him to the gates of Phu Xuan. The whole expedition was a south sea bubble, but that was not to be the last of his troubles. Devastated, he went back to France and volunteered to serve in the New World under Lafayette. He should have remained there and become a good American citizen. Instead, he went back to France to be executed during the Revolution.

In the middle of 1768, the Duke of Choiseul, the French secretary of war, had a question for Poivre: Should the French establish trade in Nam Ha by way of diplomacy or by merchant action? Poivre earnestly replied that Nam Ha had 400 elephants, ninety 60-oars junks, and 20,000 infantry scattered along the Cambodian border. Since these troops lacked food and clothing, their morale was very low. Only 2,000 were dependable. This country was rich in gold but it had no silver. To familiarize the population with French industrial products would require quite a long time and France would also have to secure the ownership of Tourane or Fai Fo. The people were basically honest but those associated with the court were scoundrels. So it was impossible not to use force to implant there. A good idea would be to storm the capital and take all the treasures; although it was protected by surrounding heavy guns, there was no ammunition. Force was the only way to deal with them but the French had to be very careful. In the first stage, they might send soldiers disguised as merchants. Twenty thousand piastres, 20,000 meters of red cotton fabrics, and a certain amount of jewelry was provided for use as gifts. Poivre also needed 2,000 infantrymen from Ile de France and some negroes because the people of Nam Ha mostly feared blacks. Actually, had France had the necessary means, it would rather have poured them into India for the sake of Pondichery. In 1770, the French East India Company was dissolved and all plans were discarded. France had missed the opportunity to penetrate Vietnam. Later it would take no appropriate action either in implementing an offensive and defensive treaty with Nguyen Anh in 1783. By the time Pigneau de Behaine succeeded in building his own fleet, it was already too late for France to claim to have made any contribution. When Pigneau de Behaine and his fleet were back to Nam Ha, Nguyen Anh had already recaptured Gia Dinh and was on his way to annihilate the formidable Tay Son.

But the colonialist faction had not given up. In 1775, a naval architect named Rothe was put in command of an expeditionary force that included the 350-ton imperial warship *Nourio*. It was armed with four battleguns and sixty men under Major Le Floch de la Carriere. Later the project was aborted.

Pigneau de Behaine and the Versailles Treaty

In comparison with Pallu, Pigneau de Behaine, despite his hot temper, remained a patrician. Born Pierre Joseph Georges Pigneau in 1741 at Behaine, in the modern department of Aisne, he was sent to Cochin China after a training at the Seminaire des Missions Etrangères. He was put in charge of the Seminaire Hon Dat near Ha Tien, "a wretched little collection of bamboos huts"[13] set up for missionary refugees from Siam at the time of the Burmese invasion. A raid from sea pirates forced the missionaries out and Pigneau came back to Ha Tien only in 1775.

When Nguyen Anh at age sixteen or seventeen escaped from the Tay Son slaughter in which his uncle and cousin perished, he took refuge in the swamps of Ha Tien where he met Pigneau, who moved him to safety at Poulo Pajang. During the following period, he resisted the temptation of accepting Pigneau's offer for help, until he was at the end of his rope after being severely mauled by Nguyen Hue four consecutive times. The French bishop journeyed to France at the end of 1787 as the special envoy of the King of Nam Ha. At that time, the French had just lost to the English in India and were looking for other bases from which to preserve their influence in Asia. The bishop met with the Count of Montmorin, secretary of foreign affairs, and the Marquis of Castries, secretary of the navy. Eminent Catholic dignitaries such as Lomenie de Brienne, Archbishop of Toulouse, and De Vermond, Archbishop of Narbonne, were among his staunch supporters. Consensus was obtained on the consideration that factories in the Far East would not only serve mercantile interests but they would also be an obstacle to English expansion in Asia. There were objections from conservative circles about the difficulty of carrying on a military defense of Nam Ha against the Dutch, who were firmly entrenched in nearby Indonesia, and the English, who were solidly implanted in Malaysia. Strategically Nam Ha was surrounded by hostile forces, and the supply route was under the control of the English.

Nevertheless, the Versailles Treaty was signed on November 21, 1788, between Count De Montmorin, representing King Louis XVI, and Pigneau de Behaine, emissary of King Nguyen Anh. It was agreed that France would send to the coast of Nam Ha four warships, 1,200 Kaffir troops, 200 artillery men, and 250 black soldiers all completely equipped. While waiting for the contingent to arrive, the king of Nam Ha granted France absolute ownership of the port of Tourane and the island of Poulo Condor. In addition, France would be allowed to establish factories throughout the entire kingdom for the purpose of promoting trade and constructing or repairing ships. Freedom of trade was exclusively reserved for the French, who would be free to travel and do business in Nam Ha with a passport delivered by the French commander of the port of Tourane. They had the right to import into Nam Ha any Western merchandise not under French prohibition and could export any Nam Ha product. They were subject to the same taxes as the natives. As for third-country vessels, whether military or merchant they had to display French flags in Nam Ha ports and possess a pass from the Tourane French commander. French citizens were subject to French laws. Both countries agreed on reciprocal extradition. In case of hostilities between France and other powers, Nam Ha would provide at its own expense assistance in infantry troops, war fleet, and logistics support. It is to be noted that not a single word gave the French freedom to preach in Vietnam. The matter was irrelevant to the agenda of Pigneau, who was acting as the representative of the king of Nam Ha, not as a Catholic missionary. The request should have come from the French officials, but they were preoccupied with military matters. Furthermore, as the religious question could turn calm negotiations into hot debate, Pigneau might prudently have decided not to force the issue.

Anyway, this "offensive and defensive treaty" appeared to be a curious instrument in which a fair deal was conspicuously lacking. While France had just thrown in the air a promise to help, Nam Ha had consented to pay in advance with land concessions. On the other hand, since only Western nations were kept out of competition, the Chinese and Japanese were still free to compete. This shows that the French government was only concerned with the idea of having the other European powers evicted from Asia. Anyhow, the accord would never be implemented because the French had ulterior motives.

They left the matter to the discretion of a man of controversial character, the Count De Conway, newly assigned governor of French India. He was promised 200,000 piastres to carry out the Nam Ha expedition. Born Irish, he had served under Lafayette, who found him an ambitious and dangerous man. Even Louis XVI himself had warned Pigneau of the possibility of troubles with Count De Conway, whose assignment abroad was the only way for the government to get rid of him. Indeed, De Montmorin writes to Chevalier d'Entrecasteaux, governor of the Ile de France and Bourbon: "I beg you not to mention to the Bishop of Adran that the King had left to Mr. De Conway to suspend or postpone the expedition."[14] Obviously, De Conway had been chosen to be the government scapegoat. Actually, he was well disposed toward the bishop's project from the outset. At the time he met with Pigneau in Paris, before his departure for India, De Conway had assured him of his total cooperation. Only the secret instructions he received later changed his perspective. Furthermore, De Conway had no experience of the Far East, but was wise enough to read between the lines of the orders he received from Paris. He put to use the French adage "Dans le doute, abstiens-toi." His personal dislike of Pigneau was another reason for his later decision to stall the expedition.

In December 1787, Pigneau and his retinue left France with four ships, the *Dryade*, the *Meduse*, the *Astrée*, and the *Calypso,* under the command of De Saint Riveul, one of De Conway's officers. When Pigneau set foot in Pondichery on May 17, 1788, he found De Conway reluctant to release the expedition funds, stating that his administration was short of cash. Under Pigneau's protests, he agreed to take care of the immediate needs of the Pigneau group. Relations between the two men became more and more strained. First, De Conway wished to meet with Nguyen Anh in Pondichery, but Pigneau opposed this as a waste of time, claiming Prince Canh could represent his father. De Conway rejected the idea, saying Canh was an irresponsible minor. He then dispatched Captain De Richery with the ship *Marquis De Castries* to Nam Ha. De Richery later reported that he could not meet with Nguyen Anh since, at that time, Nguyen Anh was still in Thailand. However, De Conway reported to Paris that he opposed the idea of taking Nguyen Anh back to Pondichery because he had no instructions to do so, and furthermore, he did not believe it was in the interest of his king.

Before long, the religious convictions of the bishop added another dimension to his personal conflict. Pigneau, after paying a courtesy visit to all the ladies of the governor's entourage, adamantly refused to meet with the provocative Madame De Vienne, De Conway's influential mistress. He publicly criticized their adulterous relationship because she was married to the governor's aide. She wasted no time in reacting. At an official reception, she pointed to De Conway's chest and laughed. She said that the king gave this decoration to the general certainly not for his military skill but for his obedience to the Pope. If he were a good soldier, he would not be under the command of a priest.[15]

To be fair, one can not entirely blame De Conway for any excess of prudence. The secret instructions from Paris had induced him to watch his steps carefully whether he liked the bishop or not. He reported to his superior, the powerful De Montmorin, now intendant general and a personal friend of King Louis XVI, that the expedition could not start before 1789 due to the monsoon and would require six ships instead of four, with a budget of 1,500,000 francs, which his administration was in no position to provide. When Pigneau was made aware of these reservations, he reacted angrily and the two parties almost came to physical confrontation. As his supporters in France were not interested in his personal strife, they began to lend a deaf ear to Pigneau's incessant complaints. Blaming the monsoon, De Conway refused to let him sail back to Nam Ha and instead ordered De Kersaint, with the *Dryade* and the *Pandour*, to go to search for the *De Castries* and the *Calypso*, allegedly in trouble on their way to China. He also instructed De Kersaint not to allow the bishop on board and not to take Nguyen Anh back to Pondichery. Indeed, De Conway behaved as a professional soldier and a responsible politician. De Kersaint was secretly instructed to make a complete strategic survey of Poulo Condor, Phu Quoc, Ha Tien, and Tourane. He was also to assess the military potential of Macao, Malacca, and neighboring ports in view of possible intervention from the Portuguese, Dutch, and English. But their seeming indifference toward French involvement suggested that they considered the game not worth the candle and that Nam Ha had no more to offer in terms of profitable trade. This was also the opinion of D'Entrecasteaux, the governor of Ile de France, who also insisted that the English and Dutch had left because of the waning trade. Furthermore, he emphasized that in case of conflict Nam Ha was too far for any significant help from Ile de France. As for the trade exclusivity provided by the treaty, since it was aimed against European competitors, commerce remained in the hands of the Chinese and Japanese, who had long been established in Fai Fo.

Then the political situation in France deteriorated as the Revolution closed in. The French government had to give up its Nam Ha project. On March 15, 1789, De Conway was ordered by Paris to take Prince Canh back to Nam Ha and to invite Pigneau to rejoin France. As for Pigneau, he had received a final notice dated April 16, 1789, from Count de la Luzerne in response to his many complaints which said, "concerning the slowness of the measures taken in connection with the expedition to Cochin China, I can only refer to the letter in which I indicated to you that this expedition will not take place. I authorized the Count de Conway to supply you with the means to return to France, if you so desire."[16] The offensive and defensive Treaty of Versailles was virtually dead. Pigneau would have to take care of Nam Ha by his own means. He declared: "I shall make my own revolution!" Fortunately, amidst frustrations and obstacles, some news from Nam Ha brought him much encouragement. The unity of the Tay Son was seriously damaged after the clash between Nguyen Nhac and Nguyen Hue. Pigneau raised funds among the French merchants in India and Madagascar, enough to entirely equip two ships with guns and ammunitions. From the French navy, he hired many deserters. He named the two ships the *Long* (*Dragon*) and the *Phung* (*Pheonix*) and he gave their commands to Chaigneau and Vannier respectively.

Finally, on June 15, 1789, Pigneau and Prince Canh, with a retinue of twenty men, sailed back to Nam Ha on the *Meduse*, which was provided by De Conway. They were followed by two other ships and stopped for two days in Malacca to purchase more arms. There, they were quite startled to witness the efforts of an underground English agent named Cox. He was disguised as a merchant based in Canton and was collecting information on Nam Ha. After another stop at Poulo Condor, the Pigneau fleet arrived at Vung Tau on July 24, 1789. At that time Nguyen Anh had already recaptured Gia Dinh and was on his way to assault Qui Nhon, where Prince Canh would die of smallpox at the age of twenty two. Sometime later Prince Hi, another son of Gia Long, passed away at Dien Khanh.

All the French volunteers received a commission in the Nguyen forces. Jean Marie Dayot left the *Pandour* and was appointed chief of the purchasing mission, transporting military supplies on his ship the *St. Esprit.* Rosily, who took Pigneau back to Nam Ha on his *Meduse,* was in charge of recruiting troops, including the 120 soldiers and seamen who with him had previously deserted the *Meduse.* Some of them even took Vietnamese names. Chaigneau became Nguyen Van Thang; Vannier, Nguyen Van Chan; De Forcant, Le Van Lang; and De Carpentras, Ong Tin. All the French were assigned to the manufacturing of guns, construction of ships, building of fortresses, and training of troops. In spite of such an array of talents, the Nguyen would have to carry out four campaigns to subdue Qui Nhon.

Pigneau followed the Nguyen forces to Qui Nhon and died of dysentery during the campaign. Nguyen Anh presided at his funeral. On December 16, 1799, he was buried at Phu Nhuan, in the suburbs of Saigon. The entire court was conducted by Prince Canh. Twelve thousand men of the imperial guard and 40,000 civil and military mourners attended the ceremony. The emperor himself wrote a eulogy on a piece of silk and presented it during the ceremony to Monsignor Labartette, Pigneau's successor.

Despite his great contribution to Vietnam, Pigneau failed in his religious mission. He had not converted Gia Long to Christianity, but had succeeded in making Prince Canh a Catholic zealot, universally condemned for having told his mother to throw feces on Buddhist images.[17] His last hope of making Vietnam another Philippines was shattered by the death of Prince Canh. Worse, at the time of Pigneau's passing, the number of Catholics in Vietnam had dropped from an original 100,000 to 30,000.[18] But when religious conversions later reached 360,000, their impact on Vietnam's social and political structure led the Viet to regard Catholics as Western agents, devoted to the uprooting of Confucian culture.

NOTES

1. Le Thanh Khoi, *Histoire du Vietnam* (Paris: Sudestasie, 1992), p. 268.

2. Ibid., p. 275.

3. Pham Van Son, *Viet Su Tan Bien* (Reprint, Los Angeles: Dai Nam, n.d.), B. IV, p. 142.

4. The romanized transcription of the Sino-Viet Nom.

5. At that time, all Westerners commonly were called Hoa Lan (Dutch).

6. Joseph Buttinger, *The Smaller Dragon: A Political History of Vietnam* (New York: Praeger, 1958), pp. 216, 217.

7. Ibid., p. 218.

8. Le Thanh Khoi, *Histoire du Vietnam,* p. 290.

9. Buttinger, *The Smaller Dragon,* p. 219.

10. Le Thanh Khoi, *Histoire du Vietnam,* p. 291.

11. Ibid., p. 284.

12. Buttinger, *The Smaller Dragon,* p. 229.

13. D.G.E. Hall, *A History of Southeast Asia* (New York: St. Martin's Press, 1964), p. 404.

14. Buttinger, *The Smaller Dragon,* p. 263.

15. Pham Van Son, *Viet Su Tan Bien,* B. IV, p. 181.

16. Buttinger, *The Smaller Dragon*, pp. 263, 264.

17. Do Mau, *Vietnam: Mau Lua Que Huong Toi* (Mission Hills, CA: Que Huong Publications, 1986), p. 35.

18. Buttinger, *The Smaller Dragon*, p. 242.

8

THE FRENCH CONQUEST

The modern dynasty founded by Gia Long paved the way for the French conquest. It was for Vietnam an outcome difficult to avoid, given on the one hand the imperialistic tenet of Europe and on the other the backward conditions of all of Southeast Asia. Having persisted in keeping the Chinese as their role models, the Viets would have to pay for their delusion.

THE MODERN DYNASTY

Nguyen Anh, Emperor Gia Long (1802–1819)

In 1806, two hundred years after Nguyen Hoang was granted the miserable fiefdom of Thuan Hoa, his scion King Nguyen Anh took the title of Emperor Gia Long and founded the Nguyen dynasty with its capital in Phu Xuan (Hue), instead of Thang Long, the traditional abode of the Viet dynasties. He did so for two reasons. First, he wanted to conform with Nguyen Binh Khiem's prediction. Nguyen Binh Khiem had once advised Nguyen Hoang to take refuge south of Hoanh Son Mountain. Second, since the Le were not reinstalled as promised, for the people of Bac Ha Gia Long was just another usurper. Thus his choice of Thang Long might have stirred up a great deal of trouble, which he wished to avoid since at the time Vietnam needed unity and reconciliation. However, to please the Northerners he appointed Nguyen Van Thanh, a man of the North, to be the new governor of Bac Ha. But it was to no avail, for serious revolts would erupt later, threatening the existence of his dynasty. Because of this onus, he had to consolidate his military power by building more and more citadels for protection not only against foreign invaders but also against his own people. These constructions required the drafting of a huge population and a tremendous squeeze on the meager national budget. This jeopardized Gia Long's reforms in other fields, particularly the maintenance of the vital dikes and dams network. As a result, under his successor, Minh Mang, the Van Giang water system in the capital region broke down eighteen times.

Gia Long's first move was to establish his dynasty as the legitimate successor of the Le. This he did by recognizing their descendants and by preserving their land, their titles, and their privileges to carry on their ancestral worship. In a calculated move, he returned to China a number of Chinese renegades who had created havoc in South China under the banner of the Heaven and Earth secret society, an organization once financed by Nguyen Hue. At the same time, he applied for Chinese investiture. His choice of the name Nam Viet was promptly denied by China, under the suspicion that he harbored the same designs as Nguyen Hue—to recover the two provinces of Kwangsi and Kwangtung which had been part of Nam Viet under Chao To. In 1802, another embassy went to China. In 1803, the Chinese Emperor Chia Ching (Gia Khanh) issued a decree naming Gia Long king of Vietnam, against a triennial tribute detailed as follows:

Elephant tusks	100 pounds
Rhinoceros horns	2 sets
Cinnamon	100 pounds
Gold	200 taels
Silver	1,000 taels
Silk	100 pieces

In contrast to what Vietnam received from its own vassals, Laos and Cambodia, its tribute to China seemed rather symbolic. Some authors, for instance Le Thanh Khoi, have argued that, in comparison with the magnificent gifts from the Chinese emperor, investiture was closer to diplomatic recognition by modern standards than to feudal allegiance.[1] However, to Pham Van Son the investiture formalities left no doubt about the relationship between the two countries.[2] Te Bo Sam, the governor of Kwangsi was dispatched to carry out the ceremony of which he laid down all the details. Vietnam provided an escort of three high dignitaries, thirty-six musicians, ten honor guards, 2,500 troops, and thirty elephants. From Langson to Thang Long, eight rest areas offered abundant food and comfortable lodging. In Thang Long, a red carpet covered the entire way from the river landing point to the capital. At the Thang Long gate, the Chinese mission received three kowtows and nine nods from the Vietnamese dignitaries. A decorated palanquin carried the royal seal[3] and the imperial presents. Each time he was handed the seal and the presents, the Viet king elevated them to his forehead as a sign of respect and gratitude. One may remember that, in order to avoid such humiliation, Nguyen Hue had persistently refused to attend the ceremony in person and that the Chinese had had to deal with a fake Hue.

The following year, 1804, Gia Long dispatched Le Ba Pham to thank the Chinese emperor and later kept regularly sending embassies to the Peking court.

Map 18
Vietnam in 1806, with Gia Long

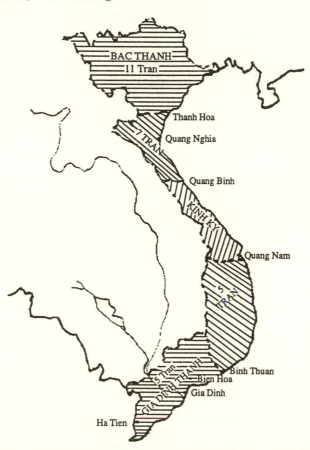

Although he owed his throne to the French, he chose the Chinese as his masters, so compelling were the Confucian bonds to which Vietnam had for centuries submitted. Despite the evidence of Western technological superiority, the Viets remained entrenched in the idea that China was the most powerful nation on the earth and that Westerners were no better than the Mongolian barbarians.

In 1806, after the completion of his Thai Hoa Palace, Gia Long officially took the title of emperor. Actually, foreign monarchs might take any title they wished, but toward China they kept the rank assigned to them as tributary vassals of the Chinese emperor. Unlike Nguyen Hue, Gia Long owed his kingdom to the French and also to a handful of loyal subjects he had to reward. By that time, he had enough political experience to refrain from reestablishing the feudal system. He created new jobs and titles. The country was then divided into four regions with twenty-three subdivisions (*tran*) (Map 18):

1. Bac Thanh (North Tonking) with eleven *tran* was placed under Nguyen Van Thanh, who had followed Gia Long to his exile in Thailand and had helped him fight the Burmese on the Thai's account. Later Nguyen Van Thanh seized Qui Nhon, one of the Tay Son capitals.

2. Gia Dinh Thanh (Cochin China) with five *tran*, was placed under the famous Marshall Le Van Duyet, who had secured the final victory by destroying the Tay Son fleet at the mouth of the Thi Nai and by capturing the capital cities of Phu Xuan and Thang Long. Ha Tien, including Long Xuyen, was still an autonomous territory under Mac Cong Thiem, the fourth grandson of Mac Thiem Tu, himself son of Mac Cuu, the original founder. Only the death of Mac Cong Thiem in 1808 enabled Gia Long to annex Ha Tien as a province.

3. Kinh Ky (from Quang Binh to Quang Nam) with four *doanh* remained under the direct control of the central authority.

4. The remaining seven *tran* were placed under various commanders. Actually, high civil servants from previous regimes were reluctant to join the new emperor, and at the beginning the administration was carried out by the military.

Political reforms were aimed first at the dynastic structure itself. Traditionally, queens and empresses were by right involved in the succession process, which often led to the downfall of the dynasty. Gia Long decided to suppress the title of empress; his concubines would take the title of imperial consort.

Also, within his administration he abolished the omnipotent post of prime minister. Six ministries would be in charge of administration, treasury, rites and education, public works, defense, and justice. The ministers themselves had no exclusive power; they could not make any decision without the concurrence of two assistants. Finally, at the top, the emperor himself and his government were subject to the scrutiny of the high censorate.

The granting of land was gradually replaced by remuneration in kind and cash. Titles became mostly honorific and were not necessarily transferable. When inheritance applied, the title was to be reduced one step down for the following generation. For example, the son of a deceased duke (*cong*) had to take the rank of marquis (*hau*) unless the continuity was maintained by imperial decree.

Tax reforms focused on produce and natural resources. Land was divided into three classes. First class land had to contribute 20 *thang* of rice (1 *thang* = 2 liters) per hectare; second class land, fifteen *thang*; and third class lands ten *thang*. Personal taxes depended on the geographical area and were paid with one to two bowls of cereal, plus from one *tien* to one *quan* in cash. Exemption was granted in case of natural disasters. Communal estates were reserved for community needs and no sale was allowed for this type of land. Natural resources, including minerals and forest products, continued to be taxed.

In 1803, Gia Long opened the Central Coin Factory in Bac Thanh to produce gold and silver ingots (*nen*) and copper and zinc coins (*tien* and *dong*). The basic weight was the tael or ounce representing 37.7831 grams of gold. Silver was valued at 1/34 the weight of gold. But on the current market, transactions were based on the sapeque or zinc *dong*. A square hole in the center of the coins enabled people to assemble 60 *dong* for 1 *tien*. A set of 10 *tien* was worth 1 *quan* or 600 *dong*.

During the war, the cadastral register was totally distorted by numerous manipulations related to illegal sales of public properties. Entire villages even disappeared from the records. To put an end to the chaos, Gia Long prohibited the sale of communal lands unless the sale was to support the development of some public project. As for those territories recently annexed from Cambodia, ownership was easily obtained upon proof of cultivation of the land. Among the forest products, cinnamon and bird nests were on the top of the list of taxable items, followed by sandalwood, ginseng, and other precious woods. Chinese teams were allowed to continue to dig their copper, tin, and zinc mines, but gold exploitation was reserved for Sino-Viet joint ventures. Also, for the first time the Chinese population, now called Minh Huong, appeared on the census records. Import taxes depended on the region, and ships were taxed according to their tonnage. Until 1819, the French paid reduced taxes. But afterward, the loss of that privilege was the last straw and caused the departure of Jean Baptiste Chaigneau, the leader of the French Volunteers.

Any new ruler coming to power enacts new legislation as an affirmation of the existence of his dynasty and an expression of his philosophy of government. As Hsun Tzu put it, "Should a true King arise, he must certainly follow the ancient terms and make the new ones."[4] In this respect, Gia Long cannot be seen as a "true king." In 1815, Nguyen Van Thanh, the governor of Bac Ha whom Gia Long had commissioned to write new legislation, came out with a code of 398 articles in twenty-two volumes. It was a mere copy of the Ch'ing code without any reference to Vietnam's culture and traditions. Indeed, all the liberal provisions of the Hong Duc Code had been wiped out, including its remarkable attention to women's rights. But the backward clauses forbidding convicts, singers, opera actors (*hat bo*), and their descendants from taking part in any examinations remained. Gia Long had not followed the ancient terms and had failed to make new ones. In the field of justice, he was carrying out the law of the Ch'ing as if Vietnam continued to be a Chinese province. The failure to promote a national code of conduct would undermine Vietnam's spirit and prepare the country for further renunciation.

In the field of education, in 1803 Gia Long opened the National College (Quoc Tu Giam) which was accessible to the best commoners. He also resumed the *thi huong* (doctoral degree) national examination, based for the most part on the Chinese format.

In the military field, the draft was revised. The *trans*, from Quang Binh down to Binh Thuan, were required to provide one soldier for every three peasants. In Gia Dinh Thanh, the rate was one to five, and in Bac Thanh and Kinh Ky, it was one to seven. The *doanhs* were responsible for recruiting sailors. In the aftermath of the war Gia Long's army numbered a total of 113,000 men, including 42,000 who were Western trained, 200 elephants, and a transport unit with brigades of buffalo. As for the navy, there were 18,800 men serving on 200 warships and 500 oarboats. Shipbuilding employed 8,000 workers.[5] The traditional system of rotation enabled soldiers to take time for rice cultivation. In spite of the creation of two new military academies and the French help in training, the building of a modern army was an unusual task for a Vietnam where Confucian and Taoist values dominated a society divided into four classes. On the top were the landlord-scholars (*si*), followed by the farmers-peasants (*nong*), the artisans (*cong*), and, at the bottom, the merchants (*thuong*). As for the soldiers, they were a species apart from the mainstream, and the tradition ran so strong that even in the government hierarchy, for those of relatively equal position, a scholar was always ranked one step over a military man. Furthermore, for the civil mandarins promotions were scheduled twice a year, while a military officer would have to wait three times as long. So to be able to build up a modern national defense, it was necessary to promote the military to a proper social status. In other words, society had to be remodeled. Of course, China was facing the same dilemma. Numerous fortresses and citadels were erected under French supervision. The quality of the Hue citadel, for instance, was reported to have been even better than that of the English forts in India. But these constructions required a substantial squeeze on the budget and diversion of the population from other programs.

Public works were performed throughout the country, but under the care of each village. The people were called upon to build roads and bridges against payment in rice, based on the mileage of the completed construction. Ninety-eight rest areas were also constructed along the main roads. However, dams and dikes were not properly maintained since later on many broke down, causing widespread discontent.

In foreign policy, in 1807 Gia Long again assumed the protectorate of Cambodia. The Khmer had to pay a three-year tribute, which is listed below to allow comparison with what Vietnam had to pay to China:

5-meter-high elephants	2 each
Rhinoceros horns	2 each
Elephant tusks	2 each
Almonds	50 pounds
Medicinal plants	150 pounds
Black paint	20 pots

In 1811, Siam continued to harass Cambodia by seizing the important province of Battambang, but Le Van Duyet's ultimatum compelled them to withdraw. To secure peace in the Khmer kingdom, Le Van Duyet fortified Phnom Penh, where General Nguyen Van Thuy was stationed with 1,000 troops. The protectorate was thus definitively established, and Thailand renounced further attempts to intimidate Cambodia. Relations with Laos had improved dramatically from the time when it had treacherously settled with the Ming against Dai Viet. The contribution of Laos to Gia Long's victory was quite significant. The Lao were holding the Nghe An front against the Tay Son, and in 1799 and 1800, the Viet-Lao coalition troops finally brought about the decisive capture of the Tay Son province of Nghe An. For some time longer, Laos was subject to a triennial tribute to Vietnam consisting of elephant tusks, rhinoceros horns and cinnamon.

Towards the Western powers, Gia Long's hidden xenophobia affected his foreign policy. During the war, he refrained from displaying his true feelings for fear of losing Pigneau's aid. But after receiving recognition from the Ch'ing, his first move was to restrain missionary activity. In public, he prohibited repairs of old religious temples and the construction of new ones; but in private, he was targeting the Catholic missions, which were anxious to expand.

In 1804, Gia Long rejected a request from an Englishman, J. W. Roberts to open a trading post in Quang Nam. His innate mistrust of Europeans increased as he was gradually exposed to their imperialistic machinations. If he ever applied for French help, he did so only as a last resort and because he had no other choice. The fanatical zeal of the missionaries, with their interdictions against ancestor worship, finally convinced him that it would be difficult for Vietnam's Confucian culture to coexist with Christianity. He personally experienced this fact within his own family. His heir, Prince Canh, under Pigneau's influence, had secretly converted to Catholicism while he was in France. Upon his return, he caused a national scandal by refusing to honor the cult of his ancestors. This was the catalyst for anti-Catholic sentiment in Vietnam. And so, Gia Long did not grant the French missionaries the amount of support Pigneau had expected as a just reward for his military assistance. But Gia Long maintained personal loyalty toward the bishop, which he conspicuously displayed during the nationwide mourning for him. As for the French volunteers, such as Chaigneau and Vannier, even after Pigneau's departure, Gia Long treated them with courtesy and maybe even affection, making them dukes and marquis and allowing them to dispense with the traditional kowtow. But at his death, Gia Long told his successor, Minh Mang, who was well-known for his anti-Western views: "Just treat the French well but do not grant them any prominent posts."[6]

Of course, the French did almost everything to confirm Gia Long's suspicions. After the fall of Napoleon I, King Louis XVIII suddenly dug out the Versailles Treaty and dispatched the warship *Cybele* to Da Nang under the command of the Count of Kergariou to demand implementation of the 1787 Franco-Viet treaty. The French were told firmly that since they had never implemented that agreement, it was rescinded. Gia Long was probably outraged by the French behavior, which confirmed his doubts about their probity. Nevertheless, in 1819 two French vessels, the *Rose* and the *Henri*, were permitted to trade advantageously in Da Nang. As for Chaigneau, he was disappointed by Gia Long's restrictive policy, and so he took a three-year leave and went back to France on the *Henri*. He came back later, in 1821, as consul of France, but did not succeed in securing a trade agreement with Vietnam.

In 1819, Gia Long died at the age of fifty-nine, leaving the throne to Prince Dam, who became Emperor Minh Mang. Despite his success in unifying the country, which Nguyen Hue would have done anyway were he still alive, the deceased emperor, Gia Long, was accused of bringing in the Western powers and of lacking moral principles. The way he treated the defeated Tay Son showed a total absence of humanity, and his ingratitude toward those who contributed to his rise was severely criticized. The case of Nguyen Van Thanh was a typical example of Gia Long's nature. After completion of his legislative work, Nguyen Van Thanh met a cruel fate. His son Nguyen Thien, a *tien si* (doctor), was a gregarious scholar who enjoyed building friendships with other intellectuals. In a letter of invitation to Nguyen Van Khue and Nguyen Duc Nhuan, renowned writers from Thanh Hoa, he imprudently expressed the hope that their meeting would help to bring a change in the situation. The case was brought first to the attention of Marshall Le Van Duyet, who suspected Nguyen Thien of plotting a coup. Thus he initiated an inquest leading to the arrest of Nguyen Thien for sedition. As Nguyen Van Thanh, in the presence of the entire court, begged on his knees for his son, Gia Long brutally shoved him away. The unfortunate man said: "The emperor wants me dead, as a loyal subject I must die."[7] So, he swallowed poison and died. He had been the one who brought Nguyen Anh (Gia Long) to safety in Thailand when the king was running for his life, hunted by the victorious Nguyen Hue. For Vietnamese historians, there was no excuse for Gia Long's behavior.

Emperor Minh Mang (1820–1840)

Minh Mang succeeded Gia Long as Emperor Nguyen Thanh To. His choice for the throne was not without problem, for he was not in the direct line of succession, being the son of a concubine. Crown Prince Canh had died during the Qui Nhon campaign leaving a minor son. Gia Long, fearing the complications of a regency, decided to name Prince Dam as his heir, despite the opposition of high dignitaries, among whom was Marshall Le Van Duyet himself. Later Minh Mang would, with a vengeance, desecrate his grave, thus triggering a violent revolt in the South.

At twenty-eight years old, Minh Mang was already a well-trained monarch. He would later prove himself to be a remarkable politician, for without his firm and rather cruel hand, the dynasty would have been submerged under the massive rebellion of Le Van Khoi.

It was easy for him to build up absolute power for, unlike his father, he was not subject to moral and political constraints. A generation had passed since the conclusion of the war against the Tay Son and the old soldiers and associates had begun to fade away. The death of Marshall Le Van Duyet gave Minh Mang the opportunity to bring the country under centralized command by replacing the two quasi-autonomous *Tong Tran* (governors) with *Tong Doc* (province chiefs). By splitting Bac Ha and Nam Ha into downsized provinces, he also limited the power of the *Tong Doc*. The *Tong Doc* appointed provincial officers directly, presided over examinations, and supervised public works. Under them were the *Tuan Phu* who were in charge of political affairs and education, the *Bo Chinh* who were the tax collectors, and the *An Sat Su* who were the provincial chief justices. The salaries of government employees basically depended on their examination degrees and were supplemented by a function bonus. National examinations followed the Ch'ing pattern. With the concentration of power, the *Gia Long Thi-Thu Vien* (secretarial chamber) was transformed into the *Noi Cac* (imperial cabinet).

In the field of justice, as the Gia Long code remained entirely in effect, Minh Mang made no innovations of his own and resorted to a code of conduct similar to the Le Thanh Tong code of some 400 hundred years before. It called for respecting the three social relationships,[8] between king and subject, father and son, and husband and wife, and observing the five individual virtues, human heartedness (*nhan*), righteousness (*nghia*), propriety (*le*), wisdom (*tri*), and good faith (*tin*).[9] A penal court (*Bo Hinh*) and a court of appeal (*Toa Tam Pap*) were erected in the capital. The number of prisons was increased significantly.

As Gia Long had failed to bring back prosperity, the indigent population had tremendously increased, thus compelling Minh Mang to build hospices and nursing homes.

In Cochin China, the cadastral survey was completed and taxes this time were imposed on the Chinese population at the rate of two *lang* per head.[10] The elderly Chinese paid half. The salt tax was readjusted along with the tax on mining.

There were no major changes in the reorganization of the army. In addition to the citadels more ships were built, as they were needed against the Chinese Tau O (Black Pavilion) pirates who were infesting the Gulf of Tonking. The Viet forces were now well armed with infantry, artillery, navy, and elephant units. Military hospitals were erected as they had been during the war against the Tay Son. But much disillusionment surfaced as the people pondered their sacrifices for war and their expectations of peace. Even military training had become a setting for abuses. For a shooting round, a soldier was given only three to five bullets, and if he missed his target, he had to pay back the cost of the lost munitions. Morale was such that the simple act of boarding a junk following an assignment to another area was perceived by the soldiers as a death sentence:

Bang! Bang! the drums beat five rounds.
Putting my foot on the junk, my tears pour down like
rain.[11]

Minh Mang's accession to the throne was preceded by his anti-Western reputation, which translated into a policy of nonalignment with the Western nations, including the former French allies. When Chaigneau came back as consul of France, he vainly struggled to obtain a trade agreement with Vietnam. But Minh Mang retorted very courteously that considering the friendly relations between the two nations, an agreement was not necessary. Later, in 1822, Minh Mang denied another request from Chaigneau to grant audience to Captain Courson de la Ville, commander of the warship *Cleopatra*, recently arrived at Da Nang. This time he said that having rejected a similar request from the English, he was reluctant to hold a double standard. In 1824, disappointed by Minh Mang's hostile attitude, Chaigneau, together with Vannier, went into retirement in France. In 1825, Captain De Bougainville arrived at Da Nang with the warships *Thetis* and *Esperance*. With numerous presents, he applied for an audience, but was denied on the grounds that France and England were belligerent and therefore Vietnam did not wish to get involved with them. Furthermore, since Chaigneau and Vannier had left, no interpreter was available. In 1826, Chaigneau's nephew was appointed consul in place of his uncle, but was also denied an audience. This was the end of friendly Franco-Viet relations. Vietnam entered a decade of isolation, during which Minh Mang carried out religious obstructions and persecutions.

As a result of his Confucian background, as well as his exposure to the missionaries' questionable activities, Minh Mang reached the conclusion that the Christians were agents of Western imperialism, a claim difficult to deny given the close connection between the French government and the foreign missions. The very fact that, in order to help the Nguyen, the French priests had called upon the Catholic population to revolt against the Tay Son was considered a dangerous precedent.

Moreover, for Minh Mang the despicable role the Jesuits and the missionaries had played in Bangkok in 1688 warranted nothing but troubles for Vietnam. With all that on his mind, Minh Mang set out to stop, once and for all, the overexpansion of French foreign mission influence in his kingdom. Under the pretext of having foreign books to translate into the Vietnamese language, he had all missionaries regrouped in Hue and assigned to that task. When they resisted and went into hiding, he ordered their deportation and persecution.

At that point, numerous revolts surged in the North. They were led by the many factions loyal to the Le. In the South, Le Van Khoi's case took on international dimensions as the Thais were called in to support the mutineer. In Tonking, the Nguyen were unable to secure the loyalty of the people and the scholars who remained loyal to the Le dynasty. The memory of the liberator Le Loi was still alive in the North. In Cochin China, the people had found themselves happy with Le Van Duyet's strict but benevolent rule; however, the reduction of their autonomy and the brutal behavior of his successor were the cause of major discontent.

Early in 1826, a series of revolts ravaged North Vietnam, with Pham Ba Vanh in Nam Dinh, Le Duy Luong in Ninh Binh, and Nong Van Van in Tuyen Quang all aiming to destroy the Nguyen. At that time, the Tay Son remnants who had fled to China after the fall of Phu Xuan came back with a force of 5,000 under the command of Nguyen Hanh and joined with the Chinese pirates, the Tau O. As for Phan Ba Vanh, he was by no means prepared for a revolutionary career. According to Taoist physiognomy, he had the physical features of a Son of Heaven and consequently was considered a threat to the Nguyen dynasty. Thus before government troops could round him up, he dashed to the Cao Bang jungle, where he raised an army of partisans, among whom was a man named Nguyen Huu Khoi. They captured the northeast of Tonking, threatening the capital, Thang Long. At that point Minh Mang dispatched Marshall Le Van Duyet to deal with them. Finally they surrendered in Thai Binh. Nguyen Huu Khoi escaped execution, having impressed Le Van Duyet with his martial appearance. Thus Le Van Duyet adopted the rebel and gave him the name of Le Van Khoi. Later he made him a senior officer in his own army.

In 1827, with the help of several mountain tribes, Le Duy Luong, a descendant of the Le king, captured three districts in the southwest of Tonking and threatened the important province of Hung Hoa. He was captured three years later and decapitated. All those bearing the Le name were deported to the South, to Quang Nam, Quang Nghia, and Binh Dinh. They were separated into groups of fifteen families, each with an allotment of two hectares of rice fields and ten ligatures of cash.

Before the Le Duy Luong problem was settled, the Nong Van Van case erupted in connection with the revolt of Le Van Khoi in Cochin China. Nong Van Van was chief of Cao Bang province and his sister was Le Van Khoi's wife. As that family relationship subjected him to collective responsibility for Le Van Khoi's actions, Nong Van Van chose to put up a rebellion of his own. He soon captured Cao Bang, Langson, Thai Nguyen, and Tuyen Quang. All the former province chiefs were tattooed on the forehead with the following: "This province chief took money from the people." Minh Mang had to assign generals Le Van Duc and Nguyen Cong Tru to chase Nong Van Van into the mountains, where he ended his life in a brush fire ignited by soldiers.

In the meantime, down in Cochin China, Le Van Duyet died, and Gia Dinh Province was divided into small territories under the administration of Bui Xuan Nguyen, one of Minh Mang's men. Before leaving Hue for his new assignment, Bui Xuan Nguyen received secret instructions from Minh Mang to build a case against Le Van Duyet, who had once opposed Minh Mang's enthronement. Bui Xuan Nguyen wasted no time in compiling a voluminous report in which he charged Le Van Duyet with numerous misdeeds, seven of which called for capital punishment. Since Le Van Duyet was dead, Bui Xuan Nguyen recommended that the sixteen surviving members of his family be put to death, including Le Van Khoi. As a result, only two of Le Van Duyet's nephews were executed; their wives remained untouched because they were Nguyen princesses. Also, considering that Le Van Duyet had been a eunuch, his wife, Do Thi Nham, was released. Finally, the only punishment possible was to rase his tomb and put in it a defamatory stone with the following inscription: "This is the place where the infamous Le Van Duyet was punished."

Le Chat, a lifetime friend of Le Van Duyet, was also prosecuted. An inquest led by another one of Minh Mang's men resulted in sixteen accusations, six requiring live dissection, eight requiring decapitation, and two requiring hanging. As Le Chat was long dead, his tomb was leveled as punishment. His surviving family members were imprisoned and all their property was confiscated.

But with the surviving Le Van Khoi, it was another matter. On the night of May 10, 1833, Le Van Khoi escaped from prison and, with his troops, killed all the government officials, together with their families. As for Bui Xuan Nguyen he was offered burning like a human candle, in a ritual sacrifice dedicated to the memory of Le Van Duyet. The entire Phien An district joined Le Van Khoi, who proclaimed himself general. In one single month, they took six provinces in Gia Dinh. Minh Mang dispatched a punitive expedition that succeeded in luring one of Le Van Khoi's officers. The rebel general had to take refuge in the impregnable Phien An citadel, built by Le Van Duyet. In the meantime, Le Van Khoi sent for assistance from Thailand, but shortly thereafter he was poisoned by Minh Mang's agents. He was succeeded by his eight-year-old son, Le Van Cu, which caused discord among his lieutenants and resulted in many desertions. And yet it took the government three entire years to overcome the rebels and their Thai allies. When Phien An was finally invaded by government troops, 1,831 people were executed and buried en masse in a huge pit.

Only six survivors were sent to Hue for judgement. Among them there were a Chinese man, the eight-year-old son of Le Van Khoi, and a French priest, Father Marchand. The presence of Father Marchand among the rebels and a message for help he had sent to Father Taberd in Siam unveiled the role of the Catholics in Le Van Khoi's revolt. Although all along the church denied any participation, Minh Mang knew better, for he owed his throne to the military assistance of Pigneau de Behaine. When the mission realized it was not possible to build a Christian kingdom with the Nguyen, Father Marchand was singled out to find other allies.

Anyway, no matter what crimes had been committed, the punishments were unanimously condemned for their brutality, especially when the victim was an innocent eight-year-old child. Besides the way the Nguyen treated the Tay Son and their rumored murder of Prince Canh's wife and children, the Nguyen displayed their savagery in various ways. According to a French witness: On November 5, 1835 at 5:00 A.M., five gunshots awoke the Hue populace to attend the execution. The victims were pulled out of their wooden cages and tortured one after the other. Thus the eight-year-old Le Van Cu had to witness the agony of Father Marchand before succumbing to the same fate. First, the prisoners had their vests pulled down to show their bare chests, while their pants were rolled up. They were marched to Minh Mang's tribune where they were looked upon personally by the emperor. He then coldly threw down a small flag indicating the death sentence. The victims had to kowtow five times and were led back before the justice panel for a public interrogation. The first was Marchand. By then he had his clothes removed and two soldiers held him firmly near a furnace, where several pincers were heating in the flames. On a signal from the president of the panel, five red hot pincers were applied to the thighs and the buttocks of the priest, until the instruments cooled down. While the torment progressed, the president asked a series of questions: Why in your religion do they gouge the eyes of the people? Why does the wedding ceremony have to be carried out before the altar? What kind of cake do you give people to eat to secure their loyalty?

At one point, the tortures stopped in order to spare the victims for the final execution.

The prisoners were offered a last meal, but Marchand could not eat. Finally he was attached to a cross. Each executioner was flanked by two soldiers armed with whips. Their role was to flog the tormentors when they relented or displayed sympathy for the victims. This time, the red hot pincers were applied to the chest. The pectoral muscles were torn off and thrown to the ground. Simultaneously, another executioner sliced the buttocks and yet another attacked other parts of the body. When the victim was dead, they put the corpse on the ground and continued to carve it to the bone. In the last stage, after the head was severed, the skeleton was hacked into four parts and thrown into the ocean. The head was displayed in a bamboo basket at the marketplace. Ultimately, it would be crushed to powder and dispersed.

From 1833 through 1838, religious persecutions continued while the missionaries went underground and intensified their clandestine activities in Vietnam. But political developments in Malaysia, where Singapore had been seized by the British, and in China, where the British were victoriously waging the Opium Wars against the Ch'ing, gave much concern to Minh Mang. Consequently, he dispatched information missions to Penang, Batavia, Calcutta, London, and Paris to find out European intentions about Vietnam.

When the USS *Peacock* came back in 1836 with Edmund Robert, Minh Mang saw an opportunity to build a relationship with America. He hastily granted an audience to Robert, but due to a sudden illness, Robert had to sail at once to Macao, where he died without meeting with Minh Mang's envoys. In 1841, Minh Mang passed away and was succeeded by Thieu Tri.

Thieu Tri (1841–1847)

The next emperor, Thieu Tri, was invested in 1842 by the governor of Kwangsi and Kwangtung, representing the Chinese emperor Tao Kuang. A peaceful and unassuming man, Thieu Tri did not bring innovations to his short reign, for he had enough to do dealing with Minh Mang's legacy.

In Cambodia, the Viet protectorate met with the resistance of the Khmer people, who finally rose up, aided by Thailand. As the Viet occupation troops were unable to quell dissidence, Thieu Tri denounced them and ordered them out of Cambodia. Truong Minh Giang, their commander in chief, suffered tremendous loss of face, and back in Vietnam he soon died of a broken heart. As he was one of the best soldiers of the time, it was for Vietnam not a small casualty.

After the withdrawal of the Viets, the Thais came back to reassert their rule over the Khmers. They put Nac Ong Don on the throne, but this time the Khmer people turned to the Viets for assistance. In 1847, Nac Ong Don and his Thai allies were surrounded at Oudong and had to surrender. The Viet troops took 23,000 Thai and Khmer prisoners. Then the Viets simply reappointed Nac Ong Don as the king of Cambodia. Peace came back and many of Thieu Tri's subjects wondered why they had to fight so hard against Nac Ong Don.

Thieu Tri was opposed to foreign religion, but aware of European might, he refrained from action against the French in order to avoid further confrontation. At that time, 1839, the French had a consulate in Manila to keep an eye on Asia. Actually the French fleet was also ready in Macao, Singapore, and Hong Kong. Since five priests were still in prison, Commander Favin Leveque came to Danang with his ship *Heroine*. All the hostages were released, but the missionaries kept coming back in a provocative fashion. In 1845, Bishop Lefebvre was sentenced to death. His request for French intervention was handled through Commander Percival of the USS *Constitution*, who happened to be there. This time the French Admiral Cecile dispatched the warship *Alcmene* under Captain Fournier Duplan to Danang. Lefebvre was released and brought to Singapore, from where he managed to come back again. And again he was captured and released.

With the execution of Father Marchand and the news of continuous persecution by Minh Mang, the French were prepared for a showdown with Vietnam. In 1847, as the English had by the Treaty of Nanking obtained possession of Hong Kong, the French succeeded in obtaining freedom of trade and religion in China. After all the hostages had been freed, two French officers, De Lapierre and Rigault de Genouilly, arrived in Cochin China to take possession of Tourane (Danang) in accordance with the 1787 Versailles Treaty. During the difficult negotiations, the French gave a show of strength by sinking the entire Viet fleet in the Bay of Da Nang. In protest, Thieu Tri put an abrupt end to the negotiations.

After the French sailed back, the English governor of Hong Kong, John Davis, made an attempt to fish in troubled water by offering Thieu Tri a treaty for trade and alliance. The Viet emperor rejected the offer. He died in the winter at the age of forty. After him came the deluge.

Tu Duc (1848–1883)

Tu Duc was the second son of Thieu Tri. He was nineteen years old when he was enthroned by the Ch'ing in 1849. His accession was marked by the abandoning of the primogeniture tradition, depriving his elder brother Hong Bao of the crown. The evicted prince wasted no time in mounting a coup d'etat. To keep secrecy, he had all his associates share a blood oath. This did not stop a monk from turning traitor and all the mutineers were captured when they assaulted the Hue citadel. To make matters worse for Catholics, a ship loaded with mercenaries arrived at that time, but left without fighting. Hong Bao was condemned to live dissection. Tu Duc commuted the sentence to life, but Hong Bao hung himself with a bed sheet.

This incident suggests that by Confucian standards if Tu Duc was not a sage he was at least a good man. Above all he was a devoted son, reserving fifteen days every month to report formally to the queen mother. Whenever she had good advice for the sake of the country, he recorded it in a notebook he carried around which he called *tu huan luc* (queen mother's teachings book). One day, engaged in a hunting party, he was late for a family anniversary celebration. Fearing an escort would cause more delay, he ran back to the palace alone in a heavy rain. Then he kowtowed, presenting a rod for his mother to punish him. She said: "You have my pardon. But since your escorts had to suffer the rain for you, do not forget to reward them." His compassion for his people was also proverbial. One day, the clumsiness of a servant caused a slight burn to his hand; he just rubbed the wound without a word of reproach.

Unfortunately Tu Duc had other obligations as an emperor. The legacies from Minh Mang and Thieu Tri were unquestionable, given the political context. Despite the church's denial, there was enough proof of Catholic collusion to prompt Tu Duc to order the massacre of the Catholic population, including priests. In 1851, Schoeffer was beheaded in Son Tay and Jean Louis Bonnard was executed in Nam Dinh. Later it was the turn of the Frenchmen Charbonnier and Matheron and the Spaniards Diaz and Garcia.

The Catholics were not Tu Duc's only problem. After the fourth year of his reign, the North became the center of serious disturbances. The remnants of China's Taiping Heavenly Kingdom (*Thai Binh Thien Quoc*), whose leader claimed to be a brother of Jesus Christ, had crossed the Vietnamese border and, with another Chinese group called the three T'ang (*tam duong*), was rampaging in the mountainous regions.

In 1856, Leheur de Ville-sur-Arc arrived in Da Nang with a French message blaming Vietnam for the religious executions. As the court refused to give any explanations, the warship *Catinat* bombed Da Nang in retaliation. In 1857, Louis Charles de Montigny, the French envoy based in Thailand, arrived to demand the opening of a consulate in Hue and freedom to trade and to preach. The court rejected all his requests. Finally, in 1858, upon the exhortations of his wife Eugenie, a devout Catholic under Jesuit domination, Napoleon III dispatched the China fleet to Vietnam with 3,000 troops, including Spanish Tagals from the Philippines. On September 1, 1858, after a short resistance Da Nang fell into the hands of Admiral Rigault de Genouilly. Then he moved to the South and conquered Cochin China.

While Vietnam was the largest independent nation on the Indochinese Peninsula, its economy was in shambles. Although it is always difficult for an agricultural country to convert peacefully into an industrial nation, the transformation is most difficult for a Confucian state. At the time the West faced the imperatives of the industrial revolution, Vietnam was still honoring a traditional culture, keeping economic forces in the background and focusing solely on agriculture.

In spite of rewards to peasants in the form of government subsidies and honorific titles, the state of agriculture did not improve, due to the shortage of modern equipment. New settlements in the former Champa territories showed only promises. Handicrafts centered on silk production and ceramics failed to have a significant impact on the economy. Absence of know-how kept the mining industry in the hands of Chinese specialists, who finally gave up for financial reasons. Out of the 120 mines in operation under Thieu Tri, more than half closed down under Tu Duc. Government-operated mines, with manpower supplied by convicts, operated at a loss because of lack of motivation and incentives.

After the rupture of relations with the West, external trade was carried out mainly with China, Cambodia, and Siam, in a few consumer products, which included cinnamon, pepper, areca, raw cotton, raw silk, and sugar. Water buffalo, elephant tusks, and rhinoceros horns were also exported in exchange for manufactured products such as Chinese silk, porcelain, tea, and paper. Credit was nonexistent or, if practiced, reached usurious levels without any guarantee.

Unlike Thailand and its peaceful transition, Vietnam refused to jump on the Western bandwagon. That reluctance to change was deeply rooted in the Chinese classics. As Lao Tzu said, "The sage keeps to the deed that consists in taking no action."[12] Of course the Vietnamese rulers did not see this as an order to abdicate their responsibility to rule, but as a word of prudence in their dealings with the West. Regarding the peasants, Western superiority left them unshaken, for better than anyone they knew the cyclical aspect of nature and history. In this world, rises and falls are unfathomable realities, for the Tao reversal theory applies not only to nature but also to human enterprise. "When the sun has reached its meridian, it declines and when the moon has become full, it wanes."[13] Thus there was a consensus among the rulers and the ruled alike to keep the pendulum from excessive swings, so that life could go on in traditional harmony. But the immediate concern of the peasants, and to a large extent the Confucian scholars, was rather with the prophetic words of Chuang Tzu: "The more man overcomes nature, the more there will be misery and unhappiness."[14] This belief, associated by the Vietnamese with the possible hazards of Western technology, was later a major obstacle to the French efforts at conversion. If in the cities the population was more or less adjusting to Western methods, in the villages the peasants persisted in their passive resistance.

This is not to say that the Vietnamese peasants were content with their conditions. Even the villages which they considered their traditional havens failed to live up to their expectations. The village notables who were also land owners carried the land allotment (*khau phan*) for their own profit. In 1840, the central government had to intervene to compel the wealthy landlords to give away 30 percent of their assets to the communes for redistribution to the population.

On the top of that, a new tax exemption included, besides the village notables, government dignitaries, the orphans of officials killed in action, the sons and servants of low ranking officers, the laureates of provincial examinations, the handicapped, and senior citizens over the age of sixty. Also young people from eighteen to twenty years old and adults from fifty-five to sixty years old were exempt from the draft and the corvée but had to pay taxes at half rate. The tax burden fell on people from twenty to fifty-five years old, who were called the "healthy class" (*trang hang*). They had to make up for the difference in terms of the corvée, the draft and taxes. And since according to a Vietnamese proverb the "customs of the villages prevail over the authority of the emperor," there was no way for the peasants to appeal to a higher authority.

Then there were the natural disasters and epidemics that brought the population misery. From 1820 through 1850, cholera killed 864,000 people. From 1842 through 1846, typhoons destroyed 75,000 homes and took 5,600 lives. In 1854, swarms of locusts transformed Son Tay and Bac Ninh into an arid desert. Then ruptures of dikes during the 1856–1857 period condemned tens of thousands to die of famine or to live by cannibalism.

As has already been reported, multiple mutinies erupted as a result of popular discontent. For the peasants, these calamities, coupled with the French intervention, were unmistakably signs of heaven's anger.

Finally, when Cochin China became a colony under direct French rule, the monarchic regime vanished in the South, and with it the dual transcendental function of the king. On the one hand, for better or for worse, he was the supreme priest who performed ritual sacrifices to heaven in order to obtain peace and prosperity for his subjects; on the other hand, he was mandated by heaven to lead his subjects toward moral laws. The spiritual vacuum created by his disappearance pervaded the entire population of the South and led to the emergence of new religions. The Cao Daists, through the use of mediums, established direct dialogue with heaven, thus fulfilling the people's needs. But above all, their religious syncretism was a revolutionary concept for a world then oriented towards partisanship and bigotry.

NOTES

1. Le Thanh Khoi, *Histoire du Vietnam* (Paris: Sudestasie, 1992), p. 133.
2. Pham van Son, *Viet Su Tan Bien* (reprint, Los Angeles: Dai Nam, n.d.), B. IV, p. 275.

3. The seal was given by the Chinese emperor as proof of his recognition.

4. Fung Yu-lan, *A Short History of Chinese Philosophy* (New York: Macmillan, 1953), p. 152. Citing Hsun Tzu.

5. Pham van Son, *Viet Su Tan Bien*, B. IV, p. 258.

6. Le Thanh Khoi, *Histoire du Vietnam*, p. 367.

7. Pham van Son, *Viet Su Tan Bien*, B. IV, p. 293.

8. The Vietnamese call Tam Cang (the three k'ang) the three major relationships out of the original Confucian five.

9. *Ngu cuong* (The five Confucian ch'ang).

10. One *lang* equals one tael.

11. Author's translation, Pham van Son, B. IV, p. 342.

12. D. C. Lau, *Translator Tao Te Ching* (London: Penguin, 1963), B. I, p. 58.

13. James Legge, *Translator I Ching* (New York: Bantam, 1986), Appendix I, p. 259.

14. Fung Yu-Lan, *A Short History,* p. 107.

BIBLIOGRAPHY

Audric, John. *Angkor and the Khmer Empire*. London: R. Hale, 1972.

Bain, Chester A. *Vietnam the Roots of Conflict*. Englewood Cliffs, NJ: Prentice-Hall, 1967.

Baird, Robert. *Category Formation and the History of Religion*. Paris: Mouton & Co., 1971.

Benda, Harry J. *The World of Southeast Asia*. New York: Harper & Row, 1967.

Blacker, Carmen. *Ancient Cosmologies*. London: Allen & Unwin, 1975.

Bowles, Gordon T. *The People of Asia*. New York: Charles Scribner's Sons, 1977.

Bredon, Juliet. *The Moon Year, a Record of Chinese Customs and Festivals*. Reprint. New York: Paragon, 1966.

Buttinger, Joseph. *A Dragon Defiant: A Short History of Vietnam*. New York: Praeger, 1972.

————. *The Smaller Dragon: A Political History of Vietnam*. New York: Praeger, 1958.

————. *Vietnam: A Political History*. New York: Praeger, 1968.

Cady, John Frank. *The Roots of French Imperialism in Eastern Asia*. Ithaca, NY: Cornell University Press, 1954.

————. *Southeast Asia: Its Historical Development*. New York: McGraw-Hill, 1964.

Calder, Ritchie. *After the Seventh Day*. New York: Simon & Schuster, 1961.

Capra, Fritjof. *The Tao of Physics*. New York: Bantam Books, 1984.

Chafe, William H. *The Unfinished Journey*. Oxford: Oxford University Press, 1991.

Chen, King C. *Vietnam and China*. Princeton, NJ: Princeton University Press, 1969.

Cheng Te K'un. *Archeology in China*. Cambridge: W. Heffer, 1959.

Child, Alice B., and Irvin L. Child. *Religion and Magic in the Life of Traditional People*. Englewood Cliffs, NJ: Prentice-Hall, 1993.

Chong Key Ray. *Cannibalism in China*. Wakefield, NH: Longwood, 1990.

Coedes, Georges. *The Indianized States of Southeast Asia*. Honolulu: East West Center Press, 1964.

Colani, Madeleine. "*Recherches sur le prehistorique indochinois*." BEFEO 30 (1939): 299-422.

Cotterell, Arthur. *China, a Cultural History*. New York: Penguin, 1988.

Cotterell, Arthur, and David Morgan. *China's Civilization.* New York: Praeger, 1975.

Crump, James I. *Chan-kuo Ts'e.* Oxford: Clarendon Press, 1970.

————. *Intrigues.* Ann Arbor: University of Michigan Press, 1964.

De Bary, William T. *Sources of Chinese Tradition.* New York: Columbia University Press, 1960.

Devillers, Philippe. *Histoire du Vietnam.* Paris: Editions du Seuil, 1952.

Diem Bui, and D. Chanoff. *In the Jaws of History.* Boston: Houghton Mifflin, 1987.

Dillon, Michael. *Dictionary of Chinese History, 1979.* London: F. Cass, 1979.

Do Mau. *Vietnam: Mau Lua Que Huong Toi.* Mission Hills, CA: Que Huong Publications, 1986.

Duiker, William J. *Historical Dictionary of Vietnam.* Metuchen, NJ: Scarecrow Press, 1989.

Dumoutier, Gustave. "Comptoir hollandais de Pho Hien." Hanoi: Bulletin Geographique, 1895.

————. *Etude historique et archeologique sur Co Loa.* Hanoi: Cahiers Societe Geographique, 1940.

————. *Etude historique sur Trieu Vo De et sa dynastie, fondation du royaume de Nam Viet, apres la destruction de Van-Lang.* T'oung Pao, Leiden 7, 1906.

Durand, Maurice, and Nguyen T. Huan. *An Introduction to Vietnamese Literature.* Translated by D. M. Hawke. New York: Columbia University Press, 1985.

Durkheim, Emile. *The Elementary Forms of Religious Life.* London: George Allen & Unwin, 1915.

Fitzgerald, C. P. *China: A Short Cultural History.* 3d ed. New York: Praeger.

————. *History of China.* New York: American Heritage Publishing Co., 1969.

————. *The Southern Expansion of the Chinese People.* New York: Praeger, 1972.

Fung Yu-lan. *A Short History of Chinese Philosophy.* Princeton: Princeton University Press, 1983.

Garraty, John. *The Columbia History of the World.* New York: Harper & Row, 1981.

Gernet, Jacques. *Ancient China from the Beginning to the Empire.* Berkeley: University of California Press, 1968.

Gian Chi and Nguyen Hien Le, trans. *Chien Quoc Sach (Chan-Kuo Tse)* Los Angeles: Dai Nam, n.d. Reprint.

Gittings, John. *A Chinese View of China.* New York: Pantheon Books, 1973.

Golubew, Victor. "L'age de Bronze au Tonkin et dans le Nord-Annam." *BEFEO* 10 (1929): 1-46.

Gordon, Cyrus. *Hammurabi's Code.* New York: Rinehart, 1957.

Granet, Marcel. *Chinese Civilization.* London: Routledge & Kegan Paul, 1950.

Groslier, Georges. *The Art and Civilization of Angkor.* New York: Praeger, 1957.

Hall, D.G.E. *A History of Southeast Asia.* New York: St. Martin's Press, 1964.

————. *Southeast Asian History and Historiography.* Ithaca: Cornell University Press, 1976.

Harrison, Brian. *Southeast Asia: A Short History.* 3d ed. New York: St. Martin's Press, 1966.

Hawks, Pott F. *A Sketch of Chinese History.* Shanghai: Kelly & Walsh, 1908.

Hendry, James. *The Small World of Khanh Hau.* Aldine Pub. Co., 1964.

Hickey, Gerald. *Sons of the Mountains.* New Haven: Yale University Press, 1982.

————. *Village in Vietnam.* New Haven: Yale University Press, 1964.

Higham, Charles. *The Archeology of Mainland Southeast Asia*. Cambridge: Cambridge University Press, 1989.

Hirth, Friedrich. *The Ancient History of China*. Freeport, NY: Books for Libraries Press, 1969.

Honey, P. J. *Genesis of a Tragedy*. London: Benn, 1968.

Ho Ping Ti. *The Cradle of the East*. Hong Kong: Chinese University Press, 1975.

Ho Tai Hue-Tam. *Radicalism and the Origins of the Vietnam Revolution*. Cambridge, MA: Harvard University Press, 1992.

Huard, Pierre. "Les Portugais et l'Indochine." *Bulletin de l'Institut Indochinois pour l'etude de l'homme* 3 (1940): 47-65.

Huynh S. Thong. *The Heritage of Vietnamese Poetry*. New Haven: Yale University Press, 1979.

Khong Tu. *Xuan Thu Tam Truyen*. Translated by Hoang Khoi (Los Angeles: Dai Nam, 1971). Reprint.

Kramer, Andrew. *American Journal of Anthropology* 91 (1993): 163.

Lang, Olga. *Chinese Family and Society*. Hamden, CT: Archon Books, 1968.

Lau, D. C., trans. *Tao Te Ching*. New York: Penguin, 1963.

Legge, James, trans. *I Ching*. New York: Bantam Books, 1986.

———. *The Text of Taoism*. 2 vols. Delhi: Motilal Banarsidass, 1966.

———. *The Works of Mencius*. New York: Dover Publications, 1970.

Le Quang Nhut. "*Les origines du peuple annamite*." Hanoi: *Revue Indochinoise* (September 1906).

Le Thanh Khoi. *Histoire du Vietnam*. Paris: Sudestasie, 1992.

Li, Dun J. *The Ageless Chinese*. 3d ed. New York: Charles Scribner's Sons, 1965.

Liu, James T. C. *China Turning Inward*. Cambridge, MA: Harvard University Press, 1988.

Locke, John. *Two Treatises of Government*. Cambridge, Eng.: Cambridge University Press, 1967.

Lo Kuan Chung. *The Three Kingdoms*. Translated and edited by Moss Roberts. New York: Pantheon Books, 1976.

Luro, Jean B. *Le pays d'Annam*. Paris: Leroux, 1878.

Malinowski, Bronislaw. *Magic, Science and Religion*. Prospect Heights, IL: Waveland Press, 1992.

Malleret, Louis. "*Une tentative ignoree d'etablissement francais en Indochine au XVIIIe siecle*." Hanoi: *CEFEO*, No. 29 (1941).

Malraux, Andre. *Man's Fate* (*La Condition Humaine*). New York: Modern Library, 1934.

Manich Jumsai. *History of Thailand and Cambodia*. Bangkok: Chalermit, 1970.

Marr, David G. *Vietnamese Anticolonialism, 1885-1925*. Berkeley: University of California Press, 1971.

———. *Vietnamese Tradition on Trial*. Berkeley: University of California Press, 1981.

Maspero, Georges. *L'empire khmer*. Phnom Penh Imprimerie du Protectorat, 1904.

———. *The Kingdom of Champa*. New Haven: Yale University Southeast Asia Studies, 1949.

Maspero, Henri. *China in Antiquity*. Amherst: University of Massachusetts Press, 1978.

———. "Etudes d'histoires d'Annam, 1-3." Paris: *BEFEO*, no. 16 (1916): 1-55.

———. "Etudes d'histoires d'Annam. 4-6." Paris: *BEFEO*, no. 18 (1918): 1-36.

Maybon, Charles. "Les europeens en Cochinchine et au Tonkin." Hanoi: *Revue Indochinoise* (1916).

————. *"Quelques documents inedits concernant Pierre Poivre."* Hanoi: *Etudes Asiatiques* (1925).

McLeod, Mark W. *Vietnamese Response to French Intervention, 1862-1874.* New York: Praeger, 1991.

Melling, Phil, and Jon Roper. *America, France and Vietnam.* Brookfield, VT: Gower, 1991.

Morgan, Kenneth W. *Asian Religions.* New York: Macmillan, 1964.

Myrdal, Jan. *Report from a Chinese Village.* New York: Pantheon Books, 1965.

Ngo Si Lien. *Dai Viet Su Ky Toan Thu.* Reprint. Los Angeles: Dai Nam, n.d.

Nguyen Do Muc. *Dong Chu Liet Quoc.* Reprint. Los Angeles: Dai Nam, n.d.

Nguyen Huu Khang. *La commune annamite.* Paris: Sirey, 1946.

Nguyen Khac Ngu. *Mau He Cham.* Montreal: Nghien Cuu Su Dia, 1986.

Nguyen Khac Vien. *Histoire du Vietnam.* Paris: Editions Sociales, 1974.

Nguyen T. Hung, and Jerrold Schecter. *The Palace File.* New York: Harper & Row, 1986.

Nguyen Thien Lau. *"Le port et la ville de Faifo au XVIIe siecle."* Hanoi: *CEFEO,* no. 30 (1942).

Nguyen Van Huyen. *Le culte des immortels en Annam.* Hanoi: Imprimerie d'Extreme Orient, 1944.

Nguyen Van To. "Origine des noms de Fai Fo, Tourane et Cochichine." Hanoi: *Bulletin societe d'enseignement du Tonkin,* no. 13 (1934).

Norbeck, Edward. *Religion in Primitive Society.* New York: Harper & Row, 1961.

Odegard, Peter H. *Religion and Politics.* New York: Oceana Publications, 1960.

Pham Cao Duong. *Vietnamese Peasants under French Domination.* Berkeley: University Press of America, 1985.

Pham Van Son. *Viet Su Tan Bien.* Reprint. Los Angeles: Dai Nam, n.d.

Porter, Gareth. *Vietnam: A History in Documents.* New York: New American Library, 1981.

Rice, Edward. *Ten Religions of the East.* New York: Four Winds Press, 1978.

Roberts, Stephen H. *History of the French Colonial Policy.* London: F. Cass, 1963.

Ross, Edward A. *The Changing Chinese.* New York: Century Co., 1911.

Rust, William J. *Kennedy in Vietnam.* New York: Charles Scribner's Sons, 1985.

Rutledge, Paul. *The Role of Religion in the Vietnamese Community.* Lanham: University Press of America, 1985.

Sardesai, D. R. *Southeast Asia, Past and Present.* Boulder: Westview Press, 1989.

————. *Vietnam: Trials and Tribulations.* Long Beach, CA: Long Beach Publications, 1988.

Saso, M., and D. W. Chappell. *Buddhist and Taoist Studies.* Honolulu: University of Hawaii Press, 1977.

Schwartz, B. *The World of Thought in Ancient China.* Cambridge, MA: Belknap Press, 1985.

Shaplen, Robert. *The Lost Revolution.* New York: Harper & Row, 1965.

Smith, Huston. *The World's Religions.* New York: HarperCollins, 1991.

Spencer, Herbert. *Principles of Sociology.* New York: D. Appleton and Company, 1898.

Ssu Ma Ch'ien. *Annals.* Translated by Gian Chi and Nguyen Hien Le. Reprint. Los Angeles: Dai Nam, n.d.

Stableford, Brian. *The Third Millennium.* New York: Knopf, 1985.

Steinberg, D. J. *In Search of Southeast Asia.* New York: Praeger, 1971.

Toye, Hugh. *Laos: Buffer State or Battleground*. London: Oxford University Press, n.d.

Tran Trong Kim. *Viet Nam Su Luoc*. Reprint. Los Angeles: Dai Nam, n.d.

Treistman, Judith M. *The Prehistory of China*. Garden City, NY: American Museum of Natural History, n.d.

Truong Buu Lam. *Patterns of Vietnamese Response*. New Haven: Yale University Press, 1967.

Truong Nhu Tang. *A Viet Cong Memoir*. New York: Random House, 1986.

Tu Vi Lang, trans. *Tam Quoc Chi*. Reprint. Los Angeles: Dai Nam, n.d.

Twitchett, Denis, and Michael Loewe. *The Ch'in and the Han Empires*. Cambridge, Eng.: Cambridge University Press, 1986.

Tyler, E. B. *Religion in Primitive Culture*. New York: Harper & Brothers, 1958.

Waley, Arthur, trans. *The Analects of Confucious*. New York: Vintage Books, 1938.

———. *Three Ways of Thought in Ancient China*. London: George Allen & Unwin, 1953.

Wallace, Anthony. *Religion: An Anthropological View*. New York: Random House, 1966.

Wang, Zong Shu. *Han Civilization*. New Haven: Yale University Press, 1982.

Watson, Burton, trans. *Records of the Grand Historian*. New York: Columbia University Press, 1969.

———. *Records of the Historian*. New York: Columbia University Press, 1961.

———. *Ssu Ma Ch'ien Grand Historian of China*. New York: Columbia University Press, 1958.

Watson, William. *Early Civilization in China*. New York: McGraw Hill, 1966.

Weber, Max. *The Sociology of Religion*. Boston: Beacon Press, 1922.

Werner, Jayne S. *Peasant Politics and Religious Sectarianism*. New Haven: Yale University Southeast Asian Studies, 1981.

Wilbur, C. Martin. *Slavery in China During the Former Han*. New York: Russell and Russell, 1967.

Wittfogel, Karl A. *Oriental Despotism*. New Haven: Yale University Press, 1957.

Woodside, Alexander B. *Vietnam and the Chinese Model*. Cambridge: Harvard University Press, 1988.

Wu Yi. *Chinese Philosophical Terms*. Lanham, MD: University Press of America, 1966.

Zhu Liang. *Mastering the Art of War*. Translated by Cleary Thomas. Boston: Shambala, 1989.

INDEX

About the Author

OSCAR CHAPUIS was Maritime Inspector for the French High Commissioner of Indochina. He taught at the Vietnamese Maritime College in Saigon and served as the speaker on Vietnamese culture at the Multicultural Mental Health Training Program (MMHTP), University of South Florida.

ISBN 0-313-29622-7

90000>

EAN

9 780313 296222

HARDCOVER BAR CODE